RED ROCKS COMMUNITY COLLEGE

025 465 5

D0975123

31522 -2

PR
106
W55

Wintle, Justin.

The Pied Pipers

DATE			
MAY 1 0 1983			
MAY 1 3 1983			
JUN 6 1983			
JUN 24 '91			
JUL 16 '91			
NOV 21 '90			
DEC 12 '90			

COMMUNITY COLLEGE OF DENVER
RED ROCKS CAMPUS

© THE BAKER & TAYLOR CO.

Madeleine L'Engle

Nicholas Stuart Gray

Richard Adams

Rosemary Sutcliff

Richard Scarry

Lloyd Alexander

Laurent de Brunhoff

K. M. Peyton

Maurice Sendak

Scott O'Dell

Rumer Godden

The

Leon Garfield

Dr. Seuss

Roald Dahl

Alan Garner

Charlotte Zolotow

Pied Pipers

Interviews with the influential
creators of children's literature

by Justin Wintle and Emma Fisher

PADDINGTON PRESS LTD

THE TWO CONTINENTS
PUBLISHING GROUP

31522 -2
PR
106
W55   # 1137912

Library of Congress Cataloging in Publication Data

Wintle, Justin.
The Pied Pipers.

1. Authors, English—20th century—Interviews.
2. Authors, American—20th century—Interviews.
3. Illustrators—Great Britain—Interviews.
4. Illustrators—United States—Interviews.
5. Children's literature—History and criticism.
I. Fisher, Emma, 1949–   joint author. II. Title.
PR106.W55   820'.9'9282 [B]   74–15918
ISBN 0–8467–0038–7
Library of Congress Catalog Card No. 74 15918

PHOTO CREDITS: *Maurice Sendak* by Nancy Crampton; *Edward Ardizzone* by John
Hodder; *Laurent de Brunhoff* by Anne de Brunhoff; *Charlotte Zolotow* by Sidney Fields;
Richard Adams by Peter Hirst-Smith; *Nicholas Stuart Gray* by Prue Grice; *Joan Aiken*
by Rod Delroy; *Scott O'Dell* by Rudi Rath; *Madeleine L'Engle* by Bradford Bachrach;
Rumer Godden by Crispian Woodgate; *Judy Blume* by John Blume.
Introduction and Interviews with *Maurice Sendak, Charles Keeping, Richard Scarry,
Charlotte Zolotow, Roald Dahl, Richard Adams, Nicholas Stuart Gray, Scott O'Dell,
Leon Garfield, Lloyd Alexander, Alan Garner, John Rowe Townsend, Madeleine L'Engle,
Maia Wojciechowska* and *Judy Blume* all © Justin Wintle 1973 and 1974.
Interviews with *Edward Ardizzone, Laurent de Brunhoff, Joan Aiken, Rosemary Sutcliff,
K. M. Peyton, Lucy Boston* and *Rumer Godden* all © Emma Fisher 1973 and 1974.
Letter from *Dr. Seuss* © Theodor S. Geisel 1974.
Letter from *E. B. White* © E. B. White 1974.

Printed in the U.S.A.

Designed by Richard Browner

IN THE U.S.A.
PADDINGTON PRESS LTD
TWO CONTINENTS
PUBLISHING GROUP
30 East 42nd Street
New York City, New York 10017

IN THE UNITED KINGDOM
PADDINGTON PRESS LTD
1 Wardour Street
London W1

IN CANADA
PADDINGTON PRESS LTD
distributed by
RANDOM HOUSE OF CANADA
370 Alliance Avenue
Toronto, Ontario

COMMUNITY C   ENVER
RED ROCKS CAMPUS

CONTENTS

for Hirokuni Sugahara

Preface

The purpose of these interviews has been to learn something about a relatively small but representative selection of leading children's writers: their lives, the way they write their books, *why* they write them, and the connections between their work and their experience. Along the way widely different ideas and perspectives on childhood itself have also come to the surface, reflecting the many alternative conceptions adults have of what it's like to be a child and, by extension, what it's like to be an adult.

We do not expect the authors interviewed to be everybody's choice. If we had tried to satisfy everyone we would have finished by satisfying no one. Our aim was to give extended time to those we did talk to. We were particularly concerned that both English and American writers should be included, and this necessarily shortened the list for each country. If there has been a bias, it has been towards writing for older children. This is because we believe it is not too much to expect that some of these young readers may wish to study these conversations along with their parents, teachers and librarians—we hope to the mutual benefit of all.

The Introduction draws out the dynamics of today's children's literature as a market, and sketches some of the historical developments behind it. It does not describe in any detail contemporary literary trends. For these the reader must refer to the interviews.

Justin Wintle
Emma Fisher   London 1974

Acknowledgments

The authors wish to express their appreciation of the generosity and patience bestowed upon them by each of those interviewed.

They would also like to thank the many editors of various publishing houses who supplied additional information, in particular Barbara Dicks of Harper & Row, Richard Krinsley and Walter Retan of Random House, and Kaye Webb of Puffin Books. Thanks are also due to Eric Baker of the Children's Book Centre (London), John Donovon of The Children's Book Council (New York), Jennifer Marshall of the National Book League (London), Jean Mercier of *Publisher's Weekly*, Elaine Moss, and George Woods of the *New York Times*.

Justin Wintle would like to thank Hiroko Vehara; Ruth Cavin and Leonard Shatzkin of the Two Continents Publishing Group for their professional help and friendly hospitality in New York; Ed Berman of Inter-Action Trust, who first gave him the opportunity to work with children; Richard Kenin; Ava Megna for her hospitality in San Francisco.

Emma Fisher thanks her sister Lucy for advice and help.

Our final debt of gratitude is to William Horsley of the B.B.C.; and to Hirokuni Sugahara of the Fukuinkan Shoten Publishing Corporation (Tokyo), whose enthusiasm survived the distance.

The authors and publishers would like to acknowledge permission to reproduce certain copyright illustrations from books discussed in these interviews. MAURICE SENDAK: from *Where the Wild Things Are*, Harper & Row, New York, and The Bodley Head, London; from *Seven Tales by Hans Christian Andersen*, translated by Eva Le Gallienne, Harper & Row, and World's Work, Surrey; from *Mr. Rabbit and the Lovely Present*, text by Charlotte Zolotow, Harper & Row, and The Bodley Head; from *In the Night Kitchen*, Harper & Row, and The Bodley Head; from *The Juniper Tree and Other Tales by Grimm*, translated by Lore Segal and Randall Jarrell, Farrar Strauss & Giroux, New York, and The Bodley Head, London. EDWARD ARDIZZONE: from *Tim All Alone*, Oxford University Press, London, and Henry Z. Walck Inc., New York; "The momentous interview," illustration by Phiz (Hablot K. Browne) from *David Copperfield*, by Charles Dickens, Oxford University Press; "The momentous interview," the same scene from *David Copperfield*, illustrated by Edward Ardizzone, Oxford University Press; from *Pigeons and Princesses*, by James Reeves, Heinemann Ltd., London, and E. P. Dutton, New York. CHARLES KEEPING: from *The Golden Shadow*, text by Leon Garfield and Edward Blishen, Longman Young Books, London, and Pantheon Books, New York; from *The Spider's Web*, Oxford University Press; from *Knight's Fee*, text by Rosemary Sutcliff, Henry Z. Walck Inc., and Oxford University Press. RICHARD SCARRY: from *What Do People Do All Day?*, Random House, New York, and William Collins, Sons & Co. Ltd., London; from *Richard Scarry's Busy Busy World*, Western Publishing Co. Inc., Wisconsin, and Hamlyn Publishing Group Ltd., London. LAURENT DE BRUNHOFF: from *Babar en famille*, by Jean de Brunhoff, Librairie Hachette, Paris, and Methuen, London, for the English text accompanying it; from *Babar dans l'île des oiseaux*, by Laurent de Brunhoff, Librairie Hachette, and Methuen for the accompanying English text; from *Bonhomme*, by Laurent de Brunhoff, Librairie Hachette. CHARLOTTE ZOLOTOW: see Maurice Sendak. DR. SEUSS: from *And To Think That I Saw It On Mulberry Street*, Random House, and William Collins, Sons & Co. Ltd; from *Horton Hatches The Egg* and *The Cat In The Hat*, Random House, and William Collins, Sons & Co. Ltd. K. M. PEYTON: from *A Pattern of Roses*, Thomas Y. Crowell Inc., New York, and Oxford University Press; from *Pennington's Seventeenth Summer*, Thomas Y. Crowell Inc., and Oxford University Press.

Introduction

Children's literature is traditionally divided between books of an educational and informational nature—primers, readers, grammars, historical, geographical and scientific textbooks, and so on—and books of fiction and imagination. It is with the authors of the latter that this book deals.

However, in the light of recent publishing these two categories do not appear to be as separate as they once were. There is a new body of books that bridge fact and fantasy, that endeavor to entertain while they teach. Outstanding examples are Dr. Seuss's series of Beginner Books and Richard Scarry's colorful paradigms. These are books for the very young. Further along the age scale a similar concern with the adolescent's development has led to a proliferation of what are now known as "young adult" novels. Writers of this type of book include, in America, Judy Blume and sometimes Maia Wojciechowska, and in England John Rowe Townsend. Theirs are books that openly confront the problems modern society poses to those of its members on the verge of social responsibility. At the same time works of real imaginative excellence have followed on the achievements of C. S. Lewis, J. R. R. Tolkien, and May Norton in the 1950's. These are coming out in sufficient quantity for the dream of a children's literature which offers every potential benefit to be made an actuality.

The historical development of children's books is a chapter of accidents. Education in the Middle Ages was grounded in Latin. Ideally, children were taught to read and write in a foreign language. They were force-fed with declensions and conjugations until, at a precociously early age, they could tackle the works of the masters. An understanding of literature in the vernacular was not regarded as the proper object of learning, even though popular romances had as much appeal to the young as to the old. One of the earliest English works to be printed was Caxton's edition of Malory's *Morte d'Arthur* (1485), and evidence shows that this enjoyed a considerable circulation among older children. Two other books which Caxton saw through his press deserve mention: *A Book of Courtesy* (1477), the first book to be published specifically for young readers in England; and *Aesop's Fables* (1484), which, like many children's classics, began life as a book for grown-ups.

However, the arrival of printing did not herald a revolution. Throughout the Tudor century childhood was merely an inconvenient period when one was not an adult. Edward VI was a scholar by the age of nine, and, if the necessity arose, the well-born were expected to manage their own estates by their early teens. Hugh Rhodes's *Book of Nurture* (c. 1545) fulminated against reading for pleasure, and this reflected common opinion among the literate, who were in any case still only a fraction of the whole population. The Renaissance re-celebrated the value of the classics, although translations became acceptable and widespread during the reign of Elizabeth. At the same time drama, liberated from the liturgy and accordingly secularized, became *the* popular entertainment: being a child was a matter of having to wait before one was old enough to go to the Globe Theatre on Bankside.

The seventeenth century did not substantially alter the view in England of childhood as incipient manhood. This was the age of religious publication, and faith in the Christian word: the King James Bible, *Pilgrim's Progress*, *Paradise Lost* and, from an earlier time, Cranmer's *Book of Common Prayer* and Foxe's *Book of Martyrs* (1563). "The end of learning," wrote Milton, "is to repair the ruins of our first parents by regaining to know God aright" (*Of Education*, 1644). The poet's recommended method of achieving this goal was, by today's standards, Draconian. However, there were signs of change. *The Visible World in Pictures* (a translation of *Orbis Sensualium Pictus* by the Moravian scholar John Amos Comenius, published in 1659) was an altogether more influential book than Milton's tract. For the first time in a printed work, pictures were used to convey information to children as children. Concurrently, John Locke and other European thinkers were launching their enquiries into the nature of perception, visual and otherwise. Their scientific approach to the human organism was to be an important step toward a more enlightened view of man's relationship to his world. In short, the Enlightenment. Attitudes toward children were slower in the ferment, but the essential impetus was there: adults were seeing themselves differently.

From the beginning of the eighteenth century, popular ballads, tracts and tales were brought out in small collections or chapbooks, not infrequently illustrated with woodcuts. These supplemented the family diet of scripture and saints' lives, of Bunyan and Milton. But the appearance of Defoe's *Robinson Crusoe* (1719) and Swift's *Gulliver's Travels* (1726) was the real landmark in children's literature. Both these books were speedily adapted and bowdlerized for younger readers, and became, fortuitously, the first children's classics.

It was at this point that the great John Newbery (1713–67) invented children's publishing as a viable business concern. He was a bookseller, editor and author all in one, and he had the wit to realize an original market. His motto was "Trade and Plum Cake forever, Huzza!": or, how to make profits out of virtue. *A Little Pretty Pocket Book* (1744) was his first publication, and set the standards for all his subsequent titles. He went on to produce an entire "Juvenile Library," petite volumes, attractively designed and using flowered and gilt Dutch paper. With an undeniable flare for presentation and publicity, Newbery intuited that children's books could be purely for fun. Part of his success lay in his deliberate pursuit of the parent's or guardian's interest, knowing that they were the ones to pay for his goods. Not all of Newbery's motives were philanthropic: his significance would probably be that much less if they had been.

While Newbery's experiment was in the long run decisive, the stage continued to be occupied by would-be moralists and educators. Mary Sherwood (1778–1851) was the most prolific of a number of lady authors who created a new genre in morally didactic fiction for young persons at the end of the eighteenth century and the beginning of the nineteenth. The feeling that children's reading should be informed by some nobility of purpose was more satisfactorily accommodated by Charles and Mary Lamb's *Tales from Shakespeare* (1809).

Abroad, in countries where concepts of the child as a distinct social phenomenon took root earlier than in England, new influences were at work. At the court of Louis XIV (1638–1715) there was a vogue for fairy tales. Eight of these, among them *Little Red Riding Hood*, *The Sleeping Beauty*, *Bluebeard* and *Cinderella*, were gathered by Charles Perrault and published in 1697. They were translated into English in 1729. The brothers Grimm, Jacob and Wilhelm, performed the same service for German folklore, and later Hans Christian Andersen, in a more creative and inventive fashion, for Scandinavian folklore. *German Popular Stories*, translated by Edgar Taylor and illustrated by George Cruikshank, was published in England in 1823–6; and in 1846 Mary Howitt's rendering of Andersen's *Wonderful Stories for Children*. These books set off a wide-ranging interest in fairy tales, reflected in Mary Frere's *Old Deccan Days* (1868) and Andrew Lang's collections in the eighties and nineties. A similar response in America brought forth *The Age of Fable* (1855) by Thomas Bullfinch and *Uncle Remus: His Songs and Sayings* (1880) by Joel Chandler Harris.

With an undertaking to write specifically for children, authors were being sent back to the well-springs of fantasy, no longer shackled by conventions that demanded improving qualities first, good writing second. The resonances of this new order were amplified by an array

Introduction

of incredible talents. It was the first age of great children's books: Edward Lear's *Book of Nonsense* (1846), *Water Babies* (1863) by Charles Kingsley, *Alice's Adventures in Wonderland* (1865), *Through the Looking Glass* (1872) and *The Hunting of the Snark* (1876) by Lewis Carroll; Mark Twain's *The Adventures of Tom Sawyer* (1876) and *The Adventures of Huckleberry Finn* (1885); *At The Back of the North Wind* (1871), *The Princess and the Goblin* (1871), and *The Princess and Curdie* (1883) by George Macdonald; *Black Beauty* (1877) by Anna Sewell; the works of Howard Pyle, such as *Pepper and Salt* (1886) and *The Garden Behind the Moon* (1895); *The Wind in the Willows* (1908) by Kenneth Grahame, and so on and so on. The list could be three, four times as long. There is no single explanation for such an assemblage. The accidents of genius, the dynamics of the market, cheaper printing methods, the swelling of the middle class, the increased sophistication of editors, the post-romantic sentimentalizing of the child, an abundance of literacy, the loosening of church morality, the awareness of class, the growth of advertising, and so on and so on again. Each writer requires a separate genealogy, a separate balance sheet.

The same period marked a substantial improvement in the art of illustration. English and American Victorians had an insatiable appetite to view the world in their parlors and drawing rooms. This was reflected across the board, from hyper-realism in fine art to the new-fangled illustrated weeklies. Color lithography was introduced for the first time. Not surprisingly, therefore, this was also the first age of quality children's illustration. Once again there was a host of gifted individuals. Earlier in the century George Cruikshank, John Leech and Hablot K. Browne ('Phiz') turned their skills as cartoonists to illustrating books. The enthusiasm of publishers for good children's illustrations created a new career in art, successfully pursued by John Tenniel, Walter Crane, Randolph Caldecott, Kate Greenaway and, of course, Arthur Rackham. Rackham's books are collector's items. They were handsomely produced and available only to the wealthy. Kate Greenaway was more genuinely popular. *Under the Window: Pictures and Rhymes for Children* (1878) sold over a hundred thousand copies in its first editions, and by the end of the century she was a household name in England and America.

By the early twentieth century children's literature had become an industry with discrete genres at every level. Numerous magazines catered to the interests of boys and girls at every age. Sexual discrimination had already been perpetrated by a whole string of adventure stories for young males—the works of G. A. Henty, R. M. Ballantyne, Captain Marryat and R. L. Stevenson. Girls did not do badly either, with, among others, Louisa May Alcott's *Little Women* (1868–9), and Frances Hodgson Burnett's *Little Lord Fauntleroy* (1886) and *The Secret Garden* (1909). By contrast to a hundred years before, there seemed almost a surfeit of books for pleasure and entertainment.

Introduction

Soon after the Great War conflicting theories among educationists and the impact of the invention of psychology set up a chain of reactions and counter-reactions that gave rise to entirely new attitudes toward children and what they should read. Depending on how you interpreted Freud and his successors, the child was either a precocious adult in his latent sexuality, or an inhabitant of a private world from which grown-ups are estranged. Should a child's experiences be controlled with a regard to their formative, or to their immediate effects? Should they be controlled at all? These and other confusions have never been properly sorted out. To some extent they have been taken over by a neurotic obsession with the functions of the human individual and his or her relations to society. Whether writers choose to indulge or avoid these issues, there has never been such a conscious need for a versatile children's literature.

While the twenties and early thirties produced a handful of enduring writers—A. A. Milne, Laura Ingalls Wilder, Arthur Ransome and Hugh Lofting among them—and a few new genres, there was no major breakthrough. Up until 1945 it was not the policy of the majority of general publishers to operate distinct juvenile departments. (Publishers remained conservative.) Books for the young were fitted in haphazardly and irregularly, and the dedicated children's editor was a relatively rare phenomenon. Those who did care, and were aware of the needs of younger readers, realized that there could be a profitable expansion in the juvenile book trade. But just as the paperback revolution made a dramatic growth inevitable, war broke out in Europe and, in England at least, the developing situation had to be put on ice.

By common consent we are, in the present time, entered upon the second age of children's literature. Today, the manufacture of children's books, individually or in series, has become a major concern of every large publishing interest, and the exclusive business of several smaller houses, in England and America. This radical expansion depended largely on the enterprise and determination of a relatively small group of innovators, like Ursula Nordstrom of Harper and Row and Eleanor Graham at Puffin Books in the post-war period. Conditions were not as favorable as they had been in the mid-thirties. With rising production costs, the days of the book as an inexpensive commodity were numbered. The new entrepreneurial juvenile editor was obliged both to campaign aggressively among booksellers and librarians and to defend his or her optimism in the face of directorial scepticism.

Since 1920 the number of new juvenile titles published each year in the United States has increased more than five-fold. In the late nineteen-sixties this annual figure climbed to over 2,500. Recently the output has dropped back to around 2,000, mainly as a result of the falling-off in discretionary incomes. In England, where a cutback is still to be experienced, the statistics have been equally or

15

even more dramatic, with the production of new children's titles now approaching 3,000 per year.

The take-off of the last three decades is reflected in the histories of individual publishing houses. Random House, one of the biggest of the American publishing corporations, allocated in the region of $13,000,000 of its budget to juvenile hardback and softback publication in 1973.

In 1940 Random House had no such thing as a separate children's department. Equally significant is the fact that profit percentages from this division are higher than in any other section of Random House. Entire warehouses covering many acres of land are devoted to the storage of its single most successful author, Dr. Seuss, whose books sell over a million copies each year. In England the most prestigious publisher of children's literature is Puffin Books, a subsidiary of Penguin, which started its exclusively softback operation in 1940. In 1947 as many as eight million books were sold to the retail trade. Profits are not as high as they might be—indeed they are the lowest in all the many departments of the Penguin-Longman combine. Original philanthropy has, for once, survived. Puffin Books prefers to maintain an overall image of representative quality in children's literature, publishing at least a selection of all the best authors at prices that are suited to the pockets of the young. Titles are not priced on their individual merits, but are slotted into the lowest price bracket economically possible. Kaye Webb, Puffin's general editor, insists on preserving standards. She has been known to reject books guaranteed a commercial success. Of course, children who build up a Puffin library are likely to collect Penguins when they get older, but it is a fair game to play.

The creation of a wide and sometimes mass market for children's books has gone a long way toward making writing for children a stable profession. However, the gap between the rich and the struggling author is still enormous, and there is certainly no necessary correlation between large sales and literary or instructional value.

Getting good books noticed is a perennial problem in England and in America. There is always the tendency to devote most review space to established authors, regardless of whether they continue to merit it. Furthermore, reviewers seem often to be more interested in what satisfies their own intelligence than in what will stimulate a child, possibly because there is a certain natural speciousness about one generation dictating the taste of another.

There is a distinct shortage of publications and institutions prepared to give adequate coverage for new and old children's books. The result is a suffocating concentration of influence. In America, of the four key organs of review, only one, the *New York Times Book Review*, is genuinely public. The *Horn Book Magazine, Kirkus Reviews* and the *School Library Journal*, the only other magazines to give critical opinion worthy of the name, are all specialist reviews. They can be bought by anyone, but they are not on sale everywhere. Failure to get a recommendation from at least one of the journals usually means a book will sink, unless the publisher is prepared to spend a small fortune on advertising. In England a similar situation obtains, although the voices of influence are more diffuse. A number of national newspapers—the *Guardian*, the *New Statesman*, the *Observer* and the *Sunday Times*, as well as the *Times Literary Supplement* and the *Times Educational Supplement*—regularly review children's books. Regularly does not mean enough. *The Sunday Times*, for example, fulfils its obligation once a month, with a special flourish at Christmas. Again there is a run of specialist publications: *The School Librarian* and *The Teacher, Signal, Books for Your Children, Children's Book Review* and Margery Fisher's *Growing Point;* and, in book form, *Children's Books of the Year*, a guide compiled annually by Elaine Moss. What is disappointing in both countries is the reluctance of the most effective medium, television, to take anything but a negligible notice of children's literature. In America, where most television is commercial, there is little incentive to satisfy an audience which is only an indirect consumer. In England the deficiency is partially made up by a much fuller children's broadcasting service, and more frequent dramatization of children's books.

In both countries the condition of children's literature is best appreciated by knowing who buys it. In the United States 80 per cent of the market is accounted for by libraries and schools; a mere 20 per cent of the total sales of children's books belongs in bookshops and other outlets of a relatively narrow retail trade. (Random House alone stands out as having reversed these figures.) It would be surprising if as much as 3 per cent of all children's books in America were directly chosen by children for themselves. In England, where there is a greater paperback distribution and publishers do not manufacture special library editions, there is evidence that the proportions are slightly more even.

The hegemony of the library system, both in the review and selection of books, is not necessarily an evil in itself. Librarians and teachers are not a homogeneous body. They have the autonomy to develop and express individual tastes; and being professionals, often with a deep devotion to books, they are at least in the best position for making informed choices. In America, the Newbery and Caldecott annual awards for the best children's author and illustrator (the equivalents of the Carnegie and Kate Greenaway Medals in England) are made by a Committee of the Library Association. Even so, it not infrequently happens that fierce objections to the selections are raised by non-participating librarians. Such dissent can only be healthy.

What is not so healthy is the lack of knowledge and understanding of children's literature among the second, and not quantitatively

Introduction

insignificant, body of purchasers—the parents. Without library promotions, books of genuine merit that have sold well, like Madeleine L'Engle's *A Wrinkle in Time* or E. L. Konigsburg's *From the Mixed-Up Files of Mrs. Basil E. Frankweiler*, might not have sold at all. Certainly it is no credit that the works of a writer as essentially uninteresting as Enid Blyton, whom many librarians refuse to handle, should be among the world's topmost best-sellers, with eight-five million copies already disseminated. Many parents will only buy their children a book if they have heard of it, perhaps to avoid looking foolish in the face of overworked sales assistants; the opportunities for extending their repertoire are few, and seldom exploited.

Booksellers do not make a large profit out of paperbacks, particularly children's. To avoid taking up too much space, paperbacks are frequently crammed into inconvenient corners, making way for the heavier display items. Until they are subsidized, or motivated by altruism, booksellers are unlikely to provide the best conditions for a child to make a choice of book for himself, and parents must continue to do the choosing. Certain bodies, like the Children's Book Council in New York and the National Book League and the Federation of Children's Book Groups in England, do attempt to keep adults informed by national and local campaigns, often run in conjunction with libraries, but they need more backing than they have at the moment if they are to succeed.

At the risk of being categorical, there are three sorts of erring parent: those who are not interested in books at all, those who are uncritical of what their children read, and those who are hypercritical. Of the last two, the former will simply give way to the child's craving for more and more Enid Blyton; the latter will ruthlessly banish her from the playroom before the child has had the chance to taste her books for him or herself, insisting (wrongly) that he or she should only read books of the highest literary quality.

George Woods, the children's editor of the *New York Times Book Review*, put a point succinctly when he said to us: "We have a responsibility and a right as adults to prescribe what is good for our children to read, the same as we have the responsibility to prescribe their diet and sleeping hours. However, there can be no certitude that we will be right in our predictions of their response to a given book. We can only use our judgment about their response, and allow ourselves to be wrong at least some of the time." If we do have a responsibility to choose books for our children, then that responsibility is dependent upon knowing which books to choose. What is needed among parents is more interest in the subject.

There is no reader so set apart as the child. In recent decades there has been an explosion of literature for children, a massive increase in the time, talents, energies and resources devoted to the production of books for young people. Children can enjoy a variety of reading matter that their parents never had. But there has been the parallel effect that those parents have less and less of an idea about what their offspring read, less and less knowledge of the authors who write them. Some of the old classics, many of them originally written for adults, are still taken off the shelf; but there are many new classics, written specifically for children, which are being devoured for the first time.

It is as if the Pied Piper were still alive. A child can concentrate on a book as closely as any scholar; and a good children's book can absorb its reader like a dream. While it lasts, any arrangement of images or events other than the one presented is irrelevant, non-existent. The Pied Piper took the children of Hamelin "to a joyous land" inside a mountain, away from the rats, the deceiving city councillors. In the sense that he may command the total attention of his audience, every children's author, whether he aims to provide a fairyland of escape or a down-to-earth critique of our incoherent society, is a Pied Piper. Today there are more people writing for children than there ever were before, more Pied Pipers than were ever dreamt of in Hamelin.

1 Maurice Sendak

Interviewed by Justin Wintle

Maurice Sendak is simply one of the best-known illustrators and writers of children's picture books working today. Behind the closed doors of editorial offices in both London and New York he is commonly hailed as a genius. His eminence is based on a complete fusion of talent and vocation, and a sense of freshness in his work that can transform whimsy into solid fantasy. Like many of the great illustrators of the past, he comes close to being a gallery artist.

Sendak's reputation was firmly established by the publication of *Where the Wild Things Are*, which won the Caldecott Medal in 1964. Little Max, decked in a wolf suit, is sent to his bedroom without any dinner. Defiantly the boy's imagination conjures up a forest out of the furniture; next, "an ocean tumbled by with a private boat for Max," and he sails off to the land of the Wild Things. These creatures are so effectively wild that when the book originally appeared many adults took fright and were worried that their children would be terrified. These apprehensions were wholly wrong, as it turned out: though nobody has been able to explain quite why, children have adored the Wild Things for ten years, and seem likely to continue their affection. Perhaps an answer to this riddle lies somewhere in what an admittedly precocious child said after reading the book for the first time: "I shan't mind my nightmares any more. They are no more real than Mr. Sendak's monsters."

As if one Caldecott Medal is not enough, Maurice Sendak has won the singular distinction of gaining a second, this one for his twenty-seven illustrations of *The Juniper Tree, and other tales from Grimm.* The prize was awarded him as a tribute to his versatility and unrivaled consistency as an artist.

Born of Polish descent in 1929 and raised in New York, Maurice Sendak has been an illustrator all his life. He remembers no other ambition. Unmarried, Sendak currently lives and works at his home in Ridgefield, Conneticut.

Maurice Sendak

Q   *What originally took you into illustrating children's books?*

A   Since childhood it was all I ever wanted to do. I began illustrating then, and it seemed the most natural thing in the world that I should continue to do what I enjoyed doing. I earn money from it now, but other than that nothing has changed particularly. My brother and I used to collaborate sometimes. He would write something, and I would illustrate it. Then I began to write as well, and gradually it became my profession. Truly, I guess it is like when a devoted cobbler is born and the first thing he likes to do is put a nail into a shoe. He doesn't know why, but he goes on putting nails into shoes. That's the way it was with me. I began drawing and writing, and gradually it became my work.

Q   *Were you motivated by picture-books you read as a child?*

A   I wasn't consciously aware of modeling myself, of picking professional models, until late adolescence. I don't know why I liked to make pictures as a child. It must have been something congenital. We didn't have a lot of books, although we were not "deprived." I read comic books and the junk that everybody else read. But I was not aware of the book as an aesthetic object, as a sensuous whatever, until middle adolescence, when I also began associating books with the names of the people who illustrated them. And it was only when I was sixteen or seventeen that I began looking at other people's work with a consciousness that I could learn something, or even borrow something.

Q   *How much formal artistic training did you have?*

A   Not very much. Self-education was always more important. I went to the Arts Students' League in New York for two or three years, but that was really to placate my parents more than anything else. Like all thoughtful parents they were concerned about how I was going to make a living. Going to art school at night showed them I was serious, and put the stamp of approval on my enterprise. I hate and loathe and despise schools. The only part of my childhood that was truly punishing and suffering was school. If I could have been left at home I would have been perfectly content. I couldn't see that I would have any more aptitude for art school. But I did have one very good teacher in composition—John Groth. He came in once every two weeks, made some acute criticisms of one's work, and then left one alone. This suited me much better than being obliged to accomplish a certain amount of work by the end of each week for grading purposes. Perhaps it's a rationalization because I hated it, so much, but school is bad for you if you have any talent. You should be cultivating your talent in your own particular way. I hated the competition that was forced upon me at school. There were few teachers who had any understanding or comprehension of a child. Criticism can be valuable, but not if it's incorporated in a formal system.

Q   *You do some teaching yourself, of course . . .*

A   The irony of ironies, I do, yes. But I try to give my class a maximum of freedom; that is, convey to them that they are not under the thumb of a grade or anything like that. I also tell them that I don't believe in school, and that they'd be better off outside it. It works to some degree. All I'm doing is being the older artist who is prepared to share what he has learned and experienced with a group of younger artists. They can take it or leave it.

Q   *When did you leave art school?*

A   About 1949 or 1950. I was already working by then. I love to work, meet people, do things. I took almost any kind of job I could lay my hands on, so long as it was related to art. I took jobs in display houses and similar places, and began to find my way around.

Q   *Were you interested in films as a youngster?*

A   I loved them. If I had been lucky I would have been a Renaissance child living in Florence. I would have been up early every morning to watch Michelangelo chiseling away in his back yard. But if you were an American child in the early thirties on the outskirts of a big city like New York, then you went to the movies. Movies were the great super-escape. You went with your friends, and for a good part of the day you were alone with them.

Q   *I ask because there's a film-like quality to one or two of your books, particularly* Where the Wild Things Are. *The pictures get bigger and bigger on every page, like an ordinary screen opening out to cinemascope. Was that a natural thing for you to do?*

A   I think of that as an emotional, rather than a cinematic, device. A picture-book can be very boring: you turn one page after another, and that's it. If you are an adult you'll do that without complaining. But children are not so polite. One of the reasons why the picture-book is so fascinating is that there are devices to make the form itself more interesting. In *Where the Wild Things Are* the device is really a matching of shapes. I used it to describe Max's moods pictorially: his anger, which is more or less normal in the beginning; its expansion into rage; then the explosion of fantasy as a release from that particular anger; and finally the collapse of that, when the fantasy goes and it's all over. The smell of food brings Max back to reality and he's a little boy again. A book is inert. What I try to do is animate it, and make it move emotionally.

Q   *The structure of* Where the Wild Things Are *is bridge-like; it moves from reality to an apex of fantasy, and then back to reality again. How much do you think children distinguish between those two states?*

A   They move between reality and fantasy with the greatest possible ease, without making categorical, specified lines where one stops and the other begins. That Max's room can turn into a forest is an example of that merging. He doesn't have to go into the subway to get to the forest. He's in that state of belief where it can happen in his room. Of course, I don't mean that children don't or can't distinguish between fantasy and reality. Only an insane or sick child is not going to make the distinction and stay in fantasy. When Max smells food from far away he knows it's time to go home; and he's not going home to a jungle hut: he's going back to the room he came from. He's not a dammed fool: he wants his mother. He moves back and forth. He's a pragmatist, like all kids.

Q   *Like the child who thinks riding his bicycle is flying an airplane, but still remembers to lock it up afterwards.*

A   Exactly. He's going to stop at the red light too!

Q   *Is that aspect of childhood, that description of a child's mind, based on memories of when you were young?*

A   Yes, it would have to be. I'm not describing a child's mind as a clinical psychologist would. I'm describing my own mind. I don't know children's minds. I have no training. I've read numbers of articles where I sound as though I'm a black-bearded Herr Doktor Child Psychiatrist. Bullshit! I don't know any more than you do, probably. I only know my mind and how it works, more or less. I've worked with children. Many of them are excited by what I do. There's a peculiar level of relationship that has nothing to do with age. But when I talk about children, obviously

I'm not describing a year's work in an Oklahoma clinic with disturbed kids. I don't like making grand generalizations.

Q   *What was the specific nature of your own childhood?*

A   It was decent, and I was not in any way under-privileged. I had a hard-working father, and I was sufficiently loved. But I was just that kind of child who has to live in fantasy as much as he does in reality—probably because I was very easily bored. There weren't sufficient things I could do as a child. You were stranded on a block, unless you were lucky enough to get your mother's permission to cross the street by yourself, which wasn't very often. For me that was a dull way to get through a day, so I had to fantasize. That's why the movies were so important, because I could pretend they were part of my own life.

"That very night in Max's room a forest grew." From *Where the Wild Things Are* by Maurice Sendak.

Maurice Sendak

Q *When you started to illustrate for a living, were you interested in what your contemporary illustrators were doing?*

A I was very aware of what was happening, although I can only infer that it wasn't very interesting because I do not remember very much that excited me, or that I wished to emulate. I was more intently interested in English and German illustrations from an earlier period, the nineteenth century. I greatly admired George Cruikshank. All my models came from there, not from contemporary America. Nor do I particularly keep up with what is going on now, twenty years later. There are people I admire, but I am very prejudiced.

Q *Your love, or sympathy, for German art comes across in your recent illustrations of Grimm. Is there a particular quality that attracts you?*

A Yes, but it would be very hard to define. When I was a younger man, just to look at a German illustration on a printed page was usually enough to turn me on. Artists like Ludwig Richter. I don't know why, but he just rang a bell inside me: those small clusters of children, of barns and rickety haylofts, night-skies and warmth and coziness. The appeal was purely graphic. The pages themselves were also beautifully bordered—a beauty of bookmaking true of German books and eminently true of English books. It was a sensuous pleasure in the book itself. I don't think it was anything specifically German at that time, although German music and German writing have always been unquestionably my favorite. I don't know what the link-up is. It is a very ambivalent feeling, to put it mildly, since I grew up during the war, and since I was force-fed on anti-German feeling. My father's family was totally exterminated. I belonged to what I suspect was a typical American Jewish family. One grew up with not only a loathing for things German, but also with a fear for things German. I know people today who won't travel in Germany, and who have never wanted to. I wanted to, and I did, and I have, a number of times. Perhaps it's something to do with the language. I just need to hear it spoken and I become dizzy. I just like it. There is a passion, no question about it.

Q *In addition to your fascination with German and English illustrative art, one also detects, in* Seven Tales *by Hans Christian Andersen, an appreciation of medieval art.*

A That isn't typical. It only occurs in Andersen. I have loved medieval paintings, but they have never excited me as much as other things. I find now that the illustrations I did for Andersen were inappropriate. I think I must have been afraid to do him at the time. It was very different when I did Grimm: I was older and less intimidated. Andersen threw me off balance. I didn't work by instinct, and I wasn't very careful. Also, I had just come back from a trip in Europe, which I spent mostly in France looking at Gothic cathedrals. I was passionately excited by what I had seen at Amiens and Chartres. Faced with Andersen I must have doubts about what I wanted to do, so I used what I had seen to fill a gap. My recent travels came out in the *Seven Tales*. Had I been older I would have been stricter about suppressing what came out as graphic whimsy. Beyond that, I don't think I have anything in common with Andersen—at least not in the way I have things in common with Grimm. I was so impressed by Andersen that I didn't stop to ask myself whether I liked him.

Q *Would you dismiss your work on the* Seven Tales *completely then?*

A No, not completely by any means. Looking back, there are some interesting things in that book. For example, the illustration to *The Fir Tree*. I still find there's a mystery to that picture. In the foreground there are the children and the little tree. In the background there's a stork, a traditional Danish stork, which I remember wanting to get in. But what is it doing there? He's just a creature at the top of the page, walking by himself among the dark firs. He is oblivious of the children, and the children are oblivious of him. But the stork's presence is not a complete accident. He makes the picture a double image. It's the sort of juxtapositioning of images that I took so much pleasure in later.

Q *That picture apart, I thought the other Andersen illustrations were unusually mechanical in their application of tricks of perspective and so on.*

A They were pastiches of Gothic perspectives which clung too closely to their models. I had not digested my inspiration in Europe well enough to turn it into something else.

Q *Perhaps your illustrations of Andersen were too arbitrary. But if an illustrator is to avoid being arbitrary, what is he to be?*

A Again, I can only give you my opinion, as it relates to what I want to do, or try to do. To me, illustrating means having a passionate affair with the words. I hate to say that it's akin

Maurice Sendak

Maurice Sendak's illustration for "The Fir Tree," from *Seven Tales by Hans Christian Andersen.*

to a mystic rite, but I have no other language to describe what happens. It's a densely sensual, densely important experience. An illustration is an enlargement, an interpretation of the text, so that the child will be illuminated by the picture to comprehend the words better. The images act as openings for conceptions so that the words become clearer. You are always serving the words. You are serving yourself, of course, but the pleasure in serving yourself is in serving someone else. That is what illustration is to me. It may be other things to other people.

Q   *In the introduction you wrote for the* Seven Tales *you made a distinction between functional illustration and dimensional illustration. Do you still make that distinction?*

A   Yes. I just wouldn't do the former, and I will spend my life doing the latter. It comes down to the difference between factual and non-factual illustration. Obviously a great many books require factual illustration—the How-To kind of book, for example. But I also think pictures like Ernest Shepherd's illustrations to *Winnie-the-Pooh* are factual, in the sense that they don't interpret what Christopher Robin or Eeyore look like, but tell you how they ought to look. Of course, Shepherd has invented how they ought to look, but his illustration is factual in that it is precise. I can't do that sort of thing well. My forte lies in interpretive illustration, which is what I like doing. I think I must have explained to people *ad nauseam* that to me it's like setting someone's poetry to music. You illuminate the verse, you open the lines. There's no fun in just setting a picture down. The fun is in finding out something about yourself as you do it. It's a form of miraculous self-indulgence: in everything you do you are looking for yourself. What better way of spending your life? You have to be extraordinarily careful though: you must not forget that you are looking for yourself in someone else's work, or try to find yourself by losing them.

Q   *In your recent illustrations of Grimm,* The Juniper Tree and Other Tales, *you again employed a deliberate device: each of the twenty-seven illustrations is confined to a relatively small square in the centre of the page, with the effect that the characters and objects depicted seem to compete with one another for room. A sort of claustrophobia prevails. Did you do this because of something you discovered in Grimm?*

A   I find the stories themselves claustrophobic. There's an incredible tension in each one of them. They work on two levels: first, as stories; secondly, as the unraveling of deep psychological dramas. I'm not so interested in the top layer, the story, as

I am in what I think goes on underneath. The stories are intentionally emotional, but superficialed over with a fairytale gimmick language. I was looking to catch the moment in each fairytale when the tension between the storyline and the emotion is at its greatest, so that the person reading it is in for a surprise if he thinks it is just a fairytale. I wanted my pictures to tell the readers who think the stories are simple to go back to the beginning and read again. That was my intention. I didn't want to show Rapunzel with a hank of hair hanging out of a tower. To me that's not what the story is about. A lot of illustrators have chosen that image because there seems little else to draw. But to me, Rapunzel's hair is only the gimmick in the story. I had to find out what was really underneath. It was hard. There was not one story that gave up its secret right away. I had to read and reread them for years before I could abstract the particular thing that meant something to me. Each story had an internal problem to be solved, and the device I chose happened to fit. I can't verbalize or give you an intellectual account of why it fits. I can only say that I experimented for a long time, and the way I finally did it was how I knew my Grimm should look, as opposed to anybody else's.

Q *The pictures are certainly startling. Do you think the young reader is mature enough to go back and search out the meaning you capture?*

A I think children read the internal meanings of everything. It's only adults who read the top layer most of the time. I'm generalizing again, of course, but I'll bet my last dollar that those pictures do not surprise kids. They know what's in Grimm. They know that stepmother probably means mother, that the word "step" is there to avoid frightening a lot of older people. Children know that there are mothers who abandon their children, emotionally if not literally. Sometimes they have to live with it. They don't lie to themselves. They wouldn't survive if they did. My object is never to lie to them.

Q *Much of your best work has a direct emotional appeal. The exception perhaps is the* Nutshell *Library. What was the difference there?*

A In the *Nutshell* I was writing verses, which I had never done before. Those books were also written in the early sixties, when I was interested in other things. I was interested in doing a pastiche of the Cautionary Tale, in writing an original ABC that sounded like me, and in having some simple fun. In the *Nutshell* I used what were prescribed and conventional forms—the alphabet, the counting-book, the book of months and so on. I did try to make them personal, but at the same time I realized I couldn't make them too personal.

Q   *They're certainly unlike most other examples in the same conventions, books which tend very often to be "educative."*

A   That's what I was trying to get away from. The least important aspect of *Alligators All Around* is that it is an alphabet. I wanted to see how much I could get away with from a form that is very stilted and very fixed. My alligators aren't teachers: they're like Max. They stick their tongues out and stand upside down and are very vain. They do the kind of things that all my later children do. At the moment, we're setting the *Nutshell* for a half-hour TV special for children. The verses are now about fourteen years old, but I think they are still fun. Carole King, the young rock composer, is setting them to music. She's given them a reverberation that they didn't have originally; and she's added her own emotional quality, which changes their color completely. They've taken on a new edge, a new weight. Added to that, the way I draw has changed, so that the children I'm inventing for the screen, while based on those in the *Nutshell*, will look different. They have been amplified to resemble what I am like now. I've also incorporated into the film another early book of mine, *The Sign on Rosie's Door.* I've extracted Rosie, so she's now become a kind of Fellini, inventing a movie within a movie in this very boring Brooklyn background, where I spent my own childhood. The *Nutshell* boys have become her slaves, and in return she activates their fantasies.

Q   *In the original book Rosie is eccentric and Rosie plays games. Are games as important to you as they are to some of your characters in your picture books?*

A   Rosie is not eccentric. She is just a kid who cannot get out of a fantasy as often as she probably ought to. As for games— they're more than important: they're healthy! If I have an unusual gift, it's not that I think I draw particularly better or write particularly better than other people (I've never fooled myself about that); rather, it's that I remember things other people don't recall—the sounds and feelings and images of particular moments in childhood. It seems my child-self is still alive and active. Summers were a horror. You couldn't go away, and you couldn't go to school, which at least took up a few hours of the day. For most children there was really very little to do. We lived in Brooklyn on a street with a mixed bag of kids, most of whom one had nothing in common with. Yet somehow

From Maurice Sendak's "Rapunzel," in *The Juniper Tree and other Tales by Grimm.*

you had to make do. In a situation like that children have an ability to do something, while the chances are an adult would move away. A child cannot do that. Usually he is stuck there, so he has to conform. The way he does it is to invent games and make believe, and energetically get through a difficult time. The whole point of *Rosie* was to show how a child can get through a long, boring summer's day. Her friends are not as interesting as she is, but she has to make do with them. So she turns them into vassals, and they all take small parts in her fantasies. This is healthy. It gets them through the afternoon. She is lucky to have them, and they are lucky to have her. Nothing harmful is done, and the kids have used their imaginations. It's like a muscle which is exercised in childhood, but which we do not exercise often enough as adults. We read the newspapers instead.

Q *Have you ever participated in game-orientated therapy sessions—the Esalen approach to life?*

A No, I haven't—though I've heard of them of course. The only trouble I have is in battening down my imagination and fantasy life, even at my advanced age. It's the same problem I had as a child, only now nobody's going to hit me over the head for it. They're going to pay me an advance instead. That's the only difference.

Q *Now that you have finally illustrated Grimm, what are you looking forward to doing?*

A Animating the *Nutshell* will take a long time. That's like a dream come true. For over a decade I've been toying with the idea of making an animated film. My passions for Disney when I was a child, my passion for movies, my attempts in books to simulate animation sequences: well, now here it is, baby! I'm not thinking of anything but getting this done, and getting it done as expertly as I can, despite my lack of experience. Happily, I'm working with superb craftsmen. It's an extremely exciting experience—I'm animating a film! I am making a movie! Just the way I always dreamed. Everyone, it seems, who grew up in the thirties and forties wanted to make a movie. This was the Cecil B. De Mille fantasy. You come to Hollywood to be a star. Every odious-shmodious cliche you ever heard about that unfulfilled wish to make a movie! And the feeling of my show is just that—playing at making a movie, so it's very apropos. Illustrating Grimm was a very hard job, and it took very many years of hard work. I'm a very slow worker, not flexible at all. I couldn't say "Oh, Grimm is rough. I think I'll

Cover for Maurice Sendak's *In the Night Kitchen.*

do something else this week." I could only work on Grimm, nothing else. So I'm very worn out after a long, hard project like that. It's a relief not to be doing a book right now, a great relief. I have books that are sitting there to be done, but I'm in no hurry to get to them. The only one I am in a hurry to get to is a book my father wrote just before he died, his one and only book, a fairy tale which I'm editing and translating from the Yiddish. But I need the energy of being away from books for a year before I can do well by him. So this TV thing is perfect for me.

Q   *It seems strange that you should be making an animated film of the* Nutshell Library, *rather than a book like* In The Night Kitchen, *which, in its tabloid form, seems halfway to being a film before you start.*

A   The answer to that lies in your earlier question, why the *Nutshell* doesn't have a particularly dense emotional business. That makes it easier to cope with as a first film. You're right in that *In The Night Kitchen* is laid out for a film; but it would be super-dangerous to make it into a film on the first trip out.

Q   *Now that you've begun, do you think you will make a lot of films?*

A   I think there's a fantasy of wanting to. It depends on how much pleasure I get out of animating the *Nutshell*. Whatever I do I must get a lot of pleasure out of it if I am to do it again, however good or bad it may be. I don't like to do things for a lark. When I make a book, I don't just hand it to the publisher and think to myself, "Now it's done." I like to be at the printer's, and see the whole thing right through. You go all the way to practically sewing on the binding. If making films gives me the same opportunity, then I shall go on and do several. What more could I say about it at this stage?

Los Angeles—May, 1974

Books written and illustrated by Maurice Sendak include: The Sign on Rosie's Door (1960); The Nutshell Library (1962), *comprising* Pierre (A Cautionary Tale); Chicken Soup With Rice (A Book of Months); Alligators All Around (An Alphabet), *and* One Was Johnny (A Counting Book); Where The Wild Things Are (1963); Hector Protector (1965); Higglety Pigglety Pop! or There Must Be More To Life (1967), *and* In The Night Kitchen (1970).

Among the many books by other authors he has illustrated are: Little Bear (1957); Father Bear Comes Home (1959); Little Bear's Visit (1961), *and* A Kiss for Little Bear (1968), *all by Else Holmelund Minarik;* The Happy Rain (1956), *by Jack Sendak, his brother;* Seven Tales by Hans Christian Andersen (1959), *translated by Eva Le Gallienne;* Mr. Rabbit and the Lovely Gift (1962) *by Charlotte Zolotow;* The Bee-Man of Orn *by Frank R. Stockton;* The Animal Family (1965) *by Randall Jarrell;* The Golden Key (1967) *and* The Light Princess (1969) *by George Macdonald; and, from Grimm,* The Juniper Tree & Other Tales, *translated by Lore Segal and Randall Jarrell (1973), and* King Grisly-Beard (1973), *translated by Edgar Taylor.*

2 Edward Ardizzone

Interviewed by Emma Fisher

While Sendak has many styles, Edward Ardizzone's drawings are as instantly recognizable as Kate Greenaway's, without her sugariness. Sendak delves into his own mind; Ardizzone is an observer. He tries to be as faithful as possible to the author he is illustrating. His approach is essentially innocent, and he is concerned with people rather than symbols.

Ardizzone has illustrated more than 160 books and collaborated with many children's writers, two of the most successful partnerships being with Eleanor Farjeon (*The Little Bookroom*, 1955; *Eleanor Farjeon's Book*, 1960; *The Old Nurse's Stocking Basket*, 1965) and James Reeves, whose collected poems for children, with some forty of Ardizzone's drawings, appeared in England in 1973. Other works for children illustrated by him include *The Otterbury Incident* by C. Day Lewis (1948); Philippa Pearce, *Minnow on The Say* (1955); *The Thirty-Nine Steps* by John Buchan (1964); *Daddy-Long-Legs* by Jean Webster (new edition, 1966). Among authors he has illustrated for adults are H. E. Bates, John Betjeman, G. K. Chesterton, Defoe, Dickens, R. L. Stevenson, R. S. Surtees, Thackeray, Trollope, and Shakespeare. His own children's books, with minimal text and expressive drawings, are enduringly popular; libraries stock them in tens and they are always out.

Edward Ardizzone was born in Haiphong in 1900, of an Italian father with French nationality. He was brought up in England, and after leaving school as soon as possible, worked for six years as a clerk in the London financial district. Since the thirties he has earned his living as an illustrator. He lives in Rodmersham in Kent, near other members of his large family (three children and eleven grandchildren). He is a connoisseur of good wine and has illustrated a catalogue for Harvey's, the English wine merchants. His reputation as a painter, chiefly in watercolor, is growing; there was an exhibition of his work at the Tate Gallery in 1973. He is a fellow of the Society of Industrial Artists. He has also recently published his war diaries (*Diary of a War Artist*) and his autobiography (*The Young Ardizzone*).

Edward Ardizzone

Q   *How did* Little Tim and the Brave Sea Captain *come to be written? Was it about your own childhood?*

A   My own childhood came into it, but the beginning really was that I was put on the mat by my own children—or rather my wife said to me, for heaven's sake tell them a story to keep them quiet, and on the spur of the moment I thought of little Tim. But the story I told then was very much changed and altered when it came to writing it and illustrating it.

Q   *When did the pictures come into it?*

A   Ah, the pictures came later. As usual, in those days, I was pretty broke, and I tried to think of some means of making some money. I thought this was a good story, the children liked it, so I got a large sketch book, and drew the pictures and wrote almost at the same time. With children's books, you know, the writing and the drawings go together. The story was really based on my own childhood, in the sense that I was brought up in Ipswich as a little boy, and there were the docks, and there were barges there and small sailing ships. Then later we moved to the Kentish coast where there were the pebbly beaches of Deal, Walmer, and such-like places; they all came into the book.

Q   *Did you ever want to go to sea?*

A   No, no. I'd been to sea, I'd come back from China as a small boy—I was born in China. By that time I wanted to be an artist; I can't remember ever wanting actually to go to sea, but I adored the sea, and ships and so on. My great-grandfather was a captain of one of the great sailing ships—we always said it was the Owen Glendower, but I'm not quite sure it was—she was one of the great sailing clippers going in the China trade; my grandmother was born at sea off Cape Horn. He produced the most beautiful illustrated log, and I adored that book when I was a little boy. I think it was probably one of the formative things.

Q   *When you came to write* Little Tim, *were the pictures more important than the text? That's the impression they give.*

A   You mustn't forget that if you're going to write your own children's book, the importance of the pictures is that it means you can cut the text. Now when an author writes a story, he says "There was a little boy called Tim and he wore a red jacket and one fine morning he walked down the road to the beach and he looked over the fence and saw a brown cow." If you write the book yourself and illustrate it yourself, it's all in the drawing; all you've got to say is "Tim walked down to the sea." Then you paint in the red jacket and all those things. The pictures tell you the story equally. I've always had a great love for the great simple stories like *Pilgrim's Progress*, and even a French one like *Manon Lescaut*, where no description is ever given. It's just the plain tale: "He went and did something." If you illustrate it yourself, you can do that. But if you're a wretched author you've got to say more, because you've got no pictures to help you. And even if you have your own pictures, you've still got to have a strong story underneath.

Illustration by Edward Ardizzone for his *Tim All Alone*.

Q   *Is that the ideal way of creating a picture book?*

A   Of course, for me it's the ideal way. Unless. . . there are exceptions, of course there are exceptions. And the exception is when
you are dealing with a poet, like Walter de la Mare; then, you
see, the poetry is so beautiful, you can illustrate that. It's very
difficult to explain, but it's not quite the same thing as illustrating a prose story. If it's a poem there are fewer facts, or you
come to them in an oblique manner; the sound of the words
gives you your facts. It's one of those difficult things—but I
think fine verse is a fine art; it has its own life, and it makes
you free to interpret it in your own way. Now that probably
sounds rather nonsense, but I don't think so; I think if you're
writing prose, and you're an ordinary person, you've got to give
all these details, but if you're writing verse you don't have to.
You can also in a sense do poetic drawings to match.

Q   *Don't you like being held down to details? I'm thinking particularly of Dickens, who gives detailed instructions to his illustrators.*

A   Oh no, I don't mind facts, but it just depends on how it's given
to you. Dickens is marvelous because, being a great writer, immediately he brought a character into his book he described it
from the word go. You knew exactly what Mr Micawber was
like, and you knew exactly what they were all like. You couldn't
go wrong. It makes it much easier for the illustrator.

Q   *Sometimes they don't get it quite right—in Phiz's illustrations
for* Dombey and Son *he can never decide whether Captain Cuttle's
hook is on his left arm or his right. Though some people attribute
this to the technicalities of etching.*

A   Oh, Phiz is marvelous. But do you know, Dickens hated them.
By the time he wrote *Dombey and Son* he'd much rather a Victorian RA did the illustrations. He didn't like Phiz, who was of
much earlier tradition, the caricature tradition. Dickens was
so horrified by the picture of little Paul Dombey and Mrs Pipchin
by the fire that he tried very hard to stop the production of
that monthly part. Later on, with *Edwin Drood*, when Luke
Fildes did the illustrations—and they were very good illustrations—they hadn't got that caricature element. Cruikshank and
Phiz were still in the tradition of Gillray and the cartoonists.

Q   *The technique is to seize on a characteristic, like Mr Carker's
teeth, and once you've got it in the picture you know who it is.*

A   Oh, exactly. All the way through. They were caricatures, and that's why we love them, because Dickens as a writer was a caricaturist. He was writing in that tradition, although he didn't think so. I've always loved Dickens, though my grandfather rather despised him; he said Thackeray was a man, and Dickens was a sentimentalist. He was right up to a point. To me, Thackeray wrote one great book, a book I've never illustrated—*Vanity Fair*. What a little bitch she was, Becky Sharp—what a little bitch!

Q   *Looking at your drawings for Surtees, in* Hunting with Mr. Jorrocks, *I noticed that you'd quite often chosen to illustrate the same scenes as Leech did in* Handley Cross.

A   They're much better, much better than mine. Mind you, Leech could draw horses and I'm damned if I can. It was a horse-drawn world, and a horse was an everyday object. It's very difficult for a modern illustrator to draw horses; you never see them.

Q   *Do you consciously take after Leech or Caldecott? Or is it coincidence that you often illustrate the same sort of subject? I'm thinking of one particular picture in the Surtees—of Mr. Jorrocks from the back, clambering through the mud after his vanishing horse with a whip raised in one hand. This is almost exactly the same as Leech's, in composition at any rate.*

A   I don't look up their work if they've illustrated a book before me. I don't think I did with Jorrocks. I start out on my own, but if I want to draw horses in different positions and I can't, I pinch a little bit, you know. I've learnt to draw them by looking at Caldecott and Leech. I find that the great man there is Caldecott, who's a marvelous draughtsman.

Q   *Even when the pictures are of the same scene there's a world of difference between yours and theirs—what do you think it is?*

A   Well. We live in a different age; we all draw for ourselves. Time will tell whether people will like it as much.

Q   *Do you prefer doing your own books to collaborating with other authors?*

A   That depends very much on the author. You can take it that when it comes to children's books, I'd rather illustrate my own, because I know exactly what I want. I've got the picture in my mind, don't you see; whereas if you're collaborating with an author, you've got to think of what the author thinks, and you've got to do a bit of extrasensory perception in some cases, to try and catch on.

Q   *Some don't try; Charles Keeping said in one of our interviews that he went by what he wanted, not what the author wanted.*

A   I, on the contrary, pride myself on being a professional, and I pride myself that I try very, very, very hard to be honest with the author. Whether I'm always right is another matter. But I try tremendously hard. I'll give you an example. A good many years ago I illustrated *Barchester Towers* by Anthony Trollope, a lovely book. The editor who was seeing it through the press was Michael Sadleir, the writer, and I made a drawing of Mr. Slope, of exactly what I thought Mr. Slope looked like. We had a great quarrel about that; Sadleir said I made him far too good-looking. I was struck by that, because I'd read

Illustration by Phiz (Hablot K. Browne) of a scene from *David Copperfield*.

The same scene by Edward Ardizzone.

the book so carefully, and I realized that though he was quite a good-looking man, he was a horrible man. His hands were sweaty, and he wasn't a gentleman, and I think I'd got him perfectly. He was a good-looking non-gent with sweaty hands. And Sadleir wanted him to be a caricature of a rather awful ugly person, but it wasn't true. So I do try awfully hard to get it right by the author. Whether Trollope would have agreed, I don't know, of course. With modern authors you can tell.

Q *Have any modern authors ever objected to your drawings?*

A No, the curious thing is I've never had a comeback. I've never had anybody say the character wasn't right. Ever.

Q *And some have gone overboard to say how much they liked them, like Eleanor Farjeon.*

A Eleanor Farjeon adored my drawings, said they were exactly right, but then you see we came from the same world. Her books are about life in the country before the 1914 war, and I was a little boy in the country before the 1914 war. So her world was mine; I couldn't go wrong. And then I've got a great belief that the illustrator should always suggest a character rather than draw it. In the same sense, I've always said that the best view of the hero is the back view. Because if you start putting faces in, careful, photographically-drawn faces, it doesn't work.

Q *How do you suggest character without drawing it? Do you deliber-ately keep the face rather vague?*

A I do little drawings. That's the answer. If you're going to do a large portrait with the face covering the whole page, then you're in for trouble, aren't you? I like drawing small figures in a setting, so you have the whole figure, very often; I like to think of an illustration as a scene on a stage, with me sitting in the front row, and there they all are, far away from me. So you get your portrayal of the characters by the way they behave, the way they stand—a fat man stands in a different way—back views, side views. Of course, you have to have a slight summary likeness—if a man's got a big nose, naturally it's an easy thing to suggest—but it's a suggestion rather than a portrait. The figure is the thing that matters, and how he sits in his chair—the terrible old man, you know, you can do him quite small and get him exactly, with his belly sitting out in front of him, the way his legs are apart because he's too fat to put them close to. Now that's what makes a likeness, just as much as the face.

Q *He's a type, isn't he? Everyone will know someone like that and be able to recognize him.*

A People can be described archetypally rather than personally. On the size of a page of illustration, that's the best thing to do; you can't really get a particular person, you get the type. Then the reader is happy. And the reader can add his own ideas onto it. I do think you must let the reader use his imagination too.

Q *You say that your world and Eleanor Farjeon's are the same—the peaceful, rural, unchanging world of before the 1914 war. Is that a world in which you feel particularly at home?*

A I think it's an easy world. I don't really like the modern world of mechanics very much. I'm very bad at drawing motor cars and airplanes. One illustrates to please oneself. I like drawing the old things, and quite frankly, I don't want to have an awful hard time trying to bring them up to date. You see, I'm a suggestive draughtsman; I don't want to put things down exactly as

Illustration by Edward Ardizzone from *Pigeons and Princesses* by James Reeves.

they are, I want to suggest them all the time. If that works for the people who look at it, that's all I mind. I'm giving them, I sometimes hope, a poetic idea.

Q   *One can read into it a nostalgia for the idyllic world of one's own childhood, when the center of life was the village shop.*

A   That may be so, but I'm an old man, you mustn't forget that. And you know, even today, little shops are the same, aren't they? And the people behind the counter, and the children who buy sweets, they're just the same. Most of the little girls now wear trousers, of course, but otherwise there's very little difference. Admittedly, they don't do those lovely things, where when you wanted to buy rice, they pulled a drawer out, shoveled it out in a scoop and put it into a paper bag. You could buy a twist of pepper in our village shop—you bought pepper by the twist. But the more I look at things—though I'm not talking about the enormous stores—the ordinary little shops are the same, the people are the same. The way they behave is the same, the way they move. I'm terribly keen on movement, and I try to get likenesses, and the flavor of the moment, by the movement. How they bend over, how their heads turn on one side or another. I try and get a form of artistic likeness in that way. I work frightfully hard, I take a great deal of trouble over getting my drawings like. I've got this new book, which I've nearly finished, about a little horse bus. The author makes it awfully difficult to illustrate in *my* way. The thing is, although I say I am not drawing factually in many ways, as a matter of fact I am drawing *extremely* factually; I really am working out what it would look like. The only point is that I don't do that terrible thing of being factual about faces—you know, vast portraits of two girls—I don't want to do that. I love to see two little girls among the trees, with a squirrel, a little set scene. The problem with this book is that first of all the author animates a thing called a horse bus (which is nonsense, but don't forget the horse bus is drawn by a horse). Well now, they're chasing the thieves—it's a real sort of chase thing—and they come across the Hangman's wharf, and there are grim gates in front of them, and the little horse bus says "We must break through! Charge!" and the poor little horse has to do what no horse could ever do, go headfirst at some gates and knock 'em down. But if you were a man who'd ever known a horse, you'd know no horse could have done it. Now that hurts me; I can't draw it; you're right up against a nonsense. I think many authors, even the best, have a very poor visual sense. You see, we've got to work from a certain amount of actuality, but they don't; they're just saying words, words, words. Authors do one of two things; either they make those sort of situations that factually can't be drawn, or they do the other thing and expect you to draw moods, which can't be drawn either—or very often can't be. You can do moods of Little Tim—so sad standing by the sea, with a hunch of his shoulders—but there are other more difficult abstract moods which they think are illustratable and are not. On the other hand, I will undertake anything—I don't care what it is, it's my job—and try and get something out of it.

Q   *Is Walter de la Mare an example?* Peacock Pie *is incredibly successful, but I had a look at your drawings for his* Bible Stories—

A   —and didn't like them nearly as much; no, nor did I, nor did I. It's not my cup of tea really. But I had to do it, of course. I drew the *Peacock Pie* drawings during the war; I was in "O" Mess, in Italy, and I got the job, and instead of my war drawings I sat in the corner of the tent and did those drawings. I adore drawing landscape. I love the country and was brought up in it, and de la Mare, in his poems, *was* my country. I love reading the Bible—the Authorized Version is the most wonderful language in the world—but beautifully told as those de la Mare stories were, they were not the Authorized Version. *Pilgrim's Progress*, now—that's marvelous language too. Again that to me is the perfect prose, simple, straightforward, no description, no nonsense about the color of people's clothes. You can draw them however you like. And after all, *Pilgrim's Progress* dealt with people in a way that was recognizable: we know the characters today. Mr Valiant-for-Truth crossing the waters singing, "and the trumpet sounded for him on the other side"—it's poetry, and poetry's always moved me. I've been in love with that book since a schoolboy, and it was the second book I illustrated. When I was thirteen years old and at boarding school, and was miserably unhappy, in 1913 (dear God, what a long time ago!) I was given a tiny book of *Pilgrim's Progress* with an introduction by R. L. Stevenson and a whole mass of tiny woodcuts; I adored them, I've got a copy now, and that started me wanting to be an illustrator. That really confirmed me in what I wanted to do.

Q   *You are always very meticulous about the objects in your pictures—the objects on mantlepieces, a certain kind of bow-fronted chest of drawers.*

A   Well, for me the surround is also important because it describes the character. It's part of the stage setting. For instance, in

45

my drawings for James Reeves' *Don Quixote*, which are some of my favorite drawings, you've got Sancho's wife and donkey and the farmyard set-up when they start—and that adds to Quixote. Of course there you've got a wonderful crib in Doré's illustrations. He does it very beautifully, the sandy country with thistles growing; and of course with books like that you do rely on old illustrations, for the costumes and things; you don't necessarily copy them, but you can use them. The knowledge they've put into it you can use too. The illustrator draws from knowledge. You cannot draw from life. You can't set up a scene. Do you remember an illustrator called Mantania—very bad, just before the war? He was very well paid, and had his own carpenters, and he used to make his scenes. Well now to me that's anathema; you've got to *know*. I follow Cruikshank's method. I can only describe it by saying that Cruikshank was extremely angry when Maclise did a caricature of him standing in a corner and drawing something. And Cruikshank said "it's a thing I've never done in my life; it all comes from my head." He was a born illustrator, you see. In the same way nobody saw Daumier drawing from life, nobody ever knew where he learnt to draw; it all came from his head. I do think I'm a born illustrator, and the born illustrator doesn't draw from life; he draws from knowledge, which he picks up everywhere. I've got countless notebooks, but I never use them for a drawing. I'm drawing from the body of my knowledge. If you're drawing from life you might just as well take photographs, and you know how horrible that is in a book.

Q   *Do you ever feel you've had too little time for your own painting?*

A   Well, I'm an RA and all that, but I've pushed it back in the sense that I don't paint as many pictures as I might. But on the other hand I'm an illustrative painter, so really it all adds up to the same thing. For many years I've been classed as an illustrator, and only now are they beginning to look at my watercolors and suggest that perhaps I am a painter. That's what really separates me from most illustrators. I started as a painter, and that's always my very first thing. For me the illustration comes second, but it's my way of making money. I enjoy it, but it's not so important. The more important thing is to paint pictures—but they are funny little pictures. They are not vast oils, and I think that's partly because I am a lazy man.

Q   *When you were made an official war artist in the 1939 war, did that go against the grain?*

A   No, it was very much for it. I was chosen—before the war I'd made a reputation, I'd had shows in the West End, and Kenneth Clark liked my work very much. I'd made my reputation painting pubs and tarts, and that meant ordinary life; I made a living at it and they got a certain acclaim, but they never sold very well—nobody wanted little drawings of pubs and tarts. It wasn't real *painting*. Anyhow, K got me the job, and I thought it was absolutely marvelous; I started the war as a wretched gunner, and suddenly this wonderful job sent me off to France as a war artist. But it was really doing my job as I had before; only instead of pubs and tarts, it was gunners, things happening—real life, and that's always fascinated me. I always felt there were plenty of horrors, unfortunately, but modern war is a strange thing—you've got your massacres and so on, but on the whole army life is only one-tenth fighting; the rest is boredom, lying about, the life of the army. The one thing you don't see in modern warfare is the enemy. There's a great deal of shot and shell, but if you saw the enemy you'd be dead, so you don't if you can possibly help it.

Q   *So did you try not to draw horrors? I remember one picture of a battlefield, and a man with his foot blown off.*

A   Yes, that was what we called an untidy battle; it was in Sicily. I was with a friend of mine, and we buzzed up to see what was to be seen, and got really involved in it. One of the tanks beside us got blown up, then a Bren gun carrier got hit and blocked the road, and we tried very hard to move it. The next thing, I saw our men running away; my word, they were running like the wind. That really put the wind up me. We picked up a chap with his hand blown off and got him back. From a pictorial point of view, there were only horrors to be seen; you can't draw shellbursts. But that sort of incident only happened occasionally. There were a lot of things I avoided drawing—I mean the Prima Sole bridge I just wouldn't draw. Bodies blown in half and—well, what was the point? It doesn't help. The photographers of the day did it better. But the camera does extraordinary things: it's the shot here and the shot there, and when you come to see it it's all collapsed. War's not like that a bit. The El Alamein battle—I couldn't have painted it. I was with the Rifle Brigade, and in front of us were two tanks which must have been disabled; far in front of you, looking like partridges in a stubble field, were our ring of anti-tank guns; beyond that you saw our own tanks, dots, tiny dots; and beyond that even smaller dots were the enemy tanks. Occasionally you'd see a column of smoke go up when one was hit, and all the time there was the tracer shot from the tank gunners, bouncing across the desert; and of course you got shells, and the black air bursts in the sky; you ought to have had a painting the size of this wall, and still you'd see nothing of it. But you saw the wounded, men being hit, you saw the close things; you could draw those. I remember at the time wishing it had been Waterloo; there'd have been something to see then—serried ranks of the thin red line, and so on. But there was nothing to see.

Q   *What sort of effect did the experience have on your later drawings? Did you go home and thankfully draw something else?*

A   Of course. What I did in the war was what I've always done. I've always been the illustrator, it's always come out of my head; so during the war I kept a diary, and made lots of little notes, and I used to dig myself in and recreate it—I think fairly truthfully too, according to the soldiers that have seen it. I tried very hard to be honest, one has to do that. I take things as they come; I'm a very simple man. Many of the great painters have had philosophical ideas behind them, but I haven't. I just see something. I have one thing which is to me all-important, which puts me slightly apart from the ordinary run of illustrators, and that is that I make pictures. Each little drawing of mine in a book is a picture in its own right, without any connection with the event, though I hope it's a double thing. But all of them, all these little things, have been very very carefully composed. You see that poor old woman sitting there—that one of the women by the bed? That old man was dying. I saw that in hospital, but I didn't draw it on the spot. I was so moved that I had to go and do something about it later. But even then it was very carefully composed, to give the punch to it. If I'd taken a photograph of it it wouldn't have looked *like* it. Finally, it's saying something about something which you feel about it. And the same with the war things; I had to make them up first of all as pictures, and secondly to say something that I feel about it all. One doesn't always succeed, unfortunately, but still that's the ideal. I'm not trying to make a philosophical comment—perhaps a profound comment may creep in by mistake, but it doesn't set out to be that, it sets out to say "Oh God, what a thing!" or "How beautiful!"

Kent, 1973

Edward Ardizzone's own children's books include: Little Tim and the Brave Sea Captain (1936); Tim and Lucy Go To Sea (1938); Tim to the Rescue (1949); Tim and Charlotte (1951); Tim in Danger (1953); Tim All Alone (1956); Nicholas and the Fast Moving Diesel (1959); Johnny the Clockmaker (1960); Paul the Hero of the Fire (1962); Tim's Friend Towser (1962); Peter the Wanderer (1963); Diana and her Rhino (1964); Tim and Ginger (1965); Sarah and Simon and No Red Paint (1965); Tim to the Lighthouse (1968); Johnny's Bad Day (1970); Lucy Brown and Mr. Grimes (1970); Tim's Last Voyage (1972).

3 Charles Keeping

Interviewed by Justin Wintle

Charles Keeping is perhaps the most exciting, but probably the most provocative, children's illustrator working in England since the Second World War. Often a stylist for style's sake, he repels as many readers as he attracts. His picture books are remarkable for their vivid, sometimes sensuous use of color. Some critics feel that on occasion, however, he over-indulges in the rainbow. *The Garden Shed* (1971) builds up to the moment when a boy watches the destruction of an old warehouse by fire, and sees the statue of a woman raked by flames first of one hue and then another. It was thought that children would identify the female masonry with their own mothers. This response was unnecessarily interpretive, but it did indicate a real problem: how does one provide a critique of a children's writer whose work does sometimes veer towards symbolism?

If powerful emotions are conveyed through color in Keeping's own picture-books, they are equally powerfully contained by line in his illustrations and drawings for other people's work. The two retellings of the Greek myths by Leon Garfield (q.v.) and Edward Blishen, *The God Beneath the Sea* and *The Golden Shadow*, provided him with an ideal metier, allowing him to create drawings that, if not abstract, are at least abstractions. They have about them a lethal, sometimes directly sexual, virility which is a welcome relief from the literal figurations that customarily adorn less unusual mythological narratives. Whether they are in any way particularly for children is another question altogether.

Charles Keeping was born in Lambeth, London, in 1924. During the Second World War he served as a wireless operator in the Royal Navy. In 1949 he attended the Regent Street Polytechnic, where he gained a National Diploma in Design. He was awarded the Kate Greenaway Medal in 1967. A lecturer in lithography at the Croydon College of Art, he lives in Bromley with his wife, Renate Meyer, and their four children.

Charles Keeping

Q   *You belong to a generation that has made illustrating children's books not only a respectable profession, but a distinguished one as well. What led you into illustration?*

A   Yes. I belonged to the generation that also served in the services in the war, and went to Art College after coming out. To be honest, I was always interested in illustration because to me it never was a dirty word. To me, some of the great artists of the past were illustrators. The whole of the Italian Renaissance was about telling the story of the Bible and biblical illustration. So you've got a form of illustration all along the line, haven't you? I think that when you come to painting pure and simple you've taken out the element of storytelling, and that's very rare. As a boy, and living right across from the Tate Gallery, Sunday afternoon was always a quick nip over to have a look at some pictures. I had a great love of Turner. But Turner I think I liked more for the fact that one thought of him as a Londoner, like oneself—a known Cockney Londoner. One identified with him as one of the great London painters. But the actual influence for most of the kids at that time was illustration—children's books, comics, that sort of thing. So the influence was very much illustration—and storytelling of course. When I was a kid my sister and I used to make stories up between the two of us and do drawings for them. I think this is how it came about. Also you have to bear in mind that when I left college—the old Marylebone School of Art, which was part of the Regent Street Polytechnic—the attitude, to be honest, was very much that we had to earn a living. I worked with a fellow for about two years, and we did a daily cartoon for a newspaper, the Daily Herald. Better forgotten now, though I did quite a few drawings and political cartoons, which also interested me. This was before I more or less drifted into illustrations as such. I also exhibited lithos and that sort of thing. But illustration was the thing I felt most strongly about, although it was first a question of needing to earn a living. I was very lucky. The first publishers I ever did a black-and-white book for was the Oxford University Press, which of course is one of the best publishers in the world, I would say, and with one of the best editors in Mabel George. But I didn't realize that at the time. I just remember Mabel George saying: this is a book about Romans, are you interested? And I thought: Oh no, I couldn't care less about the Romans. It was a thing—I just thought, I'll do the bloody Romans, even though I wasn't interested. But afterwards, looking back, it was a very good publisher to have started with.

Q   *Many of your early illustrations were very dramatic and stagey.*

Charles Keeping

Were you interested in the theater?

A   Oh very much, yeah, drama, yes, very much so. The whole drama scene—I like dramatic things, but with a certain element of realism, I think. You see, what I didn't like about some illustrations is that they were stagey in the worst sense: in other words they were literally costume drawings, more interested in whether they got the Roman gear right than in what the story was about. I think it's very important to think what the story is about. True, we can say for example what the Romans wore. . . But you know, there were an awful lot of people in those days who would have worn all sorts of things. I just don't believe they were as stereotyped as is made out. Look at us today. We live in an age of mass production in the way of clothing, and yet we're very varied. In those days I'm sure many people would have made their own clothing, so they would have been very inventive to suit themselves.

Q   *Not the same variety of cloth though?*

A   No, there wouldn't have been the same variation in cloth, but I'm still sure the styles weren't always as hard and fast as people like to think. I don't believe, for example, that all Vikings wore horns on their heads. Some might have done, some might not. Of course, I was never very interested in historical work anyway, although I was tied up with it for a while. I always saw them more as good stories. The great thing about Rosemary Sutcliff is that she's a bloody good writer, and what she writes about isn't, to me, so important.

Q   *Did you become an illustrator of children's books because you had a fascination with children's literature? Or was it the only kind of illustration in regular demand?*

A   I think the latter's nearer the truth. I didn't have a great interest in children's literature as opposed to any other kind. If you gave me the choice, naturally I would choose an adult book to read. Let me say it the other way round—I've always had an interest in children, and in the child in all of us. I don't like this great division (between child and adulthood), although there probably are some people who grow up and become adults and nothing else. But I think that for most of us there will always be something in life we can go on dreaming about, something we liked as a kid. Maybe it's houses, in which case we ought to go on with the excitement of looking inside a house for the first time. I think a lot of magic goes out of life if you're not too careful. So from that point of view I've always been interested in working in a children's field, though I wouldn't say I was the perfect children's illustrator by miles. There are those who think that the perfect illustrator thinks in children's terms, so that their work is almost like a child's, with utter simplicity. Well, this may be true, though I certainly wouldn't fit into that category. Also I always try to make every book something that I'm personally thinking about at that moment. That doesn't mean it will be good. I'm always trying to impress upon my students that you have to produce an awful lot of bad stuff before you're capable of producing something that's good, and capable of recognizing it. The idea of producing something good every time could become producing something mediocre every time. There's a book I did about three years ago called *The Garden Shed*, which a lot of people didn't like. Some took active exception to it, saying it was kitsch, and encouraged children to kill their mothers, because I made a child see a statue burn, having decorated it with flowers beforehand. I suppose you could level all these things at it. The thing is though, the book was about many things that one had seen. It was, if you like, a mixture of a funeral and the sickening habit butchers have of putting pigs' heads outside their shops and decorating them with plastic flowers. So you see, there's an awful lot of kitsch in life—how can you run away from this sort of thing when it's happening and everybody's seeing it all day? I'm like many people in life: I'm influenced by what goes on around me. And if I'm influenced, it's quite likely that whatever book I'm doing will take in the character of what I see. The flower has been used in the most horrific symbolism. I've seen films of soldiers in Vietnam with flowers stuck on the end of their bayonets, and films of people showering Hitler's feet with flowers after Austria. There's nothing more horrific than a corpse, and yet we shower the coffin with flowers. O.K., you can say, does it have to go into children's books? And I can say, why not? It's a recognizable symbol.

Q   *But you don't try to satisfy the pretense that your perception is the same as a child's?*

A   No, I don't believe one should—I don't believe one can. You can only use your perception and your ideas, and leave each child to pick them out for himself. Anyone who sets out saying, "I am going to please X number of children"—if they succeed, then good luck to them. But I don't believe that's the way you can do it at all. It's like walking into a classroom and saying "I am going to hammer mathematics into all this lot," while obviously there's going to be at least half that class who aren't in the least sensitive to mathematics. So at the best what you can say is "I'm going to teach mathematics well to maybe three or four children in this class of thirty. Those that get nothing out of it may get more out of the English teacher." So my idea is, if a few kids get something out of it, then fine; and those that don't find it in me may find it in Brian Wildsmith or John Burningham or somebody else.

Q   *You often seem to express, in your picture books and other illustrative work, a nostalgia for old London—a London that is rapidly disappearing, and which many kids who read your books won't have experienced.*

A   I think a lot of that London does still exist. I wouldn't 100 per cent go along with the nostalgia idea; otherwise I'd still live there. I had a very happy, very good childhood, comfortable in everything, although I have to say there was a lot of poverty in the area around where I lived.

Q   *Where was that?*

A   Lambeth. I was born in Lambeth Walk. We were "working comfortable" as opposed to "working poor." Certainly at the school I went to though, I used to have my sandwiches snatched away by other boys. They asked what was in them, and when I said butter, they said I was a liar. Obviously a load of kids didn't have butter, and were therefore offended. I can remember having my tie torn off because other boys didn't have ties. Maybe when you say nostalgia you're thinking of *Charley, Charlotte and the Golden Canary.* I had birds on the mind, in particular canaries, which we always seemed to have when I was a boy. I was walking through the market when I noticed these high-rise flats. I saw these kids stuck up on the balconies, and thought: They could never come down; there they are, stuck up in the modern flats, in their tiny caged balconies. Then I looked at all the kids running wild about the streets. And I thought to myself, What is best? A canary or a sparrow? You drive your car out and you see sparrows splattered over the road. But even if the sparrow gets run over, is its short life much happier than the canary's, stuck in its cage, unable to move? The book was about that, posing the question.

Q   *Perhaps as an artist you find that older London has more going for it visually?*

A   This is true to a point. I think there's no doubt about it, that there are things we are attracted to in youth that we don't get over. Horses is my particular love, and you don't see many of those about.

Q   *Given your urban upbringing, it's odd the number of animals you depict.*

A   A lot of animals, yeah. But when I was a kid there were a lot of animals in London. Even today you find them in pet shops. I'm not a great animal-lover, oddly enough. I couldn't possibly love an animal; even the word animal-lover I find obnoxious. I don't like or dislike them. I like to draw them, and I like the shapes they make. As for horses, it would be simple enough to say it's because I like the sheer smell of stables and straw and hide. In a way this does become nostalgia for one, in the same way that I've always liked the smell of printer's ink. There are certain smells you get hooked on as a child.

Q   *The cage is obviously an important symbol in* Charley, Charlotte and the Golden Canary. *One way or another it recurs in nearly every one of your picture books. In* The Spider's Web *it's there in the form of a fence, if not the web itself, operating as an ingenious artistic device and, I suspect, as much more. Again, in almost all of them, there's some form of barrier between the child-perceiver and what he sees—a window, a fence, or the cracks in* The Garden Shed. *What's the reason, do you think?*

A   I think that very strangely we do tend to look at things in that light, don't we? In *Through the Window* I actually kill

The vulture from *The Golden Shadow* (Leon Garfield and Edward Blishen), illustrated by Charles Keeping.

a dog, or *suggest* as much. I've often been struck by how we can look at a thing in the current way of describing it—television for example: we run from Vietnam to some shoot-up in Belfast to the Arab-Israeli war straight into some film, an American fantasy on violence. We run everything together in our lives. Unless you are directly involved, you are only an observer. Put it another way: very few things are adventurous when they're actually happening. A young American student was asking me about the war the other day, thinking it must have been fantastic. I told him it was thoroughly mundane and boring at the time, because one didn't think in those terms. I used to live in terror as a boy, being told how London was bombed in the Great War and how it could happen again. But when it did happen, you were just as likely to be eating an ice cream. The bombs dropped and you went on eating your ice cream. I also have the idea that we are in a way imprisoned within ourselves. Supposing you're driving home and you see a man run over. You get home and tell your wife about it, and she'll say: "Shocking was it? I've got you a steak for dinner, and have a sherry first." And in five minutes it's as though it had never happened. It's gone. That man's dead, and yet we can't contain everything, can we? I feel we observe through our own window, constantly, all the time.

Q   *I'm glad you made the analogy to television. To me it seems that* Through the Window *was a major turning point in the development of your picture books. Suddenly you were using what could be called a telly-graphic technique, a mature visual language*

which, at the same time, every modern child could understand. It's as if you were using a zoom lens, constantly adjusting the focal length from close-up to mid-shot to long-shot, from a fixed point—one side of the window. Are you interested in photography?

A   Interesting point. That book should have gone further—it was in fact originally drawn for a television film. That goes for three books that were done that way—*Joseph's Yard*, *Through the Window* and *The Garden Shed*. They were drawn on a sort of plastic, which is what gives them a slightly different look. *Joseph's Yard* and *Through the Window* were made into films by the BBC, *The Garden Shed* wasn't. In the films they really were zoomed in on—which is why they had a lot of detail. But to be fair to them, they were also written as books.

Q   *Your work is film-like, but it has a literary quality too—a stream of visual perceptions equivalent perhaps to the stream of consciousness one finds in some English writing. Did the parallel even occur to you on a conceptual level, or was it just a matter of how you were working?*

A   I would say it's always how I happen to be working at the moment. Right now I'm working on a book that started off as a comedy, and yet it has taken on one or two pathetic bits. In that I shall only use color as it happens to be a symbolic thing. In other words, most of it will be in brown, black-and-white brown, and the color will only be used to express the things the person likes or is interested in. So if you like the dog, the dog will be the only thing in color. This has happened purely because I couldn't see any color in the rest of it. It's also the first book where I am concerned with a lot of old people, which is rare for children. But I don't see why not. Take *Joseph's Yard*, done in the same film-like way we mentioned. A very simple text, which only refers to one object, one yard, one barrenness. Nothing happens except the elements.

Q   *How experimental are your books?*

A   To the extent of making books. *Joseph's Yard* almost has a symbolism of life and growth and everything about it. I could have done it simpler if I'd wanted to, but I was also thinking of the film. On one page there are three flowers, each one of which was supposed to fill the television screen. Unfortunately, I didn't have enough pages in the book, so they all had to go on one page. Right down to splitting the boy in half. And having wind at the top and snow at the bottom was another way of gaining a page, which I could ill afford to use.

Charles Keeping

Q   *With several of your books one could take two pages with several in between, and, although they would obviously be by the same artist, they wouldn't necessarily appear to be from the same book. Each page is so new and fresh.*

A   Naturally I can't see it that way. They are attempts to express something in the long run. I know though there are some people who can't stand the sight of them.

Q   *Some people have criticized you for being over-didactic—though I can't see it myself. Do you, though, ever pursue "messages"?*

A   Not that I know of—I've not tried to, that is, although everyone obviously is moralistic. It always amuses me because some of those old stories, so beloved by librarians and English teachers, are full of morals—and many of them weren't done for children anyway. It's funny how you see Grimm's stories offered to children—stories collected round the countryside and told to adults. Nearly all ancient tales and morals, and yet they all tell morals that have no possible relevance today. Everybody thinks the tale of Little Red Riding Hood is lovely stuff—Don't talk to wolves in the street! But nobody is likely to see a wolf in the bloody street, are they? If you were to do a book now in which a little girl, on her way to visit her grandmother, is offered a sweet by a man in a motor car, and is then raped and battered to death, they'll say "Oh you can't put that in a children's book!" But why a wolf? The idea of that tale was originally probably to warn people against wandering about in the woods, because you'll be eaten by a wolf. And that was probably true at the time. What people want now is an illustrator who prissies up all the morbid stories. I'm not that sort of illustrator, and I'm not going to be. What annoyed me all along in illustration for years was that nine times out of ten you had extremely good illustrators to stories that weren't as good as the drawings. What you want from each person is the best he can do at that moment, and the bigger the variety the better. That must be exciting—and for librarians I know it's exciting. What's the good if you've got nothing to hate? It's no fun.

Q   *How do the authors of the books you've illustrated react to your drawings?*

A   I don't know about all of them. I know Henry Treece liked my drawings; and I'm pretty sure Rosemary Sutcliff does, because I've always done her books; and I know Leon Garfield does, but then I've worked much closer with him than's usual between illustrators and authors.

Q   *What about Alan Garner?*

A   I only ever did the one book, *Elidor*; and of course Alan and I also won the Carnegie and Kate Greenaway awards in the same year. We tended to out-talk each other at the presentation.

Q   *I thought that the picture of the grandfather at the end of* The Garden Shed *had an uncanny resemblence to Garner.*

A   There must be something Freudian there somewhere. Yes, I suppose it does.

Q   *Almost every page of* The Garden Shed *was less dependent than the one before on the verbal text. Would you like to do picture books for children which had no words at all?*

A   It's been done of course, quite often. I think it can upset a lot of people who then read all their own thoughts into it. I think you have to have a few words if only to give some direction.

Q   *I'm sure though sometimes the words you do provide are far more shaking than any one might provide for oneself. In* Through the Window, *for instance, there is that magnified close-up of a bit of pavement and a drain in the road, with the caption "People got married there—or buried." As an adult I suppose I found that poetic, but even though it is presumably a bit of pavement next to the church, I'm sure a child, if he comprehended anything at all, would take fright.*

A   I look at things and think, what happens there? I'm not a churchgoer, except for weddings and funerals. So that is what a church means. I can't leave my feelings out of my books.

Q   *I find it's not just that you're distrustful of leaving things out; it's as much what you're insistent should be included. Take* The Spider's Web. *The words have less to do with describing the visual content, which explains itself, and more to do with establishing the shy, isolated, almost paranoic personality of the child who's seeing all these things. "I like spiders, but not on me."*

A   I laugh at those people who have a positive dislike for the child. Well, what sort of child do they like then? Do they have some set stereotype? They don't like a child who may be afraid. That boy has got a definite character. At least, to me he's not a nobody; and a lot of people are just like him, only liking things so long as they are safe from them. Why do we have to keep reproducing the tough image, the boy who always goes round being the best at everything? The bulk of people aren't like that. My boy's happy to hide behind the little girl. It annoys me that people take offense at that.

Q   *What do you do when you're not working or lecturing?*

A   I spend most of my time with my family, very little else. I like talking to friends in the pub. I've always been a great lover of the pub. Very very simple. And I like walking. I think nothing of starting here and walking over to Greenwich, and then across the river and all through the East End and half way back again. Walking has one great side to it. You can take the car, but you're so intent watching the road it's no good. If you're walking along you can absorb everything. And I can stroll into a pub for a cheese roll and listen to people. I don't like actually to get involved with them. It's suprising the things that you hear that become of use in a children's book. I like to talk about everything to a child. I don't believe in just having one thing. My famous stamping ground is the Isle of Dogs, where I walk a lot. I've always wanted to use a lovely pub there, that stands on its own and is painted red all over, and advertises Nightly Topless Go-Going. And there's a nice playground there which says "Children of Poplar's Playground—Totally Un-State-Aided." It's a bloody great bomb site. Wonderful humor round there.

Q   *Where do you get your colors from? The world just isn't as colorful as you make out.*

A   I don't use so much color now. I used a lot of color in the past. I think I was trying to put over a certain jazziness about London, the garishness of neon lights and so on. I had a weird idea that color, especially tarty color, gave it all a certain edgy vulgarity, which was a part of the London scene. But lately I've been going back to a more London color of just brown— though I don't know how I'll be thinking next year.

Q   *Your work's also been criticized for being over-sophisticated. We've touched on that criticism peripherally; but directly, how do you react to it?*

A   It's a word I've never really liked—sophistication. It's meaning-less. I don't recognize it as a valid attitude. You just do what you want, and you don't think in those terms. If other people want to, then fair enough.

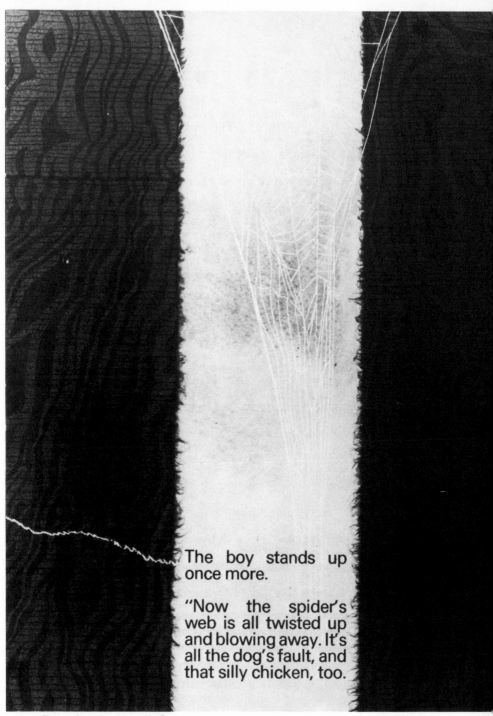

The boy stands up
once more.

"Now the spider's
web is all twisted up
and blowing away. It's
all the dog's fault, and
that silly chicken, too.

From Charles Keeping's *The Spider's Web*.

"There's that girl again. She's seen me. She's looking over at me. She wasn't afraid of the man, or the dog, or that big horse. Well, I wasn't afraid, either, really. I like that girl. I wonder whether she'll come over and play with me? I wonder what her name is?

Q   *I can see how one could formulate criteria for judging whether a piece of writing was too sophisticated for a certain age of child simply by testing its vocabulary: either it's within the child's grasp, or it's not. But visually it seems to me that you can possibly hope to push much more at a young person because his visual perception of the world isn't as stabilized as an adult's. Would you agree?*

A   Absolutely. Yes, of course you can. Because people have a built-in dislike of some things. "I know what I like"—it's the oldest saying in the world, isn't it? For instance, I'm very fond of Charlie Parker, the jazz musician, and I often play the record of "Those Foolish Things." So my daughter, who's seventeen, has grown up with that version. Just recently she heard the original Gershwin arrangement and detested it. She said it was nothing like it should be.

Q   *In your last two books,* Richard *and* The Nanny Goat and the Fierce Dog, *you seem to have gone back to a crossroads. To put it pompously,* The Spider's Web *seems to have led you into an existential trap. With* Richard *you've retreated to a simple unidentified observer situation. Has this been a deliberate step?*

A   Yeah, it's a deliberate step, very much. This was something that the publisher and I felt it was necessary to do at the moment. Slightly back to the junction. Then after that, as you said, we thought we'd go back a bit and look at what was happening. I think one can walk too far. It is a conscious step back, though the next book you see from me won't necessarily be a conscious movement in any direction.

Q   *Would you like to do adult picture books?*

A   Yes—this would be very interesting, if it could be done. There are one or two picture books I've done where I would have been able to use the full idea if I hadn't known it was being done for children. One of the first things I wanted to do was the slaughter of a horse, but it wasn't allowed.

Q   *It happened in* Black Beauty.

A   Yes, but that was Victorian times. It can't happen today. I hope people in the future will go much further than I've done—otherwise young people aren't going to come into illustrating, but they'll go somewhere else where they can do what they want. If it wasn't for a few people doing things that everybody could get annoyed about, think what a dull world it would be. The one thing that has given children's literature a kick in the last few years is the few people who've livened it up a bit—so they've all got something now to holler and shout about. This can only be good for them; and it can only be good for children's books.

Bromley, 1973

Charles Keeping's books include: Shaun and the Cart-Horse (1966); Charley, Charlotte and the Golden Canary (1967); Alfie and the Ferryboat (1968); Joseph's Yard (1969); Through the Window (1970); The Garden Shed (1971); The Spider's Web (1972); Richard (1973); The Nanny Goat and the Fierce Dog (1973); Railway Passage (1974).

4 Richard Scarry

Interviewed by Justin Wintle

If Maurice Sendak and Charles Keeping feed the young imagination, Richard Scarry, by way of complete contrast, caters to the child's need to know and understand the world around him. If the reader of Scarry's books is not already a social animal, he or she will quickly become one, although not in a deep or philosophical way.

Scarry's technique is best represented by a book like *Richard Scarry's What Do People Do All Day?* In a section called "Mother's Work Is Never Done" a matronly pig keeps a very human house clean and feeds her family in nineteen pictures of busy domestic bliss. The piglets, Sally and Harry, dressed in smocks and braces, give a helping trotter, and are generally responsible for the aura of instant, but happy, mess. Daddy Pig comes home from work, eats too much, reads his children a book of bedtime stories, and finally pulverizes the piglet's bunk when he climbs up to kiss Sally goodnight. But not to worry! Sally and Harry climb in with Mummy while Daddy snores, or snorts, his head off in his own bed. "What would we ever do if we didn't have mummies to do things for us all day—and sometimes all night?" In another section, "The Story of Seeds and How They Grow," Harry piglet learns to plant sweet-corn after a demonstration by Farmer Alfalfa, a friendly neighborhood goat, who assures Harry he has "grown the best corn I have ever seen."

Scarry's happy and numberless human animals are strangely fetal, and would doubtless feel quite at home in Enid Blyton's Toyland. But Scarry, unlike Blyton, is not afraid to throw long, interesting words at his young audience; and the evidence of teachers and parents suggests that his works offer real nutriment to their young readers.

Richard Scarry is married and has a grown-up son. He was born in Boston, in 1919, and currently has two residences in Switzerland: a modern apartment in Lausanne, close to Lake Geneva, and a chalet at Gstaad in the mountains.

Richard Scarry

Q   *Would it be fair to say that the books for which you are well known started appearing in the early to middle sixties?*

A   My major books, yes—let's say around 1962, 1963. My first big success was the *Best Word Book Ever*, which is still my best seller. It's sold over a million copies in the States as of this date, and it has also been sold in many other editions throughout the world—in Great Britain, Japan, France, Germany, Holland, Spain and so on.

Q   *Was there a takeoff point for you, a moment when you found yourself artistically?*

A   Let me go back to when I first started doing books, which was around 1947. For many years I illustrated other people's stories. My normal procedure was to illustrate a book, take it to the publisher and be given another assignment. At one point I returned a completed book and at that particular time there was no other book for me to illustrate. I was out on the street, more or less, with no work to do. So I went to another publisher, who looked at my samples and became interested in the idea of my creating my own stories. That was Doubleday's. I worked with them for a few years, writing and illustrating my own books. Then there was a change of personnel—when the art director left I left. I went back to the Golden Press of Western Publishing, and with me I took the rough outline of the *Best Word Book Ever*, which they immediately took and which immediately became a best seller. From then on I've written and illustrated all the books I've done.

Q   *Was it simply economic need that made you realize you could do the words as well as the pictures?*

A   I don't know. You just have the feeling that you can do as well as some of the stories you're illustrating. The first books I did were very "simple," though even to do that was a very difficult thing, as you probably well know. Even to make a "simple" book for children you have to be able to reach their level, and not talk above them or beneath them. You have to be able to have rapport with children of that age group, I don't think it is any different from having rapport with an adult. I get many letters from parents who say their children love my books; they say they don't mind reading them to their kids over and over again because they enjoy them themselves and also sometimes learn something from them.

Q   *Were you ever involved directly in teaching children?*

A   No, and I don't think creating books has anything to do with that at all. I am in contact with children a great deal, naturally, and not just American children. My books seem to be popular with all of them, whatever their culture.

Q   *When you do meet children, do you find yourself projecting a special Richard Scarry for them?*

A   I'm always completely my own self. I've met kids on television shows and in department stores and that sort of thing, and I treat them and talk to them exactly as if they were adults. The same is true of writing a book. Whether your reader is three years old or ninety years old, you treat them with the same respect as you'd treat anybody. By the time children are five years old they have most of their basic learning behind them, though not of course their experience. You don't use words they won't comprehend, naturally. You have to speak to them within the framework of their learning and experience. But you're polite to them as you would expect them to be polite to you.

Q   *The reason I asked if you had been a teacher is that so many of your books are built around alphabets and calendars, and things like that.*

A   When I start out on a book I want to make it as much fun as possible, whether it's a dictionary or a word book or whatever it is. In that way anything that I have in an educational manner to teach a child is going to be assimilated that much more easily. I think that the trouble with so many so-called educational books is that they tend to be dull, cut-and-dried, without a certain lightness. In past years I have worked for textbook publishers—an unfortunate period in my life. It was necessary when I didn't have other books to do. It was just so dull. Very often I was illustrating textbooks for an older age-group than I am accustomed to, and therefore necessarily more technical, less imaginative.

Q   *Are you basically an educational writer disguised as a fun-man, or a fun-man disguised as an educator?*

A   I would say a fun-man disguised as an educator. The thing is, now I only do books that I myself find fun. There's a lot of research and hard work, of course, but basically it is fun. I've done some mystery stories, which are pure fun. Those don't have any educational factors in them, except of course that they help teach a child to read. Everything has an educational value if you look for it. But it's the fun I want to get across. The fun will then carry your educational factors along with it.

Q *Even so, in nearly all your own books words are used to define the illustrated object.*

A My feeling is that if I have the space I might as well stick a word in for the child to learn. Perhaps artistically I violate a lot of laws. I tend to cram as much as I possibly can into a page. That is true.

Q *Unlike most of your contemporary illustrators, who try to have as few words as they can to accompany the artwork. The first time I opened one of your books I thought, "What a fantastic doodler!" The Danish Castle in* Busy, Busy World, *for example— lots of fun things going on in the different rooms and chambers, with nothing in particular to connect them. Would you accept that definition of your style?*

A Yes, I would go along with that. I try to put as many things onto a page as I can because I know that kids like that. They can constantly find new things that they haven't seen before. One of the things I would regret is if one sold a child a book and he read it just once. The greatest compliment I can receive is to be told that some of my books are held together with more Scotch tape than there is paper in the original book. They've been used so much that they've been torn to pieces— accidentally, of course. Children like to read things over and over again.

Q *A reaction you deliberately pursue? In one of your alphabet books,* Find Your ABC's, *on each page each letter is printed many times in red and once in black, so the reader has to search and search.*

A Here I had another ABC, and what I wanted to do was make a story out of it. So I provided these two detectives, Sam and Dudley, who go through the alphabet making a game out of it, which will hopefully teach the child to recognize the letters.

Q *Do you write your books to be used in classroom situations?*

A Not necessarily, although I know they are used in schools. To me they're simple statements of what should be said. I'm currently working on a book of numbers, grouped in fives: one to five, and six to ten. It's trying to give the concept of how numbers add up. I don't think of it as a schoolbook. I am doing

A CASTLE IN DENMARK

Here are some rules that you must obey if you live in a castle; or even if you live in a house.

Keep a light burning, so that the witches who live in your castle can find their way home at night.

Don't run in your castle or house.

Behave yourself at the dinner table.

Don't lean out of windows. You might fall out.

When they meet the King and Queen, boys should bow and girls should curtsy.

Wipe your muddy fe before you enter the ca

Do not fish in the moat.

Feed the dragon when he is hungry.

Don't be naughty. Naughty people must sit in the dungeon.

"A Castle in Denmark," from *Richard Scarry's Busy Busy World.*

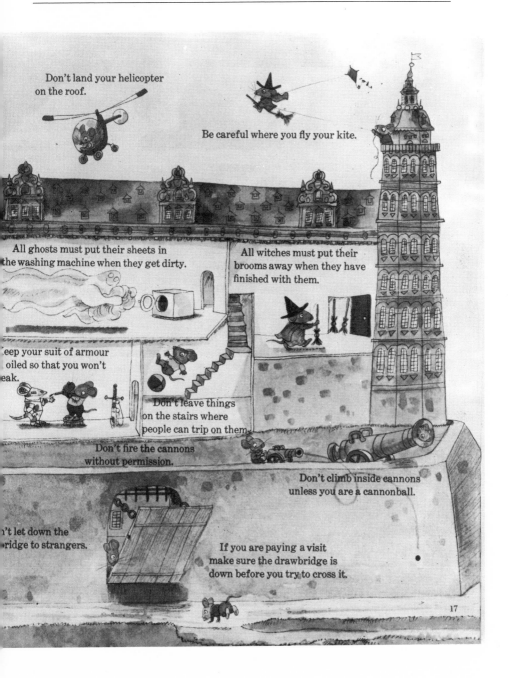

Don't land your helicopter on the roof.

Be careful where you fly your kite.

All ghosts must put their sheets in the washing machine when they get dirty.

All witches must put their brooms away when they have finished with them.

eep your suit of armour oiled so that you won't eak.

Don't leave things on the stairs where people can trip on them.

Don't fire the cannons without permission.

Don't climb inside cannons unless you are a cannonball.

't let down the ridge to strangers.

If you are paying a visit make sure the drawbridge is down before you try to cross it.

17

69

it the way I feel I can tell a child how to count. Naturally I'd like to think it's going to be used at school as well as in the home.

Q *I've always felt that there's something faintly paradoxical about an alphabet book on its own. The writer uses words to demonstrate the alphabet, yet the child needs to know the alphabet before he can understand the words.*

A The alphabet in itself means nothing until you use it to make words. Let's face it, there are thousands of thousands of alphabet books and most of them are not necessary.

Q *The ABC is used as an excuse to produce yet another book?*

A Very often it is. The thing is, you can start off and teach a child A-B-C, and the child can learn that backwards and forwards, but it won't mean a thing until you can show that "A" can be in a word like "apple" or a word like "banana." Someone, either a teacher or a parent, has to do the initial explanation. A good alphabet book will supplement what has already been learnt. I would hope that my ABC's are a stimulant, and more fun than other ABC's. If you can get that feeling of fun into it the child is going to want to grasp more and more, learn more and more.

Q *Learning the alphabet is probably the fundamental step in a modern person's education. All one's memories before then are a myth—but who actually remembers learning it? Do you?*

A I can't recall at all. I have my doubts whether anybody does. I can remember incidents that happened to me in the fourth grade, but nothing earlier than that. Little kids pick up a language just like that, and perhaps it's the same with the ABC. Living in Switzerland I've had problems, first with French, then with German. After five years or more I'm not at all fluent in either. If I'd studied them when I was very little there'd be no trouble.

Q *Why did you come to Switzerland?*

A I had spent several summers traveling in Europe, and also I'd been over here skiing in the winter. At some time I just thought I'd like to move over and live here. It's in the nature of my business that I was able to. My work is done in Switzerland and sent to New York for publication. A lot of people have the impression that I came to Switzerland for tax reasons. Apart from a concession for living overseas, I pay my taxes the same as any other American. I also pay a Swiss tax which amounts to a few thousand dollars a year, so tax is hardly my reason for living here. I like the country and I like skiing.

Q *You didn't come here out of any positive distaste for the States?*

A No, I'm not running away from America. I'm very concerned by what's happening there, as everybody else in the world should be. After all, what our president does affects everybody in the world. It's just unfortunate that not everyone has the chance to vote for the presidency. I still retain my citizenship, but I have no immediate intentions of going back.

Q *Is being an American in Europe really as analogous to being a Roman in Judea or some other province as some writers make out?*

A I don't think it's possible to avoid American society or American economic power anywhere. Right now we're in not the best financial situation, but there is no doubt that American influence is tremendous throughout the globe. Europe is different because it has a class system in a way that America doesn't. But this is changing, and I think largely because of the on-going Americanization of Europe.

Q *One thing I find very un-American about your books is that, while they reflect tenderly an essentially bourgeois society, they do not reflect the competitive idiom one tends to associate with American civilization.*

A Perhaps because in my books I do a Polyanna. Everything is rosy, everything is fine! I have very few bad characters in my books. I sometimes try to put them in but it just doesn't seem to work with me. There are a few bullies here and there who get their comeuppance. But really I'm just not interested in villains.

Q *Is that a reason why you naturally illustrate and write for very young children?*

A I don't know why I write for young children. Perhaps it's just the fact that I like to draw and use animals. I'm not interested in—or capable of, you might say—writing a teenage story. It just wouldn't appeal to me.

Q *In one book at least,* Nicky goes to the Doctor, *your Polyannaish-*

71

ness seems to overreach itself. A young rabbit goes through a series of medical tests, and, far from being ill, he is most pointedly healthy. I could see how a determined critic might accuse you of rabbity Aryanism.

A   That book was designed to be read by a child who is going to be going to doctors. I was trying to let it be known that there is nothing to fear about going to a doctor.

Q   *If you're a perfectly healthy rabbit. . .*

A   Well, so many of us have a fear of getting a shot in the arm—the anticipation is much worse than the injection itself. I was anxious to reassure a child in this situation. You tell him the doctor is his friend and there's nothing to worry about. In *What Do People Do All Day?* there is a little girl rabbit who has to go to the hospital to have her tonsils out. I try to show that this is relatively nothing. There's a dog in the next bed who tells her "I've had my tonsils out too!" He shows her it is something to brag about. Obviously, if you're having a major operation, then that is something entirely different. I don't think any book is going to help in a case like that.

Q   *Why are there never any humans in your books, but only animals? Is it just because you prefer drawing them?*

A   That's one reason, yes. I have drawn people a long time ago, but I didn't care for it. I have this feeling—and it may not be very scientific—that children find it easier to relate to animals at that age. If you have a picture of a little girl with long blond hair, then a dark-haired girl isn't going to relate to it as well as she might to a picture of a bunny rabbit. Also, a girl can relate better to a picture of a boy bunny rabbit than to a picture of a little boy. I could be wrong, but this is my feeling and this is what I am going to go along with.

Q   *Are children conditioned to react and respond to picture-book animals simply because so many picture books contain them?*

A   It's a question of which came first, the chicken or the egg. Any child who goes out and sees a bird or a bunny or a kitten will be fascinated by them.

Q   *Were you fascinated by animals when you were little?*

A   I can't recall. I can recall some of the early books I was exposed to being animal books, like the books of Thornton Burgess:

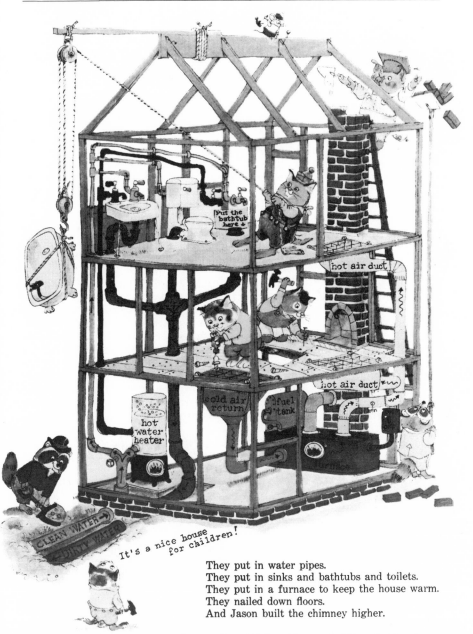

They put in water pipes.
They put in sinks and bathtubs and toilets.
They put in a furnace to keep the house warm.
They nailed down floors.
And Jason built the chimney higher.

Fixing the plumbing in a new house; from Richard Scarry's *What do People do all Day?*

73

Richard Scarry

The Adventures of Buster Bear, The Adventures of Jerry Muskrat and all the different woodland characters.

Q *Is your interest in animals entirely in what they look like, not how they behave?*

A Yes. All my characters act and dress as if they were human beings. If I have an owl and it wants to fly, then it takes an airplane. The animals have none of the particular characteristics we attribute to animals. My rabbits are not timid creatures. They are all just people, parents and children. They're completely human to me. If I was to see one running around without any clothes on I would think: There goes a streaker!

Q *What kind of training did you have to become an illustrator?*

A As a child I always drew World War I airplanes and that kind of thing mostly. I went to an art school on Saturday mornings while I was at school. After high school I went to business college for a year. Then I decided to go to an art school full-time, and studied drawing and painting for three years, after which I was drafted into the army. After I got my commission I went into Special Service School—troop entertainment, information and education. There was a request for an officer to be an art director in Algiers, so I volunteered and went. I spent my time designing army news publications, maps and other materials for the troops. After the war I went back to New York and started to freelance. For a year there was no money, but after my first assignment the work was more or less continual.

Q *Your* Storybook Dictionary *contains more than a thousand separate pictures. Do you work terribly quickly?*

A The *Best Word Book Ever* took me about three months, the *Storybook Dictionary* a little longer. *What Do People Do All Day* I think was the longest, eight or ten months, but then two months of that went into research. If I don't have a particular book in mind my publisher will say, "We think we could use a book on counting" or something like that. I say O.K., and get a big pad of paper and figure out a forty-eight page book on counting. You sit down before a piece of white paper for a few days and just doodle, trying different things out. Stories are more difficult because there's more to think of—there's a plot to be found as well. I'm confident that when I start on something I will go right through and resolve it. I've been able to do so many books that I know I'll eventually come up with something.

Q   *Your books often use the same animals again and again—Sergeant Murphy, Lowly Worm, Sam and Dudley, Huckle, et al. Do children prefer to have the same characters?*

A   Yes, I believe they like to see their familiar friends again and again—like in real life.

Q   *Do you ever get bored with the same animals?*

A   No. It's always fun.

Q   *You've mentioned research. How important is it for your books? I know a child who was reading, and loving,* What Do People Do All Day?, *all except your illustration of a house's plumbing. She could see from your picture that the pipes carrying dirty water from the bath and from the toilet were joined up. She was worried that next time she had a bath the toilet would come into her water. It was an over-simplified diagram. . .*

A   All of the things such as that, which I do research on, are factually accurate. It may be that the two pipes don't link up until they've left the house, but they still link up eventually. The basic concept is there. In that book all the technical information was presented to an expert who went through it to make sure it was perfect.

Q   *How important to you is it that children should know how these everyday things work?*

A   I think anything in life that you learn about can be interesting. For example, I was going to do something about television in that book, only we didn't have the space. How television works is a terribly complicated thing, which you could never show completely in a book of that sort. It's the same as a telephone. How does a voice travel along a wire? You can't explain it in pictures. All you can do is say, "There's a power source, and it comes over the wires." It's just one of those things you have to believe in, like How does Santa Claus get down the Chimney? I'm being a bit facetious, but it's about the same thing. You just know that Santa Claus can get down the chimney.

Q   *Do you like children to be well-behaved? Your work is full of constant reminders and exhortations to them to wipe one's feet and say thank you and all those other proper, polite things.*

A   Oh, well, yes. I try not to be pedantic about good behavior, but I feel children should be well-behaved, just as adults should be well-behaved. Everyone should treat everybody else as they would like to be treated.

Q   *Is there anything more to good behavior than convention?*

A   Good behavior is to have respect for another person, whether it's physical or mental or what have you. It's having respect for somebody else's opinion as well as opening the door for them. That's everything in life.

Q   *Finally, now that Richard Scarry books have practically become an industry, do you ever feel exploited? Do you feel hampered from waking up tomorrow morning and wanting to do something completely different?*

A   I could be taking things a lot easier than I am. I'm behind schedule on a couple of books, and there's always a certain amount of pressure on me to get things done. But I sign contracts to do books because I want to do them. Obviously it puts me under some obligations. But basically I am anxious to keep up as well as I can with my schedule and keep turning out new books. That, for me, is the most fun.

Lausanne, 1974

Richard Scarry's numerous books include: Richard Scarry's Best Word Book Ever (1964); Richard Scarry's Busy Busy World (1965); Richard Scarry's Storybook Diction-ary (1967); What Do People Do All Day? (1968); Richard Scarry's Great Big Mystery Book (1969); Richard Scarry's Great Big Schoolhouse (1969); Richard Scarry's ABC Word Book (1971); Richard Scarry's Great Big Air Book (1971); Nicky Goes to the Doctor (1971); Richard Scarry's Funniest Story Book Ever (1972); Richard Scarry's Please and Thank You Book (1973); Richard Scarry's Find Your ABC's (1973).

5 *Laurent de Brunhoff*

Interviewed by Emma Fisher

Babar the elephant, the nostalgic emblem of an idyllic middle-class existence, was created by Jean de Brunhoff in 1931. His books were quickly translated and have had a particular impact in England and America. The first Babar books were very large, beautifully drawn, colored and printed, with a simple text written in clear round calligraphy. There had been nothing quite like them before. The story of the genial elephant who escapes from the forest, meets the Old Lady, buys an outfit (including shoes and spats) at the department store, and finally becomes king of the elephants, was an immediate success. The books gave impetus to the genre of large illustrated books for young children, which have since proliferated so fantastically. *The Story of Babar* (1931), *Babar The King* (1933), *Babar's Travels* (1934), *Babar's Friend Zephir* (1936), *Babar at Home* (1938) and *Babar and Father Christmas* (1939) make up Jean de Brunhoff's *oeuvre*. He died in 1937.

Since 1946 his son Laurent has carried on Babar's adventures, taking him to America and outer space. From the original conception a thriving industry has sprung up—Little Babar Books, Babar language books, Babar on television. Inevitably, editions of the old Babar books have got successively smaller and less beautiful, and the new books do not attempt to recapture the luxuriousness of the early ones. Nevertheless they continue to be immensely successful, selling in millions all over the world. From being an innovation, Babar has become an institution.

Laurent de Brunhoff was born in 1925 and lives in Paris. He is now at work on new Babar books, and has also branched out with *Serafina the Giraffe* (1960) and *Bonhomme* (1965); a new Bonhomme book is just out in France. Laurent's elephants are astonishingly like his father's, though he himself admits that the difference between their personalities comes through. In his latest books, *Bonhomme* in particular, he has been evolving a freer, less solid, more nervous line of his own.

Laurent de Brunhoff

Q *Did your father write the Babar books for you as a child?*

A He never had it in mind to write a book for children. He was a painter, and it just happened one day that my mother narrated a story about a little elephant to us, my brother and me. We were five and four. We liked this story of the little elephant and we told my father about it. He simply had the idea of making some drawings for us. Then he became very excited about it and made a whole book, and that was the first one. Everybody around him, friends and relatives, told him he must publish it, and afterwards he continued with the same character, inventing stories himself. My mother was just the spark. He changed the first story of course, and made it his own way.

Q *He had his own printing press, didn't he? Did he publish them himself?*

A No, the four first books were published by the Condé Nast organization. Afterwards, when Babar grew, Hachette took it over. This was in 1936.

Q *And he died soon after that?*

A He died in 1937, when I was only twelve years old; so two of his books were published after his death. They were published first by a British magazine, the weekly of the *Daily Sketch—Babar at Home* and *Father Christmas—*in black and white. Then there was the war, and in 1946, I started to continue the series.

Q *In* Babar the King, *the elephants create an elephant Utopia, where everything is convenient and everybody is happy, and there are no problems like nobody wanting to collect the rubbish, but each elephant has a trade and no niche is unfilled. Did he mean this at all seriously?*

A It was a little bit serious. Because, you see, it was the time of the Front Populaire in France. French politics were very socialist and idealistic. And I think he was a bit influenced by that atmosphere, at least in making Babar a democratic king and Celesteville a place of equal opportunity. I think he had that in mind. Of course, he didn't want to make a thesis out of it. It would be a mistake to say that Jean de Brunhoff was a revolutionary. Yes, all the houses in Celesteville are identical; yes, the elephant doctor is as good as the elephant mechanic—but Jean de Brunhoff was a traditionalist. The fact that Babar is a King and his friend Cornelius is a general doesn't mean, either, that Jean de Brunhoff was a royalist.

Laurent de Brunhoff

Babar dived in and groped about with his trunk.
He felt something!
Thank goodness! It was Alexander's ear!
Quickly pulling him to the surface,
he revived him.
As for the crocodile, he swam about frantically,
but he could not free himself
from the anchor
or from the boat.

Babar saves his son from the crocodile. From *Babar at Home*, by Jean de Brunhoff.

Laurent de Brunhoff

Q   *As well as being a serious artist, your father was something of a cartoonist. There is an element of satire in the books.*

A   Yes. He had a subtle sense of humor.

Q   *For instance, the elephants' statuettes and figurines and public statues are always of elephants.*

A   No question about it. That is typical of Babar: in my last book, which is Babar going into space, I had to invent some creatures on a planet, and of course it had to be a sort of elephant. When we draw a Martian, we give him a sort of human shape; so in an elephant book, the creatures from outer space must have a sort of elephant shape.

Q   *When you started drawing your own Babar books, did you try to make them as like his as possible?*

A   Of course, yes. It was the only way to do it. Furthermore, I was used to this character; he grew up with me and I did lots of little elephants all over my copybooks at school. It was later that I understood that it was actually a bit difficult; because the personality of my father was different. I believe he was more naive, more innocent, than I am.

Q   *How does that come out in the books?*

A   For instance, when my father drew a jampot or a flower, it was the essence of the jampot, of the flower.

Q   *That's an artist's vision—making the flower into the ideal flower.*

A   I mean he was not conscious of it. He didn't *want* to make the ideal flower. But we are trying very hard to find differences between Jean and Laurent; actually there are also differences of graphic style from one book to another in my father's series as well as in my own. Anyway the essential thing to notice is, on the contrary, the similarity of the styles. I have met I don't know how many people who tell me "Is it possible that two people have drawn the different Babar books? No one can see any difference."

Q   *The technique of drawing is remarkably alike. But the difference is in the subjects.*

A   Times have changed. Then too, I am very interested by fantastic decors. I am thinking for instance, of *Babar's Visit to Bird*

Laurent de Brunhoff

They found Babar at last.
Pom, Flora and Alexander
rushed up to him in great excitement,
to bring him the visitors
who were Piros and Cardombal, Ambassadors
from the King of the Birds.
"Welcome to Elephant Land," said Babar. "I have
heard a great deal about
your Island
and your King.
What news do you bring me?"

Babar meets the bird ambassador, in *Babar's Visit to Bird Island* by Laurent de Brunhoff.

Island, where there are large spreads full of birds, which might be called fantastic. I don't think my father would have had the idea of making such a picture.

Q   *He was more interested in French bourgeois life—going to the shops, having children.*

A   Yes, very simple things. However, he also made monsters for the dream in *Babar the King.*

Q   *But they are moral monsters; they have a meaning. The monsters are disease—sloth, and other bad things—and the angelic elephants who chase them away are happiness, hard work and perseverance.*

A   Yes, his monsters represent evil. In another of his books, *Babar and Zephir*, which is more like fairy tale, there are also frightening monsters: they could change the little monkey into a stone if he was not amusing. Evil again. When I create monsters—I haven't done it in Babar yet, but in other books—they are not frightening moral monsters; and ethics of good and evil have nothing to do with the fantastic genre. For me the fantastic is normal, an everyday matter.

Q   *Isn't this true of Jean de Brunhoff also, for instance when he draws an elephant riding on a camel?*

A   Babar and the elephants act like men, so the absurdity of an elephant riding a camel disappears; it is merely a simple thing to do.

Q   *I have always been worried by the philosophy the Old Lady propounds in* Babar the King, *that one must work and play and then one will be happy. It doesn't stop anyone from being bitten by snakes.*

A   This is a characteristic of Babar, I think. Bad things never happen, or if they do, we have to rub them out. There are no horrors or ogres, as in Struwwelpeter for instance. Dramas take place, but they are never treated in a frightening fashion. There are no "bad" characters, except for the rhinos, but they are not so bad. They just have bad tempers.

Q   *There is death in some of the books, isn't there?*

A   In the first book only. Jean de Brunhoff never used that theme again. The death of Babar's mother has provoked numerous commentaries; it is a very interesting question. First you will observe that the majority of children love to be a bit frightened and even to cry, thinking that the horrible thing *could* happen to them, but fortunately it doesn't. Moreover, without cheap psychoanalysis, I could say that his mother's death is a second birth for Babar: he leaves his family, he is free, ready to face the world. When later he meets the Old Lady he actually finds a second mother, but again he leaves, and returns to the elephant country. Concerning the death of the old elephant king, I do not want to be cynical, but he dies for the purpose of the plot, to make room for Babar! It is also done in a way to show death as a natural thing.

Q   *When I was reading the books before coming over, they were always out of all the libraries. Why do you think children love Babar so much?*

A   Different things: first, an elephant is very popular, because at the same time it's funny because of the trunk, and then the big, big fat animal is somehow reassuring—children feel security with him. That is the basic thing. And the way the story is presented, this combination of imagination and real life, makes it appealing. The most bizarre things are presented just as normal; I think children like that also. An elephant going on the river in a hat, for instance, it is completely silly and crazy, and yet it is not.

Q   *Would you be able to sum up what makes a good children's book?*

A   There is no rule; if you have the ability to think and to dream in a way which is close to children's minds, you have it. Essentially you have to transmit an emotional sympathy, and to manage to give the children the possibility of identifying with the characters. I love children; they are always ready to follow you into a dream. For them there is no border between dream and reality.

Q   *Some people say that Babar has been exploited. How would you answer them?*

A   I think it is because they have seen Babar on TV, and on tee-shirts, dolls, everything. But I personally don't think that's bad. There are two ways: either you keep Babar as a very special book for a happy few, and that's all, a bibliophile's book; or you believe that Babar is for everybody, and in that case you have to use different media. And I thought it was just silly not to try something on TV. I strongly prefer animated cartoons for that sort of work; but this is so expensive that in France we tried to do something else, with puppets at first, but we were not happy with that. So then we tried live actors with masks. The result is not bad; some of those five-minute films are very funny, very nice. But the possibilities were limited. Inside Babar there was a man, he had an arm in the trunk; and he was so enormous, with this mask and costume, that we could only use one elephant, Babar surrounded by human beings. That's why we chose the part of the story where Babar stays at the Old Lady's home. No Celeste, no Arthur, no other elephant. For these films he was not King of the Elephants, he was just a little Babar. But in America they made animated cartoons for TV, and these are beautiful; I made a scenario out of the first three books, and this made a twenty-five-minute

Emilie and Bonhomme under a tree, from *Bonhomme* by Laurent de Brunhoff.

film. Peter Ustinov was the narrator, and he did all the voices: Babar, Celeste, the Old Lady, the dromedary, the fish—marvelous! They made another film from my book *Babar Comes to America*, and that was very funny also. But we are diverging; I didn't answer completely your question about the exploitation of Babar. I had begun to answer—that I think TV was a way to bring Babar to everybody. Of course there are some things I am not happy to see—Babar as a little plastic doll for instance. But it's not always very easy to control this because there are commercial and technical imperatives that you have to go along with to a certain extent. But in the long run the minor marginal things fall by the wayside and the best remain.

Q *How much money does Babar bring in a year?*

A I don't know how to talk about money.

Q *Do you find it hard to think up new adventures for Babar?*

A Sometimes, yes. I always think at the same time in drawings and in text, because I am so used to do both. So I start with an atmosphere, or a rapport, a sympathy between two characters, and it grows like that. Or it is an incident in my own life, which I think could be funny in a story. I always pick up some detail or some object, even traveling or going to the seaside, and I have my notebook with me.

Q *When you began to write your own children's books, how did you move away from your father's style?*

A *Serafina the Giraffe* was still a bit in the Babar style. But what I am doing now is more sophisticated, if you want to put it that way. I have done another book with much more text, *Gregory and the Turtle*, a story of a rabbit and turtle in a special machine, getting into a strange valley where all the animals are making music. But the character I like most is Bonhomme. I call him Bonhomme; he is neither an animal nor a man. I have just done a second book with him. In the new book he meets a big beast with scales on its back, the scales open and out come a telephone, wings, flowers, and all sorts of other crazy things. This is what I meant before when I talked about a fantastic way of telling stories. . . There is a sort of balance in my work now, a balance between these two kinds of books; always children's books, though. Between Babar, with all the atmosphere of the elephant land, always the same with different adventures; and this new style, which is more fantastic and elaborate. Maybe it is also a question of time, I mean historical time.

Laurent de Brunhoff

Babar was the expression of the bourgeois society of the 1930's and even now while I am making a Babar book the background remains the same. But nowadays, I think anxiety is more important in this world than it was in the 1930's. And maybe it is shown in this new Bonhomme. It is not only a question of personal temperament, though of course there is that also; now the world is a harder place to live in. We no longer know what is the best way of life.

Q   *I would have said that your books are an escape from that anxiety.*

A   If you dream, you escape; but at the same time there are things in my books which are essential in life, even today, and which are not at all an escape—I mean friendship and love, the search for harmony and refusal of violence. And I believe that these traits are common both in my father's books and in my own.

Paris, 1974

Laurent de Brunhoff's Babar books include: Babar and That Rascal Arthur (1947); Picnic at Babar's (1949); Babar's Visit to Bird Island (1952); Babar's Fair (1954); Babar and the Professor (1956); Serafina the Giraffe (1960); Babar Goes to America (1965); Bonhomme (1965); Babar's Birthday Surprise (1970); Babar and the Secret Planet (1972). *The first Little Babar books were excerpts from Jean de Brunhoff's large Babar books. These Little Babar books include:* Babar's Childhood (1951); Babar's Coronation (1952); Babar's Kingdom (1952); Babar at the Circus (1952); Long Live King Babar (1952); Babar and His Children (1952); Babar and the Crocodile (1952). *And since then Laurent de Brunhoff has written many new titles for the series, including:* Babar the Gardener (1966); Babar in the Snow (1966); Babar at the Seaside (1969); Babar the Sportsman (1969); Babar Goes Camping (1969); Babar and the Doctor (1969); Babar the Musician (1971); Babar the Pilot (1971); Babar the Cook (1971).

6 *Charlotte Zolotow*

Interviewed by Justin Wintle

Charlotte Zolotow writes rather than illustrates picture books; indeed, she has written over fifty texts for Harper & Row, who have given her work to nearly every illustrator of repute over the last twenty years. Her first book, *The Park Book*, was published as long ago as 1944, and is still in print.

Mrs. Zolotow is concerned almost exclusively with children. Some of her books portray their everyday experiences, both inside the family and outside, and their gradual discovery of the world around them. Others create mood pieces out of incidents which, though trivial to the adult, are central to the tentative emotions of the young person. Her success, like her work, has been quiet but sustained.

Excepting ten years taken off to raise a boy and a girl, Mrs. Zolotow has worked in the juvenile department of Harper & Row since the war. She began initially as an assistant to Ursula Nordstrom, and has continued as an outstanding editor in her own right. Among her many achievements as a publisher has been to persuade Paul Zindel to write directly for children. In 1974 she was presented with the Harper Gold Medal Award for Editorial Excellence, an honor that is not necessarily automatic with long service.

Mrs. Zolotow was born in 1915, and lives in New York with her husband, Maurice Zolotow.

Charlotte Zolotow

Q   *How did you become interested in writing and editing books for children?*

A   I've always loved the physical appearance of a book, and the only field where you can get a beautiful book and a beautiful text is in the children's book field. The illustrations and the format are as important as the text; there is a collaboration between the physical and the verbal. Even with the good editions of adults' classics you rarely get this anywhere else. I do love picture books. When I first got into the field there weren't that many lovely ones around. There were some old fashioned ones. I came to work here at Harper's right from college.

Q   *As a junior editor?*

A   As a stenographer really, an assistant to someone's assistant in the adult department. Then Ursula Nordstrom took over the children's department and asked me to join her. There were just the three of us—Ursula, myself and the secretary. Now the department employs forty-four people, and Ursula herself has just retired from her administrative duties and resumed her full editorial function again. The administrative side has become really immense. With Ursula I think a lot of breakthroughs in children's books were made on every level—picture books, and the books for older kids. While the picture book is my special writing field, as an editor I go all the way up through the junior high books, which I love.

Q   *One's heard quite a lot about Ursula Nordstrom, particularly as the editor of E. B. White's books. What are her special qualities as a publisher?*

A   I think she is a unique person, an absolute genius. She combines the ability to spot even potential talent with being able to draw it out of the person. She gave Maurice Sendak his first children's book to illustrate, and she discovered Tomi Ungerer. People come in with things that in themselves aren't applicable to young readers, but she recognizes a talent that can be drawn out and connected with the field. Just recently a young black artist, John Steptoe, came in with some portfolios of adult oil paintings. I saw his work and thought it was just beautiful. I knew Ursula would find a way of utilizing it. It was half past four and she was leaving for home, but she took off her hat and sat down with him. Although he said he didn't have any ideas for children's books she started talking to him and asking him questions about his life. At the end of it she told him he had the makings of a wonderful picture book with him. It would be oversimplifying it to say that he went home and came back the next day with a picture book, but that's roughly what happened. Anybody who can draw people out like that is extraordinary. It's the same thing when she's working with a writer. She won't tell you what to do, which is what a lot of bad editors do, but if there's a weakness in the manuscript, she'll keep asking the author what he was trying to do at that point. She can show where a manuscript isn't working and where it fails. I've learnt a great deal both about writing and about editing from her. She has an ability to work with young editors. She allows them the same freedom that she allows young authors. She allows them to work at their own pace, and she allows them to make their own mistakes, so they can learn from them. She never wants her juniors to become stereotypes or copies of herself.

Q   *Is the involvement of so much talent in children's literature over the last ten or fifteen years due to Ursula Nordstrom and one or two other editors like her? Would there have been such a flowering without them?*

A   I'm sure there wouldn't have been, and I think Ursula was the primary force in doing unconventional children's books. She has great respect for the child, and she knows that children's emotions are very intense; and she also respects their ability to handle well-done things, artistic things. She thinks they will appreciate the very best you can do for them. She's had the courage to do things that were never done before. There'd be a tremendous outcry when some of them first came out, but after two or three years they were accepted and became a way of publishing.

Q   *For example?*

A   An example would be when she started doing Margaret Wise Brown's books. She encouraged Margaret's wild fantasy and lyrical sense, and made some incredibly beautiful books out of some of Margaret's things. Ursula really loves the beauty of language, and recently she isn't afraid to publish books where the meaning isn't easily accessible, like Sendak's *In The Night Kitchen*; but the sounds and imagery are so incredible that children love them. When *Where The Wild Things Are* (Sendak) came out, a lot of adults thought kids would be afraid of those monsters, perhaps because they were frightened themselves and wanted to attribute their own adult reactions to their children. But Ursula had the courage to publish it, and children adore it. They write to Mr. Sendak and ask "Can you tell me where the wild things are? I'd like to go there."

Charlotte Zolotow

Q *Perhaps you could tell me a bit more about your early career?*

A I left the University of Wisconsin in 1936 and worked briefly at a collector's bookstore. It was the height of the Depression, and I ran alphabetically through magazines and periodicals trying to find something to do with writing.

Q *Any kind of writing?*

A At that time, anything. I preferred children's books or poetry. The collector's bookshop I worked in specialized in American poetry—the first editions of Hart Crane and things of that sort, which fascinated me. The man who ran it said I'd do better to spend my spare time practising typing than reading the books. My sister worked at Harper's though, and an opening came up. I think the salary was twelve dollars a week, which was two dollars more than I was getting at the store.

Q *Why was Ursula Nordstrom anxious for you to join her in the children's department?*

A I had lunch with her and tried to persuade her to do some Emily Dickinson for children. I think it must have been the way I spoke that persuaded her to take me with her. That was one of the lovliest things that ever happened to me in my life.

Q *Did you know that you wanted to write for children then, or did that come later?*

A I always knew I wanted to write, but not children's books in particular. I wasn't sure enough of my own ability to think that I would ever be published at all in any form. I'd been writing since I was in fourth grade—possibly because when I was a child I was very shy and found it difficult to talk, and writing was a way of reaching out to people I couldn't manage otherwise. Then when I was working in Ursula's department I got an idea for a book I thought Margaret Wise Brown could do, about twenty-four hours in the Park. I gave Ursula a long memo about it. As she didn't quite see what I was after she asked me to expand it a little more. I went into a little more detail and she told me I'd written my first children's book! This is what I mean about Ursula: she looks for talent anywhere. If she sees anything that has any kind of beauty or poetry or fun in it she zeroes right in. That's what she did with me—and thank God. It's been a lovely experience. That book came out in 1944 and it's still in print.

90

Q   *Since then you've published about fifty picture books of your own.*

A   Fifty-six or fifty-seven. I've done two longer books, but they were not published by Harper's. The picture book really is the field that I have the greater skill in.

Q   *Your books have been illustrated by so many different illustrators—it's difficult indeed to think of any prominent children's artist who hasn't illustrated one of your texts. Has this been a matter of choice?*

A   The publisher generally arranges for the artist. Garth Williams did three of my books, and Ben Shecter did several, and Mary Chalmers did two or three. It really is a question of finding an artist who fits the particular text, and I do have several veins of writing. Again I think this is part of Ursula's genius. She can always find an artist who can get to the heart of what the author's words are. You can get two very talented people, an author and an artist, who can be mismatched. But Ursula's selections mismatch nobody.

Q   *There haven't been instances when the artist hasn't been right for your text?*

A   Not at Harper's.

Q   *And you've always been pleased?*

A   Yes. I used to wish that I could paint myself, but as I've gotten older I've realized that I was very fortunate that I couldn't because I've had a much wider range of other people's talent and imagination than my own could have given me. I feel that if I had illustrated my own books there would have been a redundancy. I would have done drawings that would literally have shown what the text already said. Ben Shecter, in a recent book of mine called *My Friend John*, took a line I had about cats—"I'm the only one who knows he's afraid of cats": he has the little boy flattened against the wall with the mother cat going by with a kitten in her mouth. Now I would simply have done a snarling cat hissing at the boy. It was a marvelous extra dimension which he contributed. All good artists do that. H. A. Rey, in my first book, has people coming into the Park in the morning and the wastebaskets are empty; when they come back at night the wastebaskets are overflowing. I didn't have that in the text. He felt his way into the story and gave it that extra reflection. A good children's book sometimes comes out as a world of its own.

Charlotte Zolotow

Q *How closely do you collaborate with the artist? Do you find your-self changing the words once he has produced a few pictures?*

A Usually I write the text and the artist does a rough dummy; then, if I like the dummy, that's fine, and the artist completes his work. Sometimes, when I finally see the pictures, I take out some of the words because the illustration has rendered them redundant. It's the same problem that movies sometimes have: the dialogue is there, and the camerawork takes over and you can eliminate the dialogue. Of course, the camera work wouldn't be there if it weren't for the original dialogue.

Q *Have you ever had difficulties with a particular illustrator's work?*

A Yes—but usually it hasn't gone very far. It takes one or two new drawings and that's it. Sometimes artists just don't have the feel for that particular book, and I've had to say no.

Q *How conscious are you of the division between yourself as a children's writer and yourself as a children's editor?*

A It has to be a very concious division because they represent totally different things. As an editor you have to turn off your reactions to the world and just react to the author and what the author wants; you have to get from him exactly what his feelings are and how he wants the book to come out. As a writer very often I would do something a totally different way, and I have to turn that side of myself off. Then, when I am writing, I have to turn off my thoughts about other people's writing and what other people might hope for me to do in a book, and come at some inner image I'm after.

Q *But has the role helped you in the other at all?*

A I think that the interrelation is the stimulation, the excitement about the field and the things that can be done. As an editor I work a lot on the teenage novels, so there's no conflict there. Even so I have to be careful if I see something isn't working: the temptation's very often there to say how it should be done, which is death to an author. You've got to let him solve his own problems. You might get one perfect book from him by suggesting actual episodes, but he wouldn't grow. It's better to get a book that isn't as strong as it might be and allow the author to develop.

Q *Do you edit books for older children by choice, or has it just worked out that way?*

A   I work with all of them, and that's how it is with most of us here. I've always read a great deal, and my criteria for children's books are much the same as they would be for an adult novel. I've had some remarkably good luck with finding some really good writers, like Paul Zindel, who when I first wrote and asked him to do a book hadn't done any novels at all. His play, *The Effect of Gamma Rays On Man In The Moon Marigolds*, had just been televized, but it hadn't been done on Broadway or won the Dramatists' Award, nor had he won the Pulitzer Prize. But the portrait of the children was so sympathetic and understanding I knew this man must know what teenagers go through. I think I'm terribly tuned in to children. Their imagery, their minds and their freshness fascinate me, and I know the intensity of their emotions is even greater than adults' most of the time, because they have no defenses the way we do. Their reactions are completely open, and feel as keenly as any adult I've ever known; and their senses are so amazing because they don't have a judgmental sense of what's good and bad. They can like the odor of manure and hate the odor of a rose. It's very much like a poet's mind, the small child's.

Q   *I've heard somewhere that you were once very involved by the work of Piaget.*

A   Not very much involved, but when I was at college I was fascinated by his books and his descriptions of the child's mind and children's verbal games. There was no special reason for this—it didn't dovetail into anything else that I was doing. Children have their own special language, and if you don't know a particular child very often you can't follow him. I remember when my son had his first day at nursery school I tried desperately to find out what had happened. It was one of the first times he had been away from me and I wanted to know whether he had liked it or not. But he always was and still is a very noncommittal person and he just wouldn't tell me. He was five I guess. Finally, when I asked for the fourth or the fifth time, he told me that the teacher had a purple skirt. If I hadn't known that he loved purple the whole thing would have been lost; but this was a way of saying, Yes, it was alright. It's this quality of children, to say something indirectly but pointedly, that Piaget understood. He was the first person I came across who took children and their words seriously. That's why I read him at college though I never really studied him. I was fascinated by his examples. I didn't follow his career or any of his conclusions.

Q   *You've implied that to write for children one has to be able to know and understand them. Did you mean to imply that?*

Charlotte Zolotow

A   I think so, yes.

Q   *But can one get inside a child's mind?*

A   I don't think you ever do get inside another child's mind, but you do get inside the child in yourself. There's a certain unresolved child in every adult. Truly I think you revert to that person inside yourself. It's a sort of double exposure, of yourself as an adult and seeing what goes on with children around you; of old memories you have inside you and your reaction to a new situation.

Q   *You've referred on and off to poetry and the poetic. Is the poetry that interests you concerned with innocence and the feelings we assume we have when we're young?*

A   My preference in poetry has always been for the lyrical, and usually that's concerned with the emotions. The concision of language in a picture book is very like the poetry form. Each word has to count because it's the connotation rather than the thing described that gets to be important in such a children's book. That's true of certain short stories as well.

Q   *In many of your books you avoid telling a story and concentrate on describing a mood—*Janey, Flocks of Birds, If It Weren't For You, The Summer Night, *to name only a few examples. Where do your books begin?*

A   A lot of my books have been generated by adult emotions—like *The Hating Book,* which came about because I was really furious at a friend of mine. We were both in our fifties and she had been misquoted to me. I was angry and couldn't understand how she could have said what she said. Going over and over that in my mind it transposed itself into the imagery of two little girls. But the intensity of it was really quite genuine. I was working with an adult emotion which I knew I'd had when I was a child as well. Any interpersonal relationship I think generates an emotion of jealousy or love or loss or hate or friendship or spite or meanness; and I think this is the crux of life for both adults and children—the way you get along with people and the emotions that come about through your relationships with them.

Q   *Are you concerned simply to reflect these emotions, or do you seek to enrich the lives of your young readers in some other way in your books?*

Charlotte Zolotow

A   I don't think I set out with the concept of expanding anybody's vision, if that's what you mean. I really get caught up in the mood and try to get it on paper; and when I get that caught up in a feeling, as an adult I usually have some form or shape to it. I do think a certain philosophy evolves from these books, but it isn't the philosophy that comes first. It's the incident that comes first, and the artistic form gives it some shape and meaning. If you set out to preach to a child you generally become rather artificial.

Q   *That takes one back to Piaget, and his critique of what he called suggestive questioning. Very often when adults ask children a question they imply what kind of answer they want or what kind of answer is "right," and thereby limit the child's self-expression. By way of contrast, your books are refreshingly open-ended.*

A   I'm glad if that happens. It's the way I feel all human beings should be with each other. If you really want to know what another person is like you musn't impose yourself on him. Even in these books I hope that nobody is wagging a finger at the children saying, *This* is how you must feel. I want them to make their own interpretations and go off in their own directions.

Q   *Do you think children are more or less impressionable than most adults allow for?*

A   Children are so different, one from the other. I don't think they ever really let you know what's going on. They carry on at one level with themselves and at another with adults. You can get a very sensitive child and a seemingly insensitive child and never know the difference on a casual encounter. They all have such different ways of protecting themselves in relating to people, and so much is conditioned by their family life. I made a study once of some babies the first weeks after they were born. I studied the way they went for the breast, the way they fell asleep or how easily distracted they were. Those patterns continued right into adult life. The kid that knew exactly how much milk he wanted the third day of his life is the one who goes straight for the kind of job he wants. I think it's a mystery how these patterns persist despite the influences of their education and the culture around them. On the other hand I think no matter how different the basic personality is, there's a common humanness that we all have, and that we can unite the most widely different personalities if we were only honest enough to say how lonely or unhappy we are. But it's pretty hard to admit to these emotions in some situations. As we get older we think it's wiser not to.

Charlotte Zolotow

Q   *You must have observed your own children closely when they were young. Were they aware that they were being observed?*

A   I don't think they were particularly aware of it because it was going on all the time. I observed not only my own children but anything that was going on around me. I've got antennae or a camera-eye I guess, but a terrible memory for facts and dates. At times when I should be paying attention something inside me is recording other things.

Q   *You certainly have a knack for recognizing structures in what children say, of making a book from a phrase.*

A   There are things that if you are exposed to children you do hear over and over again, and you try to think what they mean to them. There's always a larger significance than the single phrase. In a book of mine called in fact *Over And Over* one of the things that the little girl says to her brother is "If you have a nightmare I'll come and blow on it." This is something my daughter said to me when she was about three years old. It was just too beautiful to go to waste. So some of the very phrases I hear children use become a starting-point. My son had a big stuffed rabbit once. He came with it saying "This is a bunny looking for Easter, but he may find Wester." He thought Easter was a place instead of a time. I did a book called *The Bunny Who Found Easter*. Sometimes it's a line of poetry running through my head that sets me off—it hits some chord inside my head, even though I may not use any of the words in the original line. There are some writers who can set me off and others, even better writers, who in no way touch anything inside myself.

Q   *Whom do you particularly admire?*

A   The writer I would most like to have been is Katherine Mansfield. She could have written magnificent children's books because she was aware of every sensory thing that happened, and at the same time the intelligence played over enough to see what was going on. She had that sense of immediacy that I find terribly important. I used to like Virginia Woolf, but as I've gotten older I find I like her less. A beautiful writer, but so much intellect that covers the emotion.

Q   *You said at the beginning of the interview that you write in several different "veins." How would you enumerate them?*

A   It's easier to say what I don't do. I've never done fantasy; I've never done a plotted book; and I never do humor *per se*. I think there is humor in some of my books, but it isn't for its own sake. If it's there it's to help develop whatever idea I'm after. Very often looking at something as an adult that you felt as a child you spark off a slightly funny angle—as in *Mr. Rabbit And The Lovely Present*.

Q   *Which did in its way have a beginning, a middle and an end.*

A   Yes. Actually that was two books. It started out as some color books. Ursula saw them and said there was no emotional focal point, nothing that really made them for a child. I didn't know what to do until years later I heard my daughter ask somebody what she could get me for a present. The woman said "Why don't you go pick a bunch of flowers?" My daughter said—"Yes, I can get red ones and blue ones and green ones"; and suddenly it drew the idea together.

Q   *You must have been thrilled by Maurice Sendak's pictures?*

A   Oh yes I was. I don't think Sendak has ever done anything in that impressionistic style again. But then every book of his is completely different.

Q   *Which yours aren't. . . Can we get back to those veins?*

A   There are the interpersonal ones that deal with brother and sister, or big sister and little sister—things of that sort. Then there are the pure mood ones, like *The Storm Book*, which have to do with things in nature—books that are more sensory than emotional. And then there are a few that do have a plot—like *A Tiger Called Thomas*, though that combines the interpersonal as well. It's about a little boy who doesn't want to go out because he's shy, but behind a mask he feels he'd be able to. So on Halloween Night he goes out with his mask. I did have more of an intellectual concept in that one than I usually have—that many of us feel safer behind a mask when we go out, whereas the people who actually see under the mask like us just as well. That book required a plot and there was some fun along the way. There was also one called *Indian Indian*—that was plotted too. I don't think they're my strongest books, though some of them have been very popular.

Q   *Do you find that your kind of picture books, especially perhaps the "mood" books, have had their imitators?*

A   I think a lot of people have followed me. It is egotistic to say it, but it is true I think. Some have taken up where I leave off and gone into their own marvelous things. Many of the mood books were taken up by many other people. I did one book called *The Sleeping Book*. Well, there must be about 300 books about sleepiness on the market now. Each person does it in his own way, and of course I derived from Margaret Wise Brown. This isn't a matter of imitating. It's a matter of learning from somebody you admire tremendously. I think there have been a lot of take-offs of my interpersonal books—some of them badly done, some of them beautifully done. Often we get submissions here that are almost identical copies of things I've done. Again, we have young artists come in and you see the influence of Sendak in their drawings. But they may go on and develop their own vision of the world having shown they've got the technique. We are all a chain reaction; everybody derives something from the people that came before.

Q   *One book of yours*, A Father Like That, *which shows a little*

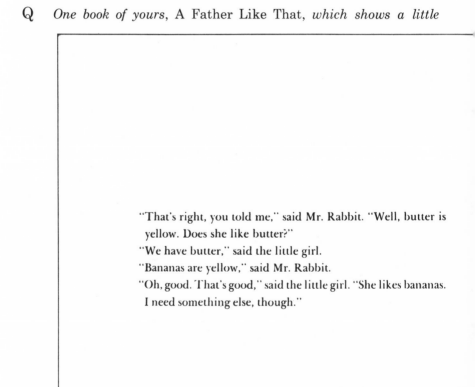

"That's right, you told me," said Mr. Rabbit. "Well, butter is yellow. Does she like butter?"

"We have butter," said the little girl.

"Bananas are yellow," said Mr. Rabbit.

"Oh, good. That's good," said the little girl. "She likes bananas. I need something else, though."

Mr. Rabbit and the Lovely Present by Charlotte Zolotow; illustrated by Maurice Sendak.

boy reflecting on what his father might be like if he had one, seemed to me a risky book to do for the very young.

A   That came out of a deep feeling that kids so often have no parent or an imperfect parent. All through that book I was working toward the ending, the feeling that if you can't create your parents you're at the mercy of them whether they're there or not there. The only way out of that is to grow up and become the parent you would like to have had. It isn't just parents—it's a thousand other things you wish other people would do or be, and which they're not going to do or be. But if you can make yourself do or be that, then at least there's one person who's fulfilling this goodness. Why did you think it was risky? Because it might upset them?

Q   *Because it gets close to a very real, very pathetic situation; because of the realism of the emotion described.*

Charlotte Zolotow

A   It's a genuine thing that kids experience, because of the war and because of so many divorces. We get a lot of books that try to explain divorce to children in a very flat-footed way. They're not really books, they're not really stories: they're a sort of preaching. A reconstruction of an emotional need I think can reach a child much better. There is no answer if there is no father, except the hope that you can get to be a father yourself. It's not a lesson, but it's a thought I would like to carry further, because I think so much of the misery in the world is caused by wanting to make other people over into the way we think they should be. If we could just settle for being that way ourselves we'd be ahead.

Q   *You manage to find sufficient poetry in the world though.*

A   I don't think it's perfect at all. Candide called it "this not best of all possible worlds"; but it's the desire for the possible world that each of my books takes off from. I think the world is a combination of absolute beauty and mystery and horror. Such dreadful things go on at every level—among humans and even in nature. The contrast of the two fascinates me. A friend of mine once got very angry when I observed that the crocuses were blooming in the middle of everything else going wrong. They thought this was an evasion. But it wasn't an evasion. It was just something to balance, however small.

New York, 1974

Among Charlotte Zolotow's many books are: The Park Book (1944: H. A. Rey); The Storm Book (1952: Margaret Bloy Graham); Over and Over (1957: Garth Williams); Big Sister and Little Sister (1958: Martha Alexander); Big Brother (1960: Mary Chalmers); The Three Funny Friends (1961: Mary Chalmers); Mr. Rabbit and the Lovely Present (1962: Maurice Sendak, a Newberry Honor Book); The Quarreling Book (1963: Arnold Lobel); A Rose, A Bridge, and A Wild Black Horse (1964: Uri Shulevitz); Flocks of Birds (1965: Joan Berg); Someday (1965: Arnold Lobel); When I Have A Little Girl (1965: Hilary Knight); If It Weren't For You (1966: Ben Shecter); When I Have A Son (1967: Hilary Knight); Summer Is. . . (1967: Janet Archer); All That Sunlight (1967: Walter Stein); My Friend John (1968: Ben Shecter); The Hating Book (1969: Ben Shecter); Wake Up and Good Night (1971: Leonard Weisgard); A Father Like That (1971: Ben Shecter); Hold My Hand (1972: Thomas di Grazia); William's Doll (1972: William Pene du Bois); Janey (1973: Ronald Himler); My Grandson Lew (1974: William Pene du Bois); The Summer Night (1974: Ben Shecter). *Mrs. Zolotow has also edited* An Overpraised Season: 10 Stories of Youth (1973).
Note: The names of her illustrators are given in brackets.

100

7 Roald Dahl

Interviewed by Justin Wintle

Having established a reputation as a brilliant adult short story writer in the fifties with collections like *Someone Like You* (1954) and the best-selling *Kiss Kiss* (1959), Roald Dahl spent the next decade establishing himself as a first-rank children's writer. While many children's authors find themselves writing for adults by default, and vice versa, his is a genuine versatility. He has turned his hand to film scripts, *You Only Live Twice* among them.

At its best Dahl's writing for children is full of zany and humorous invention. *Charlie and the Chocolate Factory*, which has already sold over a million copies in the United States alone, is the story of a good but impoverished boy who wins the fifth and final Golden Ticket to see Willy Wonka's Chocolate Factory. Each of his four companions is a caricature of a childish weakness: the spoilt Veruca Salt, the gum-chewing Violet Beauregarde, greedy Augustus Gloop, and Mike Teavee; and one by one they disappear in situations curiously appropriate to their faults. Their dismissals are celebrated by the Oompa-Loompas in songs which are strongly reminiscent of Hilaire Belloc's *Cautionary Verses*.

Charlie and the Great Glass Elevator is a follow-on, and Willy Wonka once again appears as the magician-like host to a series of wild and improbable events. Structurally this is an imperfect book, falling into two halves which seem to bear little or no relation to each other. But the speed of the narrative and the playful exuberance of the words may make this no more than a minor concern to the young reader.

Roald Dahl was born of Norwegian parents in 1916 in the Welsh town of Llandaff, and was educated at Repton. After participating in an exploration of the interior of Newfoundland he joined the Shell Oil Company who sent him to Dar-es-Salaam. When war broke out he enlisted with the R.A.F. at Nairobi, and was soon afterwards shot down in the Libyan desert. After further action over Greece and Syria, Dahl was posted to Washington as Assistant Air Attaché. In 1952, having stayed over in America, he married the Academy Award winning actress Patricia Neal. He has now resettled in England, living in Buckinghamshire with his wife and four children.

Roald Dahl

Q   *Perhaps we could begin with establishing the facts of your biography. You left school and joined an oil company. . .*

A   I went to Repton with Geoffrey Fisher as my headmaster. He later became Archbishop of Canterbury. My mother asked me if I wanted to go to Oxford or Cambridge—in those days you could get in without being particularly clever; but I said "No, I want to travel." So I interviewed and got a job with something called the Eastern Staff of the Shell Company—a good job. They train you for about two years, and then you get sent abroad—could be anywhere in the world. You wait your time until you get to the top of the list. When my turn came it was Egypt. I was summoned, but I said "No sir, I don't want to go to Egypt." "Good heavens boy, it's the best area we've got. Why not?" I couldn't think of anything, so I just said "It's too dusty." He let me off and the next fellow went. Then came East Africa, and I said "Yes, Please."

Q   *That was Tanzania?*

A   Yes. The boat stopped at Mombasa, and a man met me and said "You get on board this other little boat," which is how I got to Dar-es-Salaam. Marvelous, very exciting, those days. No airplanes. One really was a long way from anywhere. Coconut palms and beaches and crazy things, selling oil to sisal planters and diamond miners, gold miners, and learning Swahili. I was there until September 1939 when the war broke out. I borrowed an old car and made the long and wonderful drive across Tanzania, past Kilimanjaro, through the Masai country and up to Nairobi to join the Royal Air Force. We did our initial flying over Nairobi airport with Tiger Moths. Then we were sent to Baghdad, and then to a squadron in the Western Desert—Libya.

Q   *Where you were shot down?*

A   Yes—and in not too long a time. I spent quite a while in hospital in Alexandria—fractured skull and things. Then we got Hurricanes and flew to Greece just in time to have a bit of a show and then get kicked out by the Germans. It was quite a dicey exciting time. Then there was the Syrian campaign against the ridiculous Vichy French. And then my head injuries caught up with me and I was told I couldn't fly any more, so I was boated back to England—1942 I think. Next a very interesting thing happened. I was waiting at Uxbridge R.A.F. camp, trying to get medically fit enough to become a flying instructor. A man in the officers' mess, a middle-aged baldheaded fellow, suggested I went up to London with him for dinner. He took me to probably the most exclusive small club in London, a tiny little place where even in the height of wartime they were sizzling lamb chops over a wooden fire. Everyone sat together at wooden tables. I sat with my friend on one side and some other fellow on the other. Next morning I was summoned to the Commanding Officer's room at Uxbridge. I was told to go at once to see the Under-Secretary of State for Air, Harold Balfour, number two in the whole R.A.F. Without knowing it, I had been sitting next to him the night before at dinner. Apparently, he had liked me, and said he was sending me to Washington to be Assistant Air Attaché. He insisted, so I went. I suppose if I hadn't gone I might never have written anything.

Q   *How was that?*

A   Shortly after I arrived, the British Embassy, with all its concentration on getting America into the war and getting publicity for Britain, sent a man to interview me—because although I hadn't done anything particularly brave in the air, I had anyway been in combat, as they called it in America. This man was none other than C. S. Forester, the great Hornblower writer. He had a contract with the *Saturday Evening Post*. He took me to lunch and said: "You tell me your most exciting experience, and I'll write it up, and they'll take it." I started to tell him, but the story began to get a bit bogged down, so I said: "Look, would it help if I scribbled this out in the evening and posted it on? Then you can put it right." He thought that would be great. So we finished our lunch and said goodbye. I went home and wrote out my piece about getting shot down. About a week later came a letter from Forester and a check for a thousand dollars. It had sold to the *Saturday Evening Post* without being touched. They wanted as many more as I could let them have.

Q   *That story was published under your name or his?*

A   My name. He was wonderfully kind about it. He gave me the whole thing. He was a nice fellow. Then I thought, surely it can't be as easy as this, a thousand dollars. . . I sat down and wrote another, which was bought at once. I did about seventeen off the reel in the evenings, and they were all sold to major American magazines; and so suddenly I was a writer. I was making them up in the end. They were fantasy flying stories which came out in a book *(Over to You)*. Then the war ended and I went to the Shell Company and told them I would like to try to go on being a writer. They thought I was crazy. But they gave me my provident fund—about a thousand quid—and off I went to Amersham, where my mother lived, and started writing pure fiction short stories. Most of these went to the *New Yorker*, which in those days was a fine magazine with an illustrous stable of short story writers like Salinger, Collier, Cheever, O'Hara and the rest. Later, I went to New York and lived in a little flat there, pushed by some friends to do it, and got closer to my editors, who helped me greatly. Then I put together the first volume of these stories (*Someone Like You*) and looked around for a publisher. I had several offers through my agent. Then suddenly the phone went in my little flat, and a voice said: "This is Alfred Knopf." To me, and indeed to most people, this man was the greatest and most celebrated publisher in America. It flashed through my mind—What an extraordinary thing, he didn't even get a secretary to ask me to hold on a minute, or anything like that. He had dialed my number himself! I learned later that he thinks it discourteous, if he wants to talk to someone, to keep them waiting. He always calls direct, which I think is splendid. Because of the thrill of this, I gave him the book. Alfred has been a firm friend ever since and I consider myself fortunate to have found such a splendid publisher. That book, *Someone Like You*, took me five years to write.

Q   *You finished it in 1952?*

A   Yes—it was published in 1953. Then I got married, and the next eight years or so were taken up writing the next batch, which turned into *Kiss Kiss*—again I think doing nothing else. By then we had a couple of children. A short story writer does find, I think, if he's got any discrimination and he's concerned about the quality of his work, that he runs out of plots very easily. And that is why in my opinion most short story writers who are writing today are writing mood pieces, and not short stories in the true sense of the word.

Q   *What is the true sense of the word? What is your definition of a short story?*

A   The old definition—A beginning, a middle and an end. It's a definite plot which progresses and comes to a climax, and the reader is fully satisfied when he's finished it. Salinger wrote beautiful short stories—but he only did a very limited number of them, and then he ran out. After that, he had the good sense to stop. Most of the so-called short story writers of today do not really write short stories. They write essays or mood pieces.

Just look today at the fiction in the *New Yorker*. In my humble opinion, it's the most awful rubbish. The point is, it's very hard to come upon a genuine short-story plot. Anyway I had children and couldn't think of any more short stories. So I thought, why don't I write a children's book? I'd always told them stories in bed, and some of them they seemed to take a little notice of and some they didn't. So I said: Well, I must try and find some animals or creatures or something that are original. Everyone's written about bunnies and ducks and bears and moles and rats and everything else, and Beatrix Potter's done the lot. So I searched around, but there was precious little left. But I did try to pick something new—the earthworm, the centipede, the ladybug, the grasshopper and the spider. At first they didn't look very attractive, but there was a chance I could make them amusing or interesting if one gave them character. And so I wrote *James and the Giant Peach*. It was moderately successful, always selling more each succeeding year. But it was a first children's book—the fact that you're a little bit known as a writer for adults doesn't help you very much if you go into another field. In the children's book field, above all others I think, people buy books by known children's writers. You've got to break in. An exception I think is this *Watership Down* that's just come out, which got tremendous accolades and a lot of publicity. That one leaves me fairly cold, I'm afraid, but then so does Tolkien. This is probably my own misfortune, but to me those are not stories that spin you along. They're intellectual exercises. They are not children's books. They become cults for teenagers and there's nothing wrong with that. But they are not children's books. So anyway, there was *James*, and I thought I'd try to do another—*Charlie and the Chocolate Factory*—having always loved chocolate. So why not a chocolate factory? The only alternative was a toy factory. Chocolate and toys. Those are surely the two things that play the biggest part in a child's life. So I wrote the book and got it completely wrong. I remember giving it, in about the second draft, to my young nephew, then about sixteen. He told me he didn't think it was much good. That shook me. Then I looked at it and realized he was right. It wasn't very good, but I knew there was something there, so I worked and worked away at it and finally I gave it to the publishers. It did well. On its heels *James* picked up as well. Between them they did very well, and still do. I found great pleasure in doing them. Then I wrote *The Magic Finger*. After that, *Fantastic Mr. Fox*, and then, because there was such a clamor from the children for a continuation of *Charlie*, I did *Charlie and the Great Glass Elevator*.

Q *What do you mean by clamor?*

A   I get a lot of letters from children all over the world. Oh, I don't know—maybe five hundred or so a week. And very many of them kept asking for another *Charlie* book. That's what I meant by clamor. I was a bit lucky in my timing with the second Charlie. One of the characters is an idiot President of the United States. Soon after the book came out, old Nixon started going off the rails.

Q   *Were you thinking specifically of Nixon when you wrote it?*

A   Not really, no. I had in mind all Presidents, excluding Harry Truman and FDR, who I think were rather splendid. I just didn't like the whole political system and the way in which a President is appointed and the long term he lasts and the patronage he hands out everywhere. The man is treated with such tremendous respect by the children in America. There's something dangerous about the whole thing. The kids are forced to stand up and recite the pledge of allegiance every morning at school before lessons and put their hands on their hearts and all that rubbish. It really is rubbish, dangerous rubbish. Patriotism is a good thing in small doses, but it's also a rotten thing. It leads to war.

Q   *Kiss Kiss, your most celebrated collection of short stories, was thought to be very "sick" when it first appeared. . .*

A   Was it?

Q   *The book contained an unusual number of murders and mutilations.*

A   But with humor, I hope. All the nasty things were edged with humor. If there have been any imitators of this—and I think there may have been—they've usually fallen down because they've done it straight, without humor. The macabre stuff, done without humor, is terrible.

Q   *Perhaps though it's the humorous edge that makes them sick. Mutilation made to look rather bright and. . .*

A   Funny.

Q   *Yes. And from that you turned to a kind of writing in your children's books which was much more whole-heartedly entertaining.*

A   But there's quite a bit of the stuff you're referring to in the children's books. There's plenty of it in *Charlie and the Chocolate Factory* for instance—children getting mashed up in the pipes and so on.

Q *There are lots of victims of one sort or another in your children's books—the two Aunts in* James *and the Giant Peach,* Augustus Gloop in Charlie and the Chocolate Factory. *But these are caricatures, figures of fun, and entirely expendable within the stories. In your short stories the victims are far more real, far less exaggerated in their vices, and not nearly so expendable.*

A I think it's pointless and unrewarding to try to analyze someone's work like this. You should just take it or leave it.

Q *Many of your short story characters were collectors of one kind or another, people with very particular tastes. . .*

A Yes, I suppose that's because I'm enormously interested in a number of things and have a fair knowledge of pictures, furniture, wines, etcetera. They are all things I love. So I make use of them. It's no good writing about things you don't know about. That's basic. Greyhound racing was another of my loves. I used to breed racing greyhounds. I knew about them so I wrote about them.

Q *There must have been occasions when you did some kind of research.*

A Not a lot.

Q *What about "William and Mary," and all that business about excavating a living brain?*

A I discussed that one, of course, with a neurosurgeon. But I do have a fair amateur knowledge of neurology and neurosurgery.

Q *How long did it take you to write each of the stories in, say,* Kiss Kiss?

A Each story takes about four to six months, working every morning, six or seven days a week, from ten until lunchtime, and again in the afternoon from four to six. The rest of the time is spent pottering about.

Q *Six months is a long time on one story.*

A But it's the only way I can get them halfway decent. I mistrust very much facile writers who write quickly and don't work hard on revision. D. H. Lawrence was the big exception, but he was a genius.

Q *There must be a temptation sometimes to spend the rest of your life polishing one story. How do you decide when something's completed?*

A It gradually takes shape and becomes final. The important thing is not to be in a hurry. And in order to do that one needs to be under no financial pressure. Luckily before I was married, though I didn't have much money, I only had myself to support. I made roughly six thousand dollars a year, selling about two and one-half stories annually, which was enough. There has never been any pressure to finish it quickly and sell it. I don't think I could work well like that.

Q *Why then did you let yourself in for doing the film scripts, when I imagine you must have had very firm deadlines to meet?*

A Pat (my wife) had become very ill with a stroke. So, there were first of all immense expenses for hospitalization in America. There were also immense expenses with my son's head injuries. I remember his pediatrician in New York charged five thousand dollars for the first ten days, and he wasn't even the surgeon. I was now the sole source of income for five children, so I began to feel uneasy. But you are right. I did actually write one film script before Pat had her stroke. We were in Honolulu where Pat was doing a film for Otto Preminger (*In Harm's Way*, with John Wayne). I was piddling about with a story. Two fellows flew in from Los Angeles to see me—one of them was called Robert Altman, then an unknown television director (he later directed *MASH*)—with a little plot by Bob Altman they wanted me to turn into a TV series. I said—"No—please go away." They stayed around for a week getting drunker and drunker. It was a neat little plot, and in the end, I think more to get rid of them than anything else, I said I would try and do a film script. I also promised Bob Altman that if anything came of it, he would direct the film. I wrote the screenplay. Then Pat had the stroke. I needed money like hell. I offered the screenplay to the big studios. United Artists loved it. Said they would pay $150,000 for it. Okay, I said, but Mr. Robert Altman must direct it. "Robert Altman!" they cried. "Are you crazy? He's a television director!" So we were deadlocked. Altman was pretty tough about it. He said either he directed it or I could tear the bloody thing up. In the end he released me from my promise that he direct on condition I gave him half my fee—$75,000. So I did. But United Artists were silly asses not to have him. They couldn't recognize talent when they saw it staring them in the face.

Q   *So what happened to the script?*

A   They hired instead a director who had about four flops running in Hollywood—a solid old fellow. They went off to Switzerland, shot about two hundred feet of film in a month, spent a fortune on nothing and came back. Gregory Peck was in that fiasco.

Q   *What about the Bond film you did,* You Only Live Twice?

A   I enjoyed doing that enormously because Lewis Gilbert directed it. He was very competent and never went away from the screenplay at all. Quite different from shooting, ugh—*Chitty Chitty Bang Bang.*

Q   *How did you get into that?*

A   It followed right on from the Bond film. Broccoli owned the rights to *Chitty* and asked me to do it. I did the first draft after which they paid me off, to make way for the director, Ken Hughes, to do what he liked with it. He rewrote the entire screenplay and you've seen the result. And then the same thing happened with *Charlie*, which I was longing to do. I did the screenplay and they hired a director called Mel Stewart. I do not like film directors very much. They lack humility and they are too damn sure that everything they do is right. The trouble is that it's mostly wrong. Oh, what a mess that man made of *Charlie*!

Q   *And how long did it take you to write each of the children's books?*

A   Between six months and a year. The first page takes the longest, the same as a story—anything up to a month.

Q   *How long is it before you know what's going to happen in the middle of a story or a book, and how it's going to end?*

A   When I was younger, I was so confident that I would start a story with just the bare bones of the beginnings of a plot without knowing the end.

Q   *That's odd, because so many of those early stories finish with such decisive twists.*

A   This I usually found when I got to it. Just luck, I guess. Now in my older age I suddenly find I'm writing stories absorbed with sex, which didn't appear at all in the early stories, which were more or less asexual.

Q   *Except one or two like "The Landlady" in* Kiss Kiss.

A   *Yes,* "The Landlady"—that's a sort of juicy, funny story, and one called "Georgy Porgy."

Q   *Why then was the collection called* Kiss Kiss?

A   Oh good heavens, I don't know. I just liked the words.

Q   *And how do you come by your endings now?*

A   I find I now have so little confidence that I won't start on a story unless I have the whole thing plotted out first.

Q   *It seemed to me that in* Charlie and the Great Glass Elevator *the plot progressed more or less at random, almost by a casual association of somewhat disparate ideas. Did you feel the structure was weak?*

A   No.

Q   *Perhaps one of the most remarkable features of your career is your versatility as a writer—several collections of highly adult short stories, filmscripts for mass family audiences, and the children's books. Many of your contemporary children's writers, especially those writing for the adolescent age-range, have been unable to restrain themselves from exploring areas that at least traditionally have been regarded as beyond the pale of what is thought suitable for children. Some have created a licence for themselves to enter into relatively private and obsessional worlds while still apparently writing for children. You seem to have avoided this difficulty.*

A   What narks me tremendously is people who pretend they're writing for young children and they are really writing to get laughs from adults. There are too many of those about. I refuse to believe that Carroll wrote *Alice* for that little girl. It's much too complex for that.

Q   *Was there any hostile criticism to* Charlie and the Great Glass Elevator *because of the way you lampooned the President of the United States?*

A   Yes—it's banned in a number of American public libraries because it's "disrespectful."

Q   *Curious, because nothing's worth taking seriously unless it can also be taken in jest. . .*

A   Very few things are taken both ways simultaneously.

Q   *What about the Oompa-Loompas, the pigmies who work inside Willy Wonka's chocolate factory—weren't there some complaints that you were being racist?*

A   No complaints at all from children or teachers, only from those slightly kinky groups who I don't think are doing any good at all.

Q   *Is there any reason you choose to write for the younger age-range, the six-to-ten-year-olds?*

A   Yes, because after that age, by the time children are nearing their teens, they ought to be reading proper adult books, instead of a lot of rubbishy things like *Top of her Class* or *The Monitor of the Sixth Form.*

Q   *Even in your adult work, with the possible exception of some of the early R.A.F. stories, you seem always to have avoided anything personal. Have you ever wanted to make an autobiographical excursion?*

A   No.

Q   *What kind of books do you read now?*

A   I love exciting novels of any sort, but not Proust. Proust has laid beside my bed for several years and I try to read him. I can't. That, I know, is my bad luck. I just don't like it. It bores me stiff. I've never finished *Swann's Way* even. On the other hand I adore *War and Peace*, and *Madame Bovary*, real stones those.

Q   *You must have liked Rudyard Kipling.*

A   I was nurtured on him at school. Then I was profoundly fascinated and probably influenced by a book I had by my bed when I was about fourteen. It scared me a lot. It was called *Can Such Things Be?* by Ambrose Bierce. Rider Haggard I used to read a lot too, when I was young.

Q *And Henty?*

A All Henty, yes. And Captain Marryat. *Mr. Midshipman Easy*— lovely. Then later, Forester and Hemingway.

Q *And of today's children's authors?*

A I think on the whole American children's literature is more virile, if that's a good word. It's much stronger. It's faster, quicker, although there's an equal amount of rubbish published in both countries.

Q *What is it that slows up English authors?*

A They probably all have in mind that they are influenced by (a) *Alice*, (b) *The Wind In The Willows*, and (c) Beatrix Potter. They can't get those out of their minds. And those are classics. If you pick up *The Wind In The Willows* now and try to read it, you'll be astonished. It moves much too slowly. It would be lovely to rewrite it and make it go, because it's a good story; but not as it is.

Buckinghamshire, 1974

Roald Dahl's children's books include: James and the Giant Peach (1961); Charlie and the Chocolate Factory (1964); Boggis and Bunce and Bean (1970 . . . *in England,* Fantastic Mr. Fox); Charlie and the Great Glass Elevator (1973).

8 Two Letters:

For various reasons neither of these preeminent figures of children's literature was available for interview during the limited period spent in the United States. Both kindly agreed, however, to mail their answers to some written questions.

Dr. Seuss

Theodor S. Geisel, the legendary Dr. Seuss, celebrated his nativity at Springfield, Mass., in 1904. He received a B.A. at Dartmouth College in 1925, and then set sail for the University of Oxford, where he quickly decided to transfer to the Sorbonne in Paris. When his supervisor suggested that he devote two years to discovering whether Jonathan Swift wrote anything at the age of seventeen, Geisel threw in his academic towel and returned to America. For a while he worked as a cartoonist and magazine humorist, spent five years as a Hollywood screen artist, and then wound his way into advertising. He created the "Quick Henry, the Flit!" campaign for Standard Oil, and later did a series of animated television commercials for the Ford Motor Company.

Unable to find an outlet for all his energies in advertising, Geisel, having turned thirty, set about becoming Dr. Seuss. In 1937 his first book, *And To Think That I Saw It On Mulberry Street*, was published, followed by *The 500 Hats Of Bartholomew Cubbins* in 1938. These two picture books are among the most popular written this century, and deservedly so. They are masterly examples of straightforward storytelling, and their immediate success had the added virtue of convincing Dr. Seuss that he should remain Dr. Seuss. Over the next twenty years he produced a string of comparable children's classics, including *Horton Hatches The Egg*, *Thidwick The Big-Hearted Moose* and *How The Grinch Stole Christmas*.

In 1957, with the appearance of *The Cat In The Hat*, Seuss embarked on a new enterprise, Beginner Books, a division of Random House with Geisel himself as president. *The Cat In The Hat* is a lively romp with a "controlled vocabulary" of only 175 words. Over the next ten years more than fifty Beginner Books were produced, many of them created personally by Dr. Seuss, and each with a limited number of words. These books were designed to make the first stages of reading as entertaining as possible by capturing the child's attention with hilarious and occasionally sadistic art-work. The library was intended to combat the very real problem of illiteracy in the United States. Some critics have been sceptical, and feel that many children already well on the way toward literacy have been waylaid by the necessary crudities of the Beginner Books. They should not forget, however, that Dr. Seuss has continued to write excellent books in his earlier vein, and that these are certainly likely to appeal to any young child, regardless of whether he or she has been through the generally pleasant rigors of the Beginners. If anything, a recent picture book like *Did I Ever Tell You How Lucky You Are?* shows that the septuagenarian's imagination, far from slackening, is undergoing another period of growth.

Geisel has been successful in other fields as well. During the War he rose to Lieutenant Colonel in the Information and Education division of the US Army. To help the war effort he wrote and produced a film called *Your Job In Germany*, later released by Warner Brothers as *Hitler Lives* on its way to picking up an Academy Award as the Best Documentary Short in 1946. The next year he received another Academy Award for *Design For Death*, a documentary feature history of the Japanese people on which Geisel collaborated with his wife. In 1951 he was once again honored by the Academy for his animated cartoon *Gerald McBoing-Boing*. He has also made a number of animated specials out of his own books for CBS.

Dr. Seuss has probably sold more books than any other living author, so it is not surprising that he is suspected of being the richest writer alive. He lives in great style in his converted windmill (considerably added to, of course) in affluent La Jolla, near San Diego in southern California. His wife, Helen Palmer, helps Dr. Seuss with his work when not involved with her own children's books.

Dr. Seuss

Q   *What sort of childhood did you have?*

A   My childhood was normal excepting for the fact that my father ran a zoo.

Q   *Why did you leave Oxford, having come all that way?*

A   I left Lincoln College, Oxford because I had mistakenly started to take a degree in the English Schools which I found much too confining and specialized. I should have chosen Modern Greats, but it was too late to change.

Q   *Were you in Europe long enough to warrant being called an expatriate, and if so what were the benefits of that experience?*

A   Although I have spent the total of many years in Europe, I have never thought or felt like an expatriate.

Q   *When you returned to the States you took jobs in journalism and advertising. Has advertising had a responsibility for the kind of picture book you have produced for children? For instance, the ease with which you have always produced catchy jingles.*

A   Advertising experience was enormously helpful to me as a writer of children's books. It taught me conciseness and how to marry pictures with words.

Q   *Were there any specific events that made you decide to take up children's writing? What were the origins of* And To Think That I Saw It On Mulberry Street*?*

A   I wrote . . . *Mulberry Street* by accident. On a long crossing of the Atlantic the rhythm of the ship's engines got into my consciousness and I began putting words to that rhythm. The words turned out to be *And To Think That I Saw It On Mulberry Street.*

Q   *Your second book for children,* The 500 Hats Of Bartholomew Cubbins, *perhaps your most popular, conforms much more closely to the traditional notion of what a children's story is than anything else you have done. For one thing there is the familiar opposition between the peasant in his cottage and the King in his lofty palace. Did you write it as a pastiche of European fairy tales?*

A   *The 500 Hats Of Bartholomew Cubbins* was not a pastiche of European fairy tales. At the time I wrote it your fairy tales

. . . A Chinaman   A big Magician
Who eats with sticks. . . .   Doing tricks . . .

From *And To Think That I Saw It On Mulberry Street*, by Dr. Seuss.

© Dr. Seuss

A ten-foot beard
That needs a comb. . . .

No time for more,
I'm almost home.

were still popular in the USA and I decided to write one in that tradition.

Q *You have said that* Horton Hatches The Egg, *published in 1940, is your favorite. Why?*

A *Horton Hatches The Egg* is my favorite for very selfish reasons. It was the easiest book I ever wrote.

Q *When the egg hatches, an Elephant Bird is born. This is a gross distortion of the Darwinian laws of evolution, yet obviously contains a truth of a different order. What kind of truth is it that you were getting at?*

A The Elephant Bird symbolizes no great "truth." I was stuck for an ending and invented the Bird out of dire necessity.

Q *Since* Horton, *many of your books contain fantastic creations like Sneetches and Grinches, Crandalls and Zaxes. Where did they all spring from? Perhaps they have their heredity in strip cartoons.*

A My "fantastic creations" probably come into existence because I actually do not draw very well and have trouble putting together conventional animals.

Q *One is tempted to call a lot of your work a celebration of idiocy— that would certainly be one explanation of your huge popularity with children, who maybe like to feel superior in a reading situation. Is there any truth in that?*

A I would not call my work a "celebration of idiocy." I think of it rather as "logical nonsense." It seems logical to me and children, being strange, seem to find it logical.

Q *Have real children played a part in your writing? Have you tried books out on children to see how they work? Do you have children of your own?*

A I advise against any author pre-testing his books on children. It is almost impossible to get an honest reaction from kids by conducting a survey.

Q *I have read that you have not had any formal training as an illustrator. Can this be true? If so, perhaps it is one reason that your illustrations started out by being very literal (viz.* And To Think That I Saw It On Mulberry Street) *and have only slowly become more "imaginative."*

© Dr. Seuss

"An elephant's faithful One hundred per cent!" from Dr. Seuss's *Horton Hatches the Egg*.

"Look at me!

Look at me!

Look at me NOW!

It is fun to have fun

But you have to know how.

I can hold up the cup

And the milk and the cake!

I can hold up these books!

And the fish on a rake!

I can hold the toy ship

And a little toy man!

And look! With my tail

I can hold a red fan!

I can fan with the fan

As I hop on the ball!

But that is not all.

Oh, no.

That is not all. . . ."

From *The Cat in the Hat,* by Dr. Seuss.

© Dr. Seuss

A   It is true I have had no formal art training. In developing my style I have studied my liabilities and tried to turn them into assets.

Q   And To Think That I Saw It On Mulberry Street *is remarkable for its balance between words and pictures. Which usually comes first? Or does it vary, as I suspect it must.*

A   Pictures or words first? It varies. Sometimes I will "write" an entire book with pictures and add the words afterwards and vice versa.

Q   *Your most brilliant and famous contribution to the world of children's books has been the Beginner Book. How would you explain the mechanics of controlled vocabularies?*

A   Beginner Books started out with controlled vocabularies. I have since come to despise controlled vocabularies and ignore them entirely. They are completely not necessary if the writer is able to make himself clear with simple, clearly thought out sentences.

Q   *Not only did you have the initial concept for the Beginner Books, but you have consistently provided the finest examples. All this implies a great commitment on your part. What is the nature of that commitment?*

A   I am "committed" to Beginner Books primarily because there are so many illiterates running around who would not have been illiterates had they been given interesting reading materials.

Q   *You obviously love pranks. Do you play a lot of pranks yourself?*

A   I am not currently a "prankster," but have been.

Q   *One of your most recent books,* Did I Ever Tell You How Lucky You Are, *expresses something new in your work. Like your other books, it is full of absurdities in the classical sense. But if it is more recognizably satirical, it is also more visionary. Is this something to do with age?*

A

Q   *What are the most outstanding changes you have witnessed in the world of children's books, both as an industry and as a literature?*

Dr. Seuss

A The most outstanding change I have witnessed in children's books is in the finer quality of illustrators who have come into the field. I don't think the improvement in writing quality has been as notable.

Q *You are reputedly one of America's richest authors. What is your attitude toward money?*

A Money is a necessary evil. It comes in one door via the postman and goes out of the other door via the Internal Revenue Agent. Very little remains inside the house.

September, 1974

Dr. Seuss's books for children include: And To Think That I Saw It On Mulberry Street (1937); The 500 Hats of Bartholomew Cubbins (1938); The King's Stilts (1939); Horton Hatches The Egg (1940); Thidwick and the Big-Hearted Moose (1948); Bartholomew and the Oobleck (1949); If I Ran A Zoo (1950); Scrambled Eggs Super (1953); Horton Hears A Who (1954); How The Grinch Stole Christmas (1957); Yertle the Turtle (1958); The Sneetches and Other Stories (1961); Dr. Seuss's Sleep Book (1962); The Cat In The Hat Song Book (1967); The Lorax (1971); Did I Ever Tell You How Lucky You Are? (1973); A Wocket In My Pocket (1974) *and* Great Day For Up (1974).

Dr. Seuss's own Beginner Books are: The Cat In The Hat (1957); The Cat In The Hat Comes Back (1958); One Fish Two Fish Red Fish Blue Fish (1960); Green Eggs and Ham (1960); Hop On Pop (1963); Dr. Seuss's ABC Book (1963); Fox In Socks (1965); My Book About Me (1969) *and* I Can Draw It Myself (1970).

E.B.White

Elwyn Brooks White has written three books for children, each one of them a classic in its own time: *Stuart Little* (1945), *Charlotte's Web* (1952) and *The Trumpet Of The Swan* (1970). His work for adults is equally known: *The Lady Is Cold* (1929) and *Is Sex Necessary?* (1929), essays which he wrote with James Thurber, to mention but two publications. He has also been a regular contributor to the humor columns of *Harper's* and the *New Yorker* magazines.

Charlotte's Web is White's most famous contribution to children's literature. A little girl called Fern stops her father from slaughtering Wilbur, a pig who is born a runt. Bottle-fed on the best milk, Wilbur grows up strong and sturdy. It seems the question of his death, this time for the larder, must inevitably crop up again. But in the barn where he is kept Wilbur attracts the sympathy of Charlotte, a clever spider who promises to save her friend. Accordingly she spins a series of webs, into which are woven redeeming slogans, beginning with *"Some Pig."* The human community is justifiably amazed by this, and Wilbur is taken to the fair to be exhibited, accompanied of course by Charlotte. The ruse is altogether successful: Wilbur saves his bacon and lives out his days in peace. *The Trumpet Of The Swan* concerns Louis, a cygnet born without a voice. This defect is remedied when his father procures him a human trumpet. Louis quickly becomes a virtuoso, gives concerts in Boston's Public Garden, and makes a small fortune by doing so.

Far-fetched perhaps, but White has the finesse and lightness of touch to make it all work. It is this quality that links him with some of the best children's writers of the past (Kenneth Grahame is the obvious example) and gives him a particular niche in the present. One wishes that more children's writers could combine fantasy and delight in the way White does; but one knows that it is much, much harder than it looks. White himself admits that he took twelve years to write *Stuart Little*.

E. B. White was born in 1899 in Mount Vernon, New York, and

E.B.White

was educated locally. He graduated from Cornell University in 1921, after service in the First World War. He later joined the staff of the *New Yorker*, where he met his wife, a former editor. In 1938 the Whites moved to a farm in Brookline, Mass., where they have lived ever since.

To date *Charlotte's Web* has sold over three million copies in softback, and *Stuart Little* just under half that number. Hardback sales of these two books amount to over two million.

E.B.White

Q   *Many outstanding American authors have also been journalists. Why is this? And what in your view does journalism do for a writer who has other ambitions?*

A   I was a journalist first, an author second. A good deal of my life was spent with the *New Yorker*—I was a commentator, a reporter, and a memoirist. I submitted everything that came into my head and out of my typewriter, including poems. Journalism, the life of quick action and deadlines, is good discipline for a writer, and I still have the instincts and habits of a journalist, though I am no longer actively engaged in writing for a periodical.

Q   *All your books, for young and old readers alike, are characterized by elegance and humor. Where did these qualities come from?*

A   If, as you suggest, there is any elegance, any humor in my work, I haven't the slightest idea of the source of such qualities. When humor shows up in a person's writing, it seems to me it is because the writer has a natural awareness of the curious ironies and juxtapositions of life. Jane Austen seldom wrote anything funny, but her novels are masterpieces of humorous expression.

Q   *On the subject of humor, does it come out of the fantasy in your children's books? Or does the fantasy come out of the humor? If I am making an impossible distinction, could you please say why?*

A   When you ask whether, in my books for children, the humor comes out of the fantasy, or whether it is the other way round, you are asking me a question I can't answer. I would think that fantastical episodes or situations have a tendency to evoke humor. A lot depends, I suppose, on what a writer does with his material. There is a place in *Charlotte's Web* where the pig boasts that he can spin a web, and he makes a try at it. Perhaps there is something *essentially* comical about a pig trying to spin a web—I don't know. But whether there is or isn't, the way a writer develops the theme is crucial.

Q   *What are the differences between writing for children and writing for adults in your experience?*

A   What are the differences between writing for children and writing for adults? In my experience, the only difference (save for a very slight modification of vocabulary) is in one's state of mind. Children are a wonderful audience—they are so eager, so receptive, so quick. I have great respect for their powers of observation and reasoning. But like any good writer, I write to amuse myself, not some imaginary audience, and I rather suspect that it is a great help if one has managed never really to grow up. Some writers, I have noticed, have a tendency to write *down* to children. That way lies disaster. Other writers feel they must use only the easy words, the familiar words. I use any word I feel like using, on the theory that children enjoy new encounters and that I don't gain anything by depriving myself of the full scope of the language. When I mentioned a "very slight modification of vocabulary," I was really alluding to the state of one's mind—which has an effect on the state of one's vocabulary.

Q   *In* Stuart Little *the book opens with a woman giving birth to a mouse. There would be something nauseous about this if it happened in an adult novel, but in a children's book it can stand. Does this point to something essential about what a children's book is?*

A   The arrival of Stuart as the second son of Mrs. Frederick C. Little would have been completely unacceptable had I entertained any monstrous ideas about the matter, or had I introduced it gradually and in detail. It all happens in the first sentence and without the slightest suggestion of anything untoward or disagreeable. You have to make the leap boldly, if you are going to jump at all. As the story develops, it becomes clear that Stuart is a boy who happens to look like a mouse. The whole business is so fantastical as to rule out any anatomical embarrassment, such as a woman giving birth to a mouse. The first chapter of *Stuart Little* was written about fifty years ago, and in that innocent day children were not privy to the facts of life. Today, they are better informed about mammalian birth, and I suppose a few of them have moments of wondering about Stuart. But for the most part they accept the event without question, which is the happy approach.

Q   *What made you want to write your three books for children? Were they in fact written for children? And (the obvious question I'm afraid) what were the origins of each one?*

A   My first book for children was not begun with book publication in mind. I had a small son and several small nephews and nieces, and occasionally I wrote an episode in the hope of amusing them. A dozen years or more went by before *Stuart Little* emerged as a book. My second book for children was written because I had an urge to bring the characters in my own barnyard into a sustained story. I used to raise a spring pig, for butchering

127

in the fall, and I never much cared for this deliberate murder, so I invented a way to save a pig's life. *Charlotte's Web* was an easy book for me to write because of my intimate connection with the main characters. I wrote *The Trumpet Of The Swan* when I was visited by the idea of a Trumpeter Swan who came into the world without a voice.

Q   *There are two themes common to all three of your children's books. The first is the anthropomorphic one, the animal as a participant in human society. How would you compare your kind of anthropomorphism with that of other writers (e.g. Richard Adams in* Watership Down *or Kipling's* Jungle Books *or the* Doctor Doolittle *books)? Is it a means of gentle satire?*

A   I think all anthropomorphism is satirical. I can't compare my kind with the style of other writers—I'll leave that to somebody else.

Q   *The second theme is that each of your characters struggles against and masters incredible odds. Louis the Swan overcomes his muteness by learning the trumpet; Wilbur the pig is saved from slaughter when his friend Charlotte the Spider learns to write inside her web; and Stuart Little simply manages to survive. Is this a theme you have been aware of?*

A   None of my books was written to a theme. Life *is* a struggle, and there is always the question of survival uppermost. So it is not surprising that these three stories, although completely different one from the other, have a common thread running through them.

Q   *Given the similarities of your three children's books, how in your opinion have you developed as a children's writer?*

A   I don't understand your ninth question. There is some question as to my having "developed" as a children's writer. I may just have been going downhill without knowing it.

Q   *When* Stuart Little *was still in manuscript it was deplored by Anne Carroll Moore, then a leading authority on children's literature in the States. Many years later you wrote a piece claiming that her response was based on a judgment that you had broken certain "inflexible rules" when writing for children. What were those inflexible rules, and how have they changed since then?*

A   I can't say what was in Anne Carroll Moore's mind when she tried to get me to withdraw the manuscript of *Stuart Little*.

I think she was dead set against an American family having a mouse-boy. I think, too, she found my story inconclusive (which it is), and it seems to me she said something about its having been written by a sick mind. I may be misquoting her, as I haven't got the letter in my possession. There were undoubtedly some rules a writer was supposed to follow when writing for children, and I guess I smashed a few of them, knowingly or unknowingly. Today, all rules are off; the sky is the limit.

Q *When you wish to "make a point" in your children's books you do it by humorous demonstration, never by preaching. The term "low seriousness" I expect would make you jump; but what would you call it?*

A A writer who isn't "serious" isn't a writer at all. My books are serious books. But a man doesn't have to give up jumping and dancing and singing just because he is a serious man. I dive into a story the way I dive into the sea, prepared to splash about and make merry.

Q *Several critics have found that the ending of* Stuart Little *is inconclusive—in fact a non-ending. Do you ever feel the same way about it? Can something which is essentially humorous in fact have an ending?*

A There have been complaints about the ending of *Stuart Little*. Children, by and large, want to know whether Stuart ever found Margalo, and whether he got home. But I deliberately left the matter hanging. The story is the story of a quest—specifically, the quest for beauty. Life is essentially inconclusive, in most respects, and a "happy" ending would have been out of key with the story of Stuart's search. Once in a while, to my great delight, a young reader perceives this and writes me a letter of approbation.

Q *Both* Stuart Little *and* The Trumpet Of The Swan *contain school scenes, lessons in which conventional methods of teaching are sent up. Is this because you object to the way you were educated?*

A The schoolroom scenes in *Stuart* and *The Trumpet* got in there naturally. I did not introduce them, or concoct them, in order to comment on my own schooling. I was educated in a period when schoolrooms were dull and unimaginative, when discipline was firm, and when not much effort was made to give scholars free rein. If the schoolrooms in my books are a bit on the disorderly side, perhaps it is a subconscious attempt on my part to raise a rumpus and break the monotony. But I am glad I went to schools that made no bones about teaching me to read and write and spell. Too many youngsters nowadays enter college not knowing how to read and write and spell, more's the pity. Even a monotonous atmosphere has its virtues, for it compels the scholar to invent ways to lift himself out of his boredom, and sometimes this takes the form of creation.

Q   *"People believe almost anything they see in print"—the Spider's excuse in* Charlotte's Web. *Is that true? And in what sense would a child "believe" in the fantasies you have created?*

A   Children obviously enjoy fantastical events. The dullards among them soberly question the happenings and ask, "Is it true?" But most children are quite able to absorb and enjoy fantasy without questioning it, even when they are aware that they are momentarily inhabiting a world quite different from the real one.

Q   *In* Charlotte's Web *you make it a point that the girl, Fern, never talks to any of the animals, only listens to what they say. Why did you stop there?*

A   In *Charlotte's Web* there is no conversation between animals and people. Animals talk to animals, people talk to people. Fern is a listener, and a translator. This is basic to the story. It also provides a story that is much closer to reality. Animals *do* converse—not in English words, but they converse.

Q   *Perhaps* Charlotte's Web *is your most popular book because its characters are so fully blown. Did they just come from what you considered the nature of the animals in question, or were they derived from elsewhere too? Is Templeton unscrupulous simply because he is a rat, or because he reminds you of someone as well?*

A   The characters in *Charlotte's Web* were based on the animals I happened to be living among—the spider, the rat, the pig, the geese, the sheep. Templeton does not remind me of anyone—he is unscrupulous because he is a rat.

Q   *What is the appeal of writing children's books to you?*

A   It amuses me to write children's books—perhaps that is what you mean when you ask, "What is the appeal. . ." But I am not mainly a writer of children's stories. For every children's book I've written, I have written four adult books.

E.B.White

Q   *Have there been distinct influences? What was the effect of working with Thurber? Were you brought up on* Huckleberry Finn?

A   I was not brought up on *Huckleberry Finn.* And I don't recall that working with Thurber had any profound influence on me, although it was a pleasure.

Q   *Have you read the work of other contemporary children's writers? If so, whom would you single out for praise or scorn?*

A   I am not well-read in contemporary literature for children and am not in a good position to comment on other authors.

September, 1974

9 Richard Adams

Interviewed by Justin Wintle

Watership Down (1972) is a book that all the family can and often does read. Within a few months of its paperback publication in England the book had become a cult among adults as well as among children for whom it was originally intended. When it appeared in the United States this lapine odyssey shot straight to the top of the best-selling fiction lists, and lodged there for many weeks.

There is something disconcerting about the immense popularity of an epic that literally never rises more than a few inches off the ground, told in impeccable but entirely humorless English. It is the story of a few young rabbits who leave their parent warren and make their way across an enemy-infested wilderness toward the chosen land under the nominal leadership of Hazel, who resolutely pushes everything aside until his status as Chief Rabbit is confirmed. Based on the observed behavior of rabbits as recorded in R. M. Lockley's *The Private Life Of The Rabbit*, *Watership Down* is a massive novel by any standards. Set piece follows set piece, and through the introduction of a monotheistic rabbit deity, *El-ahrairah*, the author does not stop short of traditional metaphysical speculation during the slacker moments of the narrative, reflecting his own beliefs in Christianity. Like another "cult" book, J. R. R. Tolkien's *The Lord Of The Rings*, *Watership Down* creates the illusion of an autonomous world that runs itself through the only, and therefore best, means available. The options open to Hazel and his fellow protagonists are limited. It is for this reason that *Watership Down* is the opposite of escapist literature, and camp followers of any age should make themselves aware and beware of that.

Adams's vision of brutality is augmented in his second novel, *Shardik* (1974), which runs to almost twice the length of *Watership Down*. There are scenes of such real unpleasantness that his English publishers decided not to issue Adams's new novel on any children's list. The high quality of the writing, however, makes *Shardik* as accessible as *Watership Down* to anyone with the time to read it.

Richard Adams was born in Berkshire, in 1920, the son of a country doctor. During the war he served in the Middle East, and subsequently read History at Oxford University. After graduating he became a civil servant, rising to a senior position in the Clean Air section of the Department of Environment. In 1974 he retired to become a full-time writer. Adams lives with his wife and two daughters in North London and at the weekends returns to Berkshire where he has a cottage, and where, he maintains, the beer is better than anywhere else.

Richard Adams

Q   *You said over the telephone that you aren't really a writer at all, but a civil servant. And yet* Watership Down *is one of the most "written" children's books I've come across. It's certainly very literary—there are a lot of set pieces, descriptive of characters and places, and there is a relatively elaborate use of quotation. I thought—though I may be totally wrong about this—that one of the fundamental inspirations had perhaps been Vergil's* Aeneid.

A   No, I don't think that's right, because my knowledge of the *Aeneid* is not profound I'm afraid. In fact I know more of the *Odyssey* than I do of the *Aeneid*. I see what you mean now with your terms, which I think need defining. I think what you mean is that the book reflects the author's deliberate intention to make use of words as a medium, as it were, to ransack his vocabulary, and if necessary to ransack the dictionary in order to find the word he wants and to express himself by any means at all and not to be afraid, if necessary, of becoming complex and difficult. This is perfectly true. I believe that words are one way of expressing oneself—after all there are other ways of expressing oneself. I believe very strongly that one of the characteristics of a true work of art is that it's not capable of paraphrase. I think it's stupid making television plays of *Emma* or *Pride and Prejudice* because they're such fine works of art it can't be done. It only shows up what wonderful novels they are. The plays are plainly inadequate—the gaps show through at every turn. You might as well try and make a play of Beethoven's *Eroica Symphony*. Every great work of art is not capable of being turned into another medium. Now, I believe in using words, and that one should not be afraid of making it too difficult, when you're writing a novel; not be afraid of being "literary."

Q   *I mentioned the* Aeneid *because, on the one hand,* Watership Down *undoubtedly has an epic quality, both in scope and structure; and on the other because, given this epic quality, the closest comparison seemed to be with the* Aeneid. *Aeneas leaves Troy at the moment of its destruction, experiences a prolonged journey with his followers before coming to the land where he will build a new settlement, and only achieves his goals once his arch-enemy, Turnus, has been defeated. And so with Hazel in* Watership Down: *he draws off from the old warren with his companions and leads them on a dangerous and exhilarating journey across the countryside; and the safety of the new warren is only secured once Woundwort has been beaten off. The parallel could be extended, as I suppose it could be with the* Odyssey, *which is also built round a voyage; the point is, though, Odysseus is return-*

ing to his old home, while Aeneas, like Hazel, is setting out for a new one.

A   You may very well be right—though it certainly wasn't conscious. I mean, I know the *Aeneid*—I did chunks of it at school, though I never sat down and read it, either in English or in Latin. I've got a very high opinion of it, and I know that C. S. Lewis had a very high opinion of Vergil. One doesn't know what one's unconscious influences are of course. I suppose there is a certain amount of Greek versus Latin snobbery these days, and has been all my life; you know—people who like to think they're properly informed and educated prefer to talk about Aphrodite rather than Venus, Hephaistos rather than Vulcan and so on. We all like to think that we are Greek-soaked rather than Latin-soaked. Perhaps rather stupidly I rather suppose there is a certain resemblance to the *Odyssey*; but it may be the *Aeneid* is a closer parallel.

Q   *Whichever way the resemblance lies it is still one indication of the concern with literature which shows through in every chapter of* Watership Down. *In this respect one would expect its author to be someone who devoted most of his time to writing.*

A   I've never published anything before, and *Watership Down* was published when I was fifty-two.

Q   *Nothing at all?*

A   No—except the usual tripe poems in undergraduate magazines and that sort of thing.

Q   *So what suddenly prompted you to write such a large book—it must have taken you a very long time to write it?*

A   Eighteen months—between about September 1966 and the end of 1967. You don't know how *Watership Down* came to be written? This has been told so frequently now it's almost like Alice and Lewis Carroll and the boat to Godstow. When my children reached the age of about five or six I began interesting them in Shakespeare. I'd always had the idea that it would be perfectly practicable to interest young children in Shakespeare, and often wondered that it hadn't been done—although I believe Bertrand Russell did it: he used to have little five-year-olds acting Shakespeare when he ran a primary school. My method was this: I used to get tickets for a production at Stratford, and then I would say to the girls: "In six weeks' time, or two months' time, or whenever it was, we're going to see this play at Stratford. There's no nonsense about this: you're being treated as proper grown-up people. You'll have a day off school beforehand and a day off afterwards. We shall drive up in the afternoon and have a proper grown-up dinner in a hotel, and then we'll go to the evening performance—not the matinee. Now, you'll get more out of a Shakespeare play if you know it before you go, so we're going to read it, and we'll do it properly." We used to read it twice, right through, before we went. This was done at bedtime—a very good time for putting anything across because you've got a captive audience with a strong built-in desire that the lights should not be put out just yet, so they're prepared to listen quite attentively. And I would half-read, half-act the plays. I would pretend to be Malvolio picking up the letter, and then I'd go across the room and pretend to be Sir Toby looking out of the box-tree (*Twelfth Night*). They took to this—there was no compulsion—they enjoyed this very much. They were delighted: you get to the theater and the curtain goes up you find you know it all: there are Prospero and Miranda (*The Tempest*), just like Daddy said. Anyway, this was extremely successful. But it's a long way to Stratford—it's 110 miles from here—and it was necessary to while away the journey. So I used to tell stories on the way up—they slept on the way back. I told all sorts of stories—some like *Perseus and Andromeda* and the *Odyssey*, and some I made up, with all sorts of characters. I can't quite remember how I found myself telling the story of Hazel and Fiver and Fiver's vision of blood and how they set out; but this story was very popular. It lasted beyond the journey to Stratford, for which it was made up—it went on for about a fortnight afterwards on trips to school in the mornings. But when it was finally finished Juliet said "You ought to write that down Daddy"; I said "Oh don't be silly, you've no idea—it would take more than a year to write a book, you've no idea how much labor there would be in it." But she continued, she persevered. Well, I'd struck a bad patch at that time. I was working for a chap I didn't like and he didn't like me, and with one thing and another it was all very difficult. So I thought I would amuse myself by writing down this story in the evenings. I used to get home in the evenings, have supper, see the television news, and then I'd sit down at about half-past nine and write until about half-past midnight. It was a long job—it was a good night when I wrote three sides of foolscap. I write very slowly, picking my words very carefully. Nevertheless I still find the best bits are those that flowed most easily from the pen—there's no doubt about that. You write better faster than slower for some reason.

Q   *Did the story change much from the original telling?*

A   It altered a good deal from when it was first told, and I think this illustrates what I was saying earlier. A story you tell to people in a car is quite different from a story you write down to be read by people in a book. However—that's how *Watership Down* came to be written—at the specific behest of the children, and I suppose if it wasn't for the children I'd never have written the book, or had the success I have had with it. So I feel very grateful to them.

Q   *Did you read R. M. Lockley's book* The Private Life of the Rabbit, *a behavioral account of rabbits, before or after you improvised the original story for your daughters?*

A   After. This is probably something to do with my being a civil servant, but I have a strong belief in the necessity of authenticity and accuracy—I can't bear to see anything that's inaccurate or wrong. If I see anything wrong in a book I mark the margin "This is wrong." I thought I'd better know something about rabbits and get it right before I started writing a novel about rabbits. As far as I know, within the terms of reference of the anthropomorphic exercise, it is right about rabbits: I mean they do chew pellets, and they do reabsorb their embryos if they're under strain. There are various features of lapine life which I've taken the trouble to get right.

Q   *So if it wasn't Lockley's book, what led you towards rabbits initially?*

A   I was a child in the country outside Newbury before the war, and the country of *Watership Down* is my country: I was born in a fairly big house just outside Newbury with three acres of garden. My father was a country doctor. Sandleford Warren, where the story begins, was just across the fields from the bottom of this garden. I'm sorry to tell you that the house has been pulled down and the garden destroyed: it is now the site of twenty-two little dwellings—I suppose what has happened to quite a number of big houses on the outskirts of nice country towns. In a way I'm Fiver, and it's my warren that's been destroyed. I've never been back there—I don't think I could bear to see it. I didn't like the house very much, but the garden I loved passionately. When Holly describes the bulldozer that destroyed the field, so that it wasn't the same place anymore, I feel this most bitterly.

Q   *And the warren was destroyed with calcium cyanide dust?*

A   I expect it was cyanide, though I think they sometimes use phosgene. Lockley told me about this. You don't have to use cylinders of gas, you can just chuck cyanide crystals down the holes if you want to. The destruction of a warren is fundamentally as I described it in the book though, and Lockley had no fault to find with that description. In fact Lockley had no fault to find with any of the book, to be quite honest.

Q   *We've talked about the descriptive accuracy of* Watership Down—*something that all novels have to a greater or lesser degree. But at some point there is usually a changeover from a descriptive function to a prescriptive function, and this must be true of* Watership Down *if it is what you have said it is, an anthropomorphic exercise. Otherwise one would have left Lockley's account of rabbit life as it stands.*

A   I don't know what you mean by prescriptive—I'm sorry.

Q   *I mean when you begin prescribing certain forms of behavior in preference to others.* Watership Down *concludes with a tooth and claw struggle between two groups of rabbits—those led by Hazel and those led by Woundwort. These groups are distinct from each other, and their social modes are different. And yet for all their difference in behavior, both groups are living under the same conditions in the same situation in the same part of the country. It's quite clear though that we are supposed to like Hazel more than Woundwort.*

A   By prescription you mean attributing to rabbits things that real rabbits don't in fact do?

Q   *In one sense, yes.*

A   I'll talk about that for a bit. You see, the anthropomorphic fantasy is a very old genre indeed. If you go to the British Museum you can see a picture of the antelope and the lion playing chess, and of course folk tales about animals—you know, the clever spider and so on—they're so old. Anthropomorphism is a very old form of storytelling—you can trace it right down through Reynard the Fox and all manner of things. Now the interesting thing is, What's your formula? All chaps who tell anthropomorphic stories have to adopt some kind of formula, about just how to work the illusion, and how to make it convincing to the reader. The fox and the rabbit are talking like humans, but they're not humans—how much is animal and how much is human? I've studied this fairly deeply, and obviously there isn't time to go over the whole ground. But we can have a look at some of the better-known things of recent years. At one end of the scale—and you might almost call this ultraviolet, it's beyond the spectrum—is something like *Tarka The Otter*: now this is not an anthropomorphic fantasy at all; it is a perfectly straightforward account of the life and death of an otter from its birth. Now this, ipso facto, is not a novel; it cannot be. A factual account of an animal is not a novel—it's not shaped, there's no moral issue involved. It's what I call And Then He—then he did this and then he did that and then he did the other and then he died. That, I would say, is splendid natural history, but not a novel. Now, at the other end of the scale is what you might call the infrared—let's say something like *The Wind In The Willows*. Now the animals in that are just human beings who happen to be called Rat and Mole and Toad. They're hardly animals at all. Rat is described at one point as pattering about on the mud—well that's easy enough. But they have butlers, they drive motorcars, they're human beings in effect; and in fact they don't even have the natural functions of animals toward the countryside. I think it's Peter Green in his splendid biography of Kenneth Grahame (London, 1959) who says at one point that Toad's father may, as Badger says, have been an excellent animal, but he almost certainly made his money in copper. They're rather like weekenders in the country. So, somewhere along the line, you see, you poke your finger in and hit on a formula. Now I am a very pro-Kipling man, and I think Kipling was the greatest children's writer who ever lived. I think *The Just So Stories*, *Puck of Pook's Hill*, *Rewards and Fairies* and *The Jungle Books* are simply superb—they've never been beaten. Now, Kipling's formula is, I think, a very good one indeed, and I adopted it in *Watership Down*. It is this: you attribute to your animals motives and incentives and ideals that real animals wouldn't have. The animals in the *Jungle Books* have their law of the jungle, and disinterested motives which real animals obviously wouldn't have. On the other hand they are very animal to this extent: they never do anything of which real animals would be physically incapable—they don't wear clothes or smoke cigars or walk about on their hind legs or anything like that. They're allowed to keep their animalian dignity. This seemed to me a very good formula.

Q   *Because the animals don't become caricatures?*

A   No, they're not caricatures, and nor are the rabbits. Every effort is made to impregnate them with lapine authenticity. On the other hand I do reckon, with all due respect—and I hope this isn't arrogant—that in one respect I played fairer than Kipling. His animals have all sorts of rather upstage ideas about honor and the law of the jungle and so on; but my rabbits are quite unconcerned with anything throughout the whole book except food, survival and mating. Those are their only motives from start to finish. So, although they do things that real rabbits wouldn't do, like making an ally of a seagull and floating down the Test on a punt and rescuing a comrade from a snare, they do it all with the sole motive of survival. And physically they don't do anything a real rabbit would not be capable of. In fact, some young man—I think he's a lecturer at Exeter University—said it was so craftily done that many children might suppose that real rabbits would do some of these things, which is precisely the illusion I wished to effect.

Q   *But it's still an illusion of sorts; and there's still the matter of the differences between Woundwort's warren, Efrafa, and Hazel's.*

A   Well, you've got to have some goodies and some baddies or you can't write a book you know.

Q   *So there is a definite moral evaluation—that Hazel is good and Woundwort is bad?*

A   Yes, I think this is true—but at the same time you don't altogether feel unsympathetic toward Woundwort, do you?

Q   *I did.*

A   Nobody else who has read the book does—they feel sorry for him, that he couldn't help doing what he did, and they're sorry for him when he dies. Of course it's not a serious comparison, but he's a bit like Macbeth. He's a frightful bastard, but even when he's at his most bastardly you still feel a kind of sympathy for him. At least I do.

Q   *Let's say there's no compulsion to have any sympathy for Wound-wort, and move on to Hazel, toward whom there is a very clear indication to be sympathetic, both because of the moral framework of the book, and because* Watership Down *is about his success as much as anything else. However, what if one takes the line that even Hazel isn't really so very sympathetic? He's a fairer alternative to Woundwort, admittedly—but is he the fairest? For example, throughout the book he remains orientated toward having an* owsla, *or hierarchy of officers, beneath him once he has created his own warren; and he remains orientated toward being a chief rabbit. When it comes to determining what sort of warren is best, there are the beginnings of choice, but only the beginnings.*

A   It's not the way I see it. The origin of Hazel is very real to me—I was simply writing what I've experienced. I did two years in Airborne Forces during the war—I volunteered for Airborne Forces at the end of 1943. During 1944 and 1945 I was in a parachute supply company in the First Airborne Division. This was a real eye-opener after being in the ordinary army. The commanding officer was a man called John Gifford. He was a most remarkable person. He was the most unassuming man I think I've ever known in my life. He was just the reverse of what you'd expect a parachute commanding officer to be. He always seemed to be giving orders with reluctance—he detested anything that suggested rhetoric. But you noticed that whenever there was any trouble John Gifford would be there in the thick of it—just very quietly setting an example. Everybody in the company, right up from the ordinary soldiers to the higher officers, had the highest opinion of John Gifford. His every lightest word was instantly heeded. I learnt from him what real discipline and real authority are. You talk about discipline now to anybody under the age of twenty-five and they practically think it's a dirty word. They don't understand. Real discipline isn't a matter of shouting and screaming and saying "Go and do this because I say so." Real discipline is a kind of innate power that comes streaming out of the man who ought to have it, the man you're glad to follow, the man you feel it's right and proper to follow. This is what John Gifford had, and this is what I learnt from that experience: what it was to be a member of a team with the right chap in command. *Watership Down* is not a political book. *Watership Down* is about leadership, and the proper title ought to be something like *The Rabbit Leader*. But as leader is a dirty word now and sounds a bit pretentious I abandoned this idea. But this is the flow and shape of *Watership Down*. During the first part we see the hero gradually establish his authority; his problems are all within his group—he has trouble with Big-Wig, he has trouble with the mutineers on the common. During the second book we see him making his mistakes and not being afraid or ashamed to take the consequences. He makes a mistake at Nuthanger Farm and very nearly loses his life in paying for it. That takes you halfway through the book, and now the good leader is firmly established—everybody recognizes him. It's time now for the bad leader to come up against him—the chap who rules by force. In the last part we are shown how and why the good leader is better than the bad leader. This is what the book is really about—and the only extent to which it is a political book.

Q   *I'd call that pretty political.*

A   In the broadest sense of the word, in a Platonic sense, I suppose it is, in as much as any book about a society of creatures, learning to shake down and live together and evolving a system, is of the *polis*, of the city-state. Yes, to that extent you're right.

Q *I'm suspicious of this attempt to separate politics in a Platonic sense from politics in any other sense. I think somewhere you're evading a question, to do with the principle of hierarchy. The rabbits are able to question Woundwort's regime, but there the questions stop and assumptions take over—assumptions which radicals might object to.*

A I'm trying honestly to cooperate, but I don't quite know what you mean. It's as though you were to say "Monkeys are generally Friday, what do you think of that?" I can't "click" onto that at all.

Q *Try it another way. Lockley, in his book, describes a system in which some rabbits are naturally dominant because they are naturally stronger—and he depicts a picture of the survival of the fittest not unlike what Hobbes, for instance, refers to when he talks about the state of anarchy. You, however, seem to have moved your rabbits some way away from the state of anarchy—Lockley's or Hobbes's. This must be so if* Watership Down *is really about what you have just said—Hazel's responsible leadership. But you haven't moved them far enough to test whether the natural superiority of some rabbits over others justifies an automatic hierarchy.*

A I see.

Q *This is why I am inclined to call* Watership Down, *if it is at all anthropomorphic, a political book.*

A I thought it was a little story about rabbits which I wrote for my children.

Q *So you're not prepared to accept this analysis of the prescriptive function?*

A Quite honestly I think it's the most frightful piffle, like George Orwell gone mad. You might as well start inflating Jemima Puddleduck or something.

Q *The dimensions of* Watership Down *are rather different—I mean it's a long long read.*

A I don't know—they read it like mad. I'll show you some of their letters. They read it in three or four days, some of them.

Richard Adams

Q   *Others would take longer.*

A   This was the idea, you see. I wanted to write for my children what you might call a microcosmic novel. One talks about writing for children—this is all piffle. There's no such thing as writing for children—it's all bunk. People who talk about formulas and writing for children are talking through the back of their neck. Walter de la Mare said there's no such thing as a children's book—he was quite right. C. S. Lewis said much the same sort of thing—that there are books children happen to like. My object was to write something for my children to give to them and say "This is a novel. It obeys the rules of a novel. It's on the same principles as novels you'll encounter when you get older, like *Vanity Fair* and *Wuthering Heights*. The action springs from the characters of the protagonists, and the point of the book is a conflict of characters. It is an objective book, certainly, but the objectivity is, as it were, springing out of the subjectivity. If you read my little book it'll make it easy for you to read the great novels of the world, because you'll know what a novel's like." This was the idea, to preserve the child's dignity and give him something he could jolly well get his teeth into. A child who masters a Beethoven sonata can quite honestly feel "Beethoven and I created this music together—he wrote it and I played it." A novel can come to life only if someone reads it. This is what the book was intended as. Any idea of its being a mighty parable is frightful tripe.

Q   *But you said it was a microcosm. . .*

A   Of a proper adult novel, I hope.

Q   *Aren't a great number of adult novels parables and political satires and so on?*

A   I think I'm too simple, you know. I never was any good at political science. If I could have got an "A" in political science at Oxford I would have got a first. I could never see what they were talking about—the natural law and the general will—it never meant anything to me. I am an empiricist. I see the world and think and write about the world as I see it. I never think, could the world be different? Might the world be different? I could never do that at all. That's what makes me a novelist.

Q   *That must be what I wanted you to say.*

A   That's fine.

Richard Adams

Q   *Do you think your empirical approach has something to do with your being a civil servant?*

A   I'm a man who became a civil servant, and has been one for twenty-five years. But I'm a fish out of water in the Civil Service, and I think most of my colleagues would tell you this. They'd say, "Richard Adams is rather a funny sort of civil servant really—he's very unconventional. For one thing he's much too emotional and excitable." A good civil servant is never excitable. But we're all formed by our job to a certain extent. As Winston Churchill said, "First we shape our buildings and then they shape us." I've come to have a tremendous respect for the civil service, without actually being "of" it. The English higher civil servants are an outstanding body. Those at the top are very, very good indeed—their sheer intellectual brilliance is very impressive. If you want to try and do a good job at all you've got to copy their qualities, and it certainly helped me write a good novel. I don't think you'll find many loose ends in *Watership Down*. Sometimes I'm prepared to bore the reader. My new book *Shardik*—which is twice as long as *Watership Down*—is an attempt to do something that as far as I know has never been done before. It's an attempt to write a major, large-scale *tragic* novel for children. It's in seven books, of which the last book is virtually a coda. Somebody who read the manuscript said to me that he wouldn't have had the last book at all: the hero's out of danger, the villain's killed, everything's done that's necessary. I said "Well, *that* is tied up, *that* is tied up and *that* is tied up (in the last book). Had that not occurred to you . . . ?" "No," he said. "Well it wouldn't do for me." The ends should be tied up, every one of them. And if it bores the reader, the reader should have a proper sense of responsibility, like the author had. A novel ought to be a proper, responsible document of the fortunes of the people.

Q   *What sort of book is* Shardik?

A   *Shardik* is a spiritual, a religious novel. But it also takes the trouble to sort out the economic questions that arise in the reader's mind. How did these people live? What did they live on? This is what I call responsibility. And this is why I admire Jane Austen so much, and Trollope, though he in many ways is a very irresponsible novelist.

Q   *But isn't a novelist bound to be blind to some of his responsibilities?*

A   Oh, yes indeed. A novel is like a dream, do you see, and once the unconscious is let loose . . . The dreamer is very often the very last person who can see any sense in a dream. And the novelist, I suppose, is the very last person who can see the implications of his novel.

Q   *Doesn't this make it rather dangerous to talk about the novelist's responsibility as an exalted goal?*

A   It's not an exalted goal. It's a sort of by-product—you might say like a cricketer who keeps a straight eye. It's not an exalted goal, it's just something he does. The exalted goal is to try and make a century.* I started out to write an objective story. It has seemed to me that Western imaginative writing has been for a long time preoccupied—and probably always will be—with the subjective work. This goes back to *Hamlet.* The audience's interest in *Hamlet* is in the conscience of the hero. The point of the play is not whether he's going to save his life. There is an intense concern with right and wrong—and that's the mainstream of European writing for the last three or four hundred years. But there is another kind of book, equally honorable I think, which has come in at intellectual hands for undeserved contempt. This is the "objective" novel, in which the hero's problems are entirely outside himself. Fielding I suppose is a case in point. The doyen of such books of course is *Robinson Crusoe.* Robinson Crusoe's not concerned with his moral state at all; he's concerned with his survival. This is a brand of literature about which more ought to be done at the present time. Now, there is a very fine novelist writing in this vein at the moment—Mary Renault. *The King Must Die* is a superb novel, quite unsurpassed. There are other novelists as well—Saul Bellow, in *The Adventures of Augie March* and *Henderson The Rain King*—these are the kind of book that appeals to me. I'm not really interested in writing about subjective moral values unless there is a strong vein of objective action. Although there is a great deal more of moral judgments and subjective values in *Shardik*, because it is about people and not about rabbits. But primarily it is a romance. The hero's object throughout the book is to save his life and marry the heroine—which he ultimately does, though it's a tragedy because Shardik dies.

Q   *Going right back, why did you want to introduce your children to Shakespeare at such an early age?*

A   Shakespeare is a hobby of mine. Next to our salvation by Our Lord Jesus Christ, the greatest blessing that we all, as Englishmen, have in common is that Shakespeare was an Englishman who wrote in English. His work is an inexhaustible fund of beauty and wisdom. It makes you fall on your knees and weep. And what more can you do? You can't start too soon to love Shakespeare, and anybody can do it. By the time Juliet was eleven she had a fine grasp of at least ten of Shakespeare's plays, and there was no compulsion.

Q   *And you believe books do affect their readers?*

A   Of course they do! That's what's so dreadful about all the evil things that are published nowadays. They do affect their readers very badly.

Q   *For example?*

A   *Naked Lunch* (William Burroughs) I thought was very evil.

Q   *Why?*

A   It's contrary to the doctrine of Our Lord.

Q   *?*

A   I believe there are fixed moral values from the time of Plato onwards, and that right and wrong have. been revealed to us for all time by Our Lord Jesus Christ. Though what Christ said is very difficult to apply. It's very interesting to compare Christ's teaching with that in the book of *Ecclesiasticus*, which says: do this! don't do that! Christ never says that. He teaches by metaphor, by simile, by parable. He is a poet. This is why you often get two honest, devoted and sincere Christians who come to completely opposite conclusions. And He said this Himself: "I came not to bring peace but a sword."

London, 1974

century: A high individual score in cricket.

10 Nicholas Stuart Gray

Interviewed by Justin Wintle

Nicholas Stuart Gray is best known as a children's playwright. He was interviewed for this volume because his dramas are eminently readable; if they were more readily available in bookshops many children might develop a serious interest in theater.

Mr. Gray's plays are intended for professional production for young audiences. They are not pieces to be whipped up for an end-of-term performance by a classroom of juniors. On the other hand, despite the fact that his plays are full-length and elaborately worked, they generally fall well within the range of a good amateur dramatic society—ideal, one would have thought, for a Christmas or Easter family production.

Gray's subjects are mostly well known, culled from collections of Andersen's stories and other similar sources: *Beauty and the Beast*, *Puss in Boots*, *New Clothes for the Emperor*, and so on. He makes no bones about adapting these fairy tales to what he reads as the level of reasoning acceptable to the eight-year-old. His tendency to use the stage to impart an occasional lesson in moral wisdom is possibly one reason that his plays are no longer produced as frequently as they were in the fifties and early sixties; but a much more plausible explanation is probably to be found in the greater amount of time television and film companies have been prepared to devote to children in recent years, and in mounting theater costs.

Born in 1923, Nicholas Stuart Gray has spent his whole life working in the theater, at least from the age of fourteen. Not only does he write plays, but he directs and acts in them as well. In addition Gray has written several volumes of stories and novels for children. He prides himself on being an oracle on cats, and lives, unmarried, in a cottage in Somerset.

Nicholas Stuart Gray

Q   *You were sixteen when the Second World War started. What did you do during the hostilities?*

A   I ASMed (Assistant Stage Managed) various shows in London. I was also a member of the Home Guard in Sussex. I exploded hand grenades.

Q   *Intentionally?*

A   Well no, not always entirely. Our country laddies down there were very worried by the ranking regular army gentlemen who would come on the scene from time to time. I used to say to them: "Don't worry, you're all snipers, and that's really all; and if there is an invasion, then all we do is climb trees heavily disguised in leaves and try to pick off two people before they shoot us. So take no notice of them. Just laugh." They used to come, the military gentlemen, and ask: "Where is everybody?" And you'd say: "Well now, there's our Fred, 'e's gathering the hay this afternoon." These young men would come up to me and say: "Nick, I've taken the pin out. What do I do now?" I'd say: "You throw it over there as far as you possibly can and run, lovely."

Q   *What was your first professional acting experience?*

A   Oh god—it must have been at Windsor, where I also did a production. And then I wrote a play and put that on.

Q   *A children's play?*

A   Oh no. That was a whodunnit for adults, called *Judgment Reserved*. Then at the end of the War I had another play done, called *The Haunted*, at the Torch Theatre in Knightsbridge (London), and then on television.

Q   *When did you first start writing plays for children? At the end of the 1940's?*

A   *Beauty and the Beast* was first published in 1951, so that means it was written in 1949, and played at the Mercury Theatre (London) in 1950. So it *was* 1949 that I first started doing children's plays.

Q   *What decided you to turn your attention to children?*

A   Children were having special programs done for them on television, radio and films. Nobody in the theater was doing

anything. I went round to see the children's shows at Christmas
—*Peter Pan* and pantomimes, nothing else. The children were
bored sick. Only the adults were crying—I think it was nostalgic
for them, reminding them of when they were kids. And I thought
what one could do would be to write plays on two levels, so
that you have a purely adult play for the unfortunate people
taking the children, and a straightforward story for the children
themselves. And as long as I didn't make jokes that only the
adults would understand, I might be able to keep them all entertained. That's what I was trying for.

Q   *What was it that the traditional children's theater—*Peter Pan
    and the pantomimes—was lacking?

A   Pantomime wasn't giving them a story. It was giving them
    variety that was curling up dad and mum with a lot of rude jokes
    and corny modern songs and a lot of love scenes. But the children
    were all standing with their backs to the stage looking up at
    the circle, eating toffee or scrabbling about on the ground. They
    were bored to tears. And, sadly, you would hear children saying,
    "Mummy, where are the babes?" while you had the broker's
    man doing a soft-shoe shuffle. Also they were cynical. They'd
    bring people on in modern dress in the middle of something
    about Robin Hood or Dick Whittington. Funny men would come
    wandering in wearing corsets and top hats. And this threw them
    completely, because children like a story, and like to be treated
    seriously. If you're going to tell them a story, you don't break
    off on the middle and tell them: "Ah-ha-hah, I'm only pulling
    your leg, none of it is true." You've got to start "Once upon
    a time" and tell them a straightforward story. I don't think
    there's any other way of doing it. Now, unfortunately, it's gone
    back an awful lot to pantomime again because of the pop scene.
    It's a great pity. When we did the last new play of mine, a
    couple of years ago, they had to put extra seats in—the theater
    was absolutely packed, and they were an absolutely marvelous
    audience. And they weren't shrieking for pop music. It's the
    older children who demand the pop business, and they it is,
    I think, who have destroyed the scene for the younger ones.
    And what the devil is ever going to give them any feeling for
    the theater? I don't know.

Q   *What age children are you most interested in getting through
    to?*

A   About eight upwards. I know one is going to lose them at about
    fourteen because they all think they are far too grown up for
    a fairy tale; and they'll come back to it again at about twenty.

But from eight to twelve or thirteen you can hold them if you are serious about it. If you have one actor who isn't serious you can lose them while he's on stage. But if the actors play it straight, the kids will go along with it. And if they've never been to the theater before, sometimes you have to teach them to listen, because they think of it as television.

Q   *When did you begin to become interested enough in children to want to create a theatre specifically for them?*

A   I'm not the slightest bit interested in children. I don't like them—or at least a lot of them. It was just that if the theater is going to exist, where are you going to start? If you are going to throw away the children on films and television, then the theater itself is going to go down the drain.

Q   *Why in particular should the theater be preserved?*

A   Because it's got a thing that none of the others have got—it's got a rapport between the house and the stage, and if that works, it's magic. If you've got a marvelous house the whole cast goes up in the air, and you get this electric feeling between the stage and the audience. Now a child who may be too young in later years to remember even what it was about, might remember that magic, and go back to the theater again.

Q   *So you started writing for children out of loyalty to your profession?*

A   Yes—it was purely for the theatre, and not for the children. But then, of course, it's great fun playing to kids because they're such murder to play to until you can really get them. And you must never lose touch with them for a minute, because if you start thinking about something else you lose them. And this is another thing: you know with adults they're only listening to about one word in three anyway. If you get children, they listen to every word.

Q   *Was there any one episode that persuaded you that children needed the sort of theater you might be able to provide them with?*

A   I was in a bus one day and I saw children queueing up for the cinema. There was a row of eager kids waiting to go inside. There must have been a hundred of them. I was appalled. I thought, there they are, no mums or dads. And I climbed out of the bus and went to look at the cinema. It was a special matinee for the children—an assortment of special films for them. They had three or four cartoons and various things that they would enjoy. The kids were going in for very small sums, and obviously it was a cheap way of getting them out of mum's hair on a Saturday morning. But they were there, eager, happy. So I went to the manager and said: "Could I go in? I know I'm not a child, but, because I'm interested, may I sit at the back and watch their reactions?" Well, of course, they stamped up and down the aisles and they ate toffees, and giggled. But they were really enjoying themselves. And I thought, we're not doing anything like this.

Q   *That was in 1948, 1949?*

A   Yes. I thought if you're going to bring this mob into a cinema, and they're going to walk up and down the aisles chewing toffees and throwing papers about, fighting with each other over the backs of the seats, they won't half be a bloody murdersome audience when they grow up. Nobody was training them for a theater. So I went round to various people who had tried to start a children's theater and asked them what went wrong. They said that, first of all, there were no plays, once you'd done *Treasure Island*. Secondly, there was no money, because if you charge children eight pence a head to come in, as they were doing in the cinemas, what were you going to pay the actors with, and how were you going to give them beautiful clothes? And beautiful scenery? I thought there is only one thing you can do—you'll have to do it for the holiday times— Christmas and Easter—when people will take the children to the theater, and they will pay theater prices. But then you have got to be serious, and entertain the adults as well. It's been quite funny to see adults sitting there sometimes, thinking "Oh gawd, now we're going to see Noddy in Toyland," and suddenly they're all interested, and you've got them.

Q   *Do children derive the same sense of occasion of going to a theater as adults?*

A   Yes. I think so, if the adults are careful with them, and if they're telling them all about it. We had a school party come late after the curtain was up one day when we were doing a play at Stratford, and one of them was heard by an usherette to say to his master: "Ooh sir, it's in Technicolor." Now I don't know if he was just being cheeky, which I strongly suspect, or whether he had never really seen a stage play before and was thinking of it as a film. And then one night we had a terribly noisy audience. Some kind lady had gone and given the entire front two rows to children who had never been to the theater before.

And they were murder. They threw papers up onto the stage, they talked, they fought with each other. They listened in between, but they were a business. In the last scene—it was *The Imperial Nightingale,* and a very difficult last scene—and I knew that Michael Atkinson would blow his top if they started talking through his pauses. So I sent someone round to talk to them. They were so quiet. And the next day I came round and found one or two of these boys cleaning one of the actors' car. They gathered round me and said "You played Four Winds, didn't you?" I said yes and we started talking about it. I told them they had been a shocking audience. They asked me in what way, so I told them. And they said "We had no idea, nobody told us." And I said "We've got to try and remember lines. We're not just on the box, or in the cinema where you can do what you like—throw eggs at somebody and they don't know, they're not there. But we're there, and it's very hard to concentrate. And," I said, "did you notice? In one scene our leading girl came on and cleared up the stage of all the toffee papers and lolly sticks?" They said yes. "That was because a few minutes later the Emperor made a great swishing entrance across that part of the stage, and if he'd slipped and landed in the orchestra, there would have been a frightful din, and he might have broken his leg." And they said—"Ooh sir, we're sorry, we'll never do it again. Do another play for us. We'll be very quiet, and we'll tell all the others." And I went backstage where Michael had been roaring about them, and I said "Look, that's what we're doing it for. If *one* of those kids comes back to the theater of his own free will to see a show, then we've won."

Q   *So in a way your children's plays are a sort of preparation for adult theater?*

A   It's to give the children a sense of magic. Nobody attends to this enough. They give them too much realism. They can see it all on the box, they can see frightful things there. They can read it in the papers. But they're not being given a world to escape *into,* no fantasy. The said "Look, fantasy they are being allowed is—Wouldn't it be lovely if I won the football pools? But they're not being given a fantasy world. They know from the age of seven or eight upwards that there are no such things as fairies and goblins. But it's the world of imagination. You don't have to have giants and fairies when you get older. You can read Tolkien, or Kipling's *Puck of Pooks Hill,* or any good novel, and you've gone into another world that doesn't have to be a world of kitchen sinks and violence. Children must have an escape line somewhere.

Q   *Is the theater the place to do this?*

A   I think it's a place where people go to escape from reality. I don't think it should rub their noses in it. A place where people can go to get away from the monstrous things that happen to them. If you're going to have violence and tragedy, then take it into the theater and make it bigger than life. But it shouldn't be everything always being brought down to the smallest.

Q   *Do you have any teacher instincts?*

A   Only as a director. I quite enjoy teaching people to act.

Q   *I was thinking how in* Beauty and the Beast *you employ a lot of magic and so on, but the story itself is very much about the reformation of the Prince, so that at times it seems the magic takes on a secondary role.*

A   People have said so. I hope so. I think that nearly all these stories have some sort of moral behind them somewhere, except *Puss in Boots.* I had great difficulty there, not to make our hero Gerard a complete con man. After all, he *is* a con man. He allows everything to go on round him, and ends up marrying the Princess, and he doesn't do a thing. Puss does it all, and tells these terrible lies. So I had to make Gerard run round after the cat, saying Stop! Stop! And I had to make the King and the Princess gang up to stop Gerard from telling everyone who he really was. If you remember, at the very end Gerard says: "I am not the Marquis of Carabas." And the King says, "Of course not. As my future son-in-law I create you Duke of Carabas." But I had to make him protest all the time about this; otherwise he would have been thoroughly dishonest. But nearly all the other stories have got a moral. What I tried to do with *Beauty and the Beast* was to portray a reformation of Beauty as well. She begins as a very prim little thing; she wants to know what time the trains go, and bullies her father and her sisters; and she gets changed to a greater understanding. Also it was a battle for Mikey. It was very important which way he could go. Because he was copying the Beast, rushing about and tearing things, and as his uncle the Wizard had always tried to stop him telling lies, when the Wizard saw him snarling on the ground, it was just destruction: are people going to be destroyed or not?

Q   *Several of your plays and all your books are, one way or another, about animals. Is this because they are good material, or because you think they go down well with children?*

A   It's because I like writing about animals. There are far more of them in my books than in my plays, which are not so easy. To put an animal on the stage one has to be a bit careful. It cost me quite a lot of thought over Puss on how to present the cat in such a way that it didn't look like a hearth rug rushing about, like most pantomime cats. I used to say to the cast, try to imagine that you are real people, and you've got yourself into this situation. Work inside it with wonder, and suddenly do be taken aback if you meet a talking cat; otherwise nobody is going to believe in any sort of reality. Then I thought, what would one do if one met a human-sized cat? One would rush up the nearest tree and stay there. As you can't do this on the stage, I had to do this thing of making everybody see him as an ordinary-sized cat.

Q   *How did the children react to that?*

A   They thought it *was* a normal-sized cat. It was weird. We had a lovely pause on the stage once, which was broken by a child saying, "Oh mummy, can we buy Pussy?" And then they would come round backstage after the show (some of them were *very* tiny) wanting to meet the cat. I would crouch down and never speak, because I thought, to get a mask, that size, head-on and somebody talking from behind it would be very alarming. So all I did was to purr and mew for them. And they were still terrified when they came face to face with me.

Q   *Most of your plays are adaptations of existing stories, particularly Hans Christian Andersen's. What do you look for in a story?*

A   A story. A good story line, with believable characters I can work with. These plots are usually very tiny; if you boil down a story it would usually go into about half a paragraph. So you have to fill it out with two or three sub-plots. I didn't touch down on *New Clothes for the Emperor* until about halfway through the play. The introduction to that was how they, the two heroes, got to be in that country and how they started making invisible clothes.

Q   *I found* New Clothes for the Emperor *a strange play. The characters are under a spell which makes them all equally stupid, and really more or less incapable of communicating anything to one another. The play has a surface of the absurd. Were you in fact influenced by the vogue for Absurd drama, which was creeping in when you wrote* New Clothes?

A   No, not at all. As usual, I just thought: What kind of people would get themselves into that situation? It struck me that they would all have to be incredibly silly. That provided the answer—they were under a spell that made them silly. You see the invisible clothes plot happening every day, of course. You go to the worst possible art exhibition, and people say "Oh yes, that's a belief in the infinite." And nobody dares to say, "I could do that with a tube of toothpaste."

Q *Getting back to your work and the level of fantasy, are you content that all your plays should depend on a suspension of disbelief?*

A I think any play has to. You take the curtain up at one arbitrary point in people's lives and bring it down at another; and in between you present an arbitrary selection of events. If you put a tape recorder and a camera on ordinary people for two hours, they'd give away nothing—no character, no plot, no development, no background. It would just be chatting, and that isn't a play. On the stage it is always artifice.

Q *Certainly your plays are well constructed and enamored of all the traditions of the theater.*

A Yes, I would like to think so. Writing a play is very difficult, because you can't waste time on anything. You can't go in for long speeches—the sort of thing that might take up a whole chapter in a novel. You've got to do things in as few words as possible. It's got to be succinct. And every word you use has got to build a character and tell the audience what sort of person this is, and at the same time advance your plot. So many plays today are episodes, and leave you asking yourself, "What happened?"

Q *Where did you learn your theater craft?*

A I have no idea. I used to write plays for my brothers and sister in the nursery.

Q *How old were you then?*

A About ten. I wrote stories, and then I would dramatize them. We had a very big nursery with an archway at one end. My mother arranged a curtain for this, and we did plays behind it. She gave us kitchen paper and a screen or two, so we could paint our sets and pin them up. We used to knock up a play in an afternoon and do it in the evening. We charged people a penny admission, and there was no talking.

Q   *What were these plays about?*

A   Mainly rather weird dramatizations of books I had just read. We would have a go at Walter Scott—why not? So my sister, at the age of six, would teeter about in a long skirt. But I don't think that was stagecraft. As soon as I was old enough I joined an amateur dramatic school locally, and went in for drama festivals doing "scenes from" Shakespeare.

Q   *As an actor what sort of part do you prefer?*

A   Oh, Shakespeare every time. I suppose the part I always wanted to play, and was delighted to play recently, was Iago. I've never been satisfied with any Iago I have ever seen.

Q   *Is that because Iago is like a cat?*

A   Partly, and partly because it is a thing of mine about making the audience believe you. It's no good playing Iago as a moustache-wiggling villain, because it makes idiots of the rest of the cast. You've got to have the audience saying to itself that it believes him. He should be charming to them all, and terribly worried, until the moment when everybody goes off stage and he's left alone.

Q   *Do your plays change much during the rehearsals of the first production . . . when you are directing perhaps?*

A   To a minor extent, depending on the actors. Being an actor myself, when I write the plays I have a fairly detailed idea of where everybody is meant to be. I can see them as acting characters, and I can almost hear the sort of voice I need.

Q   *When did you stop thinking of writing simply for adults?*

A   When I started doing the children's plays. I thought, they are anyway partly adult because, if you get a good enough company, they'll be enjoyed by adults. I get a lot of letters from adults, saying that they hadn't enjoyed themselves so much in a theater for years. It's a challenge to do the double thing.

Q   *In a sense then, you write family entertainment?*

A   Yes. As actors we always enjoyed doing the evening shows more than the matinees because we got older children and more adults. In the afternoon they bring the youngest. In the evening they don't bring little Agie, but Dad will come instead. You really can't play serious theater to four-year-olds. A sensible six upwards.

Q   *Do you think the family is important?*

A   Yes I do. I think there is a great danger of families being broken up quite unnecessarily into age-groups. You know—that's for the youngest, that's for the older children, that's for Dad and Mum, and that's for grandfather. Apart from babies, who need special entertainment.

Q   *Is this feeling a reaction to anything in your own childhood?*

A   Yes—possibly because we were left more or less on our own in the nursery. We would have been glad of adult company. If our dreaded Mum, instead of swishing about being Morgan le Fay, had been more with us, and not left us to our ancient nanny, I think we would have enjoyed ourselves a little more.

Q   *You have called your mother beautiful and terrifying. What was particularly terrifying about her?*

A   She was a megalomaniac. This is the great penalty of somebody who is very beautiful not allowing her mind to develop. She could never believe she was no longer sixteen. Of course nobody can, let's face it, but she never got over it. I've seen her staring into her looking-glass saying, "What have they done to you?" She could never believe that all this beauty was going over. In fact it never really did go over. She was always beautiful, but not a sixteen-year-old beauty. So that once we stopped saying "Yes Mummy" and started saying "No Mummy," we were instant enemies. We were challenging her—especially me. The rest of my family was a little more peaceable. She spent the whole of her time trying to cut us down. My sister would go to her and say—"Someone at school said I was beautiful"; and she would say, "Very flattering—What did they expect to get out of you?" So we grew up terribly unsure of ourselves and doubtful of other people, always prepared to be cut down. Even a year or two ago I took her to see a play of mine. She said, "You wrote that play?" "Yes," I said. "And you directed it?" "Yes." "And you acted in it?" "Yes." "Who helped you?" We were always ugly, stupid, gullible, useless people in her eyes.

Q   *Do you feel a need to change a childhood situation?*

A   Oh yes. The witch in *The Wrong Side of the Moon* is almost a biography of my mother. So she gets into the scripts. The sad thing about people like that is they are completely alone.

Q   *Most of the older and authoritative characters in your plays are made to realize, often through magic, that their views are erroneous.*

A   Yes. Mind you, the Emperor in *The Imperial Nightingale* was like that in the story. The Wizard in *Beauty and the Beast* is not in the original story. But I was trying to show their mistake, although I have seen a lot of productions where they have missed the point. The Wizard is made nervous of the arrival of the Prince by Mikey, who is just putting it on. Mikey is not really frightened at all. He's only pretending to be. A child who was really frightened would retire to a dark corner and keep quiet.

Q   *Do you identify with any of the characters in* Beauty *and the* Beast?

A   Yes, I suppose so. If I had to play any of the parts it would be the Wizard.

Q   *What in all your plays is your favorite part?*

A   The parts I enjoyed playing most were Puss in *Puss in Boots* and Piers in *New Clothes for the Emperor*, because they were fun.

Q   *Taking up Puss, you have a very strong rapport with cats. What enchants you about their company?*

A   The fact that they are so thoroughly independent, and when they come to you they come of their own free will. If a cat comes and sits on your knee or rubs its head against you, it's because it wants to—not as a dog often does, because it feels it should. It's flattering if a cat likes you. When it's had enough of you it goes away. I find this admirable. I also find it admirable that of all the animals that have lived with man since time immemorial the cat has maintained its absolute independence. It will sit swaying in front of the fireside—and no fireside is complete without a cat—and it is the epitome of domesticity. Then something moves in the corner and you've got the jungle. Instant, something from the dawn of time. And if it gets whatever is moving in the corner, you've got a shocking spectacle— something snarling and growling and not to be touched, not to hold or bind. I find it interesting whether, on the stage, you can put that across, whether you can make people see this about cats. I was very delighted when, after *Puss in Boots*, a critic wrote an article about all the animals that have ever appeared on stage. And he said, Gray has the last word with the cat. He also said that after seeing the play he went out and bowed to the first cat he met. That pleased me, because somehow one had put over the character of a cat.

Q   *You talk about using the theater to give escape routes to children. All the same I find that in some of your plays there are some very real, very terrifying moments. There's a moment in* Beauty and the Beast *in his castle. Beast tells Beauty that he has been out hunting a doe, and he tells her that she has the same color eyes as the doe.*

A   The point about that scene is that she was showing fear of him, which she shouldn't have done.

Q   *But it was his line.*

A   Yes—I put it in deliberately, because he was saying to her that she musn't show that she fears him. He was trying to make her say whether or not she feared him. So he says "Your eyes are like the eyes of the doe. Do you hate me Beauty?" And she says "Yes." Then she drops on the floor and tells him he forced her to say it—she wouldn't have said it if she hadn't been frightened into saying it. Then he says again, very gently, "Do you hate me?", and she doesn't know. This is a man trying to get her to tell him her feelings about him, and frightening her into telling him the truth.

Q   *How did the audience take it?*

A   The adults were alarmed. But the children weren't. They were interested in what he was trying to do.

Q   *Are you pleased when the children in your audiences are pleased?*

A   Yes—that is because the children are more difficult to satisfy.

Q   *Do you think they make a more intelligent audience?*

A   They have become less intelligent over the last ten years—I think because of the influence of television. They have also become far less sophisticated. I think it is a great pity that there aren't so many of those plays around at the moment. Not just from my point of view, but from theirs as well. They aren't getting their escape routes open. I am watching a niece who is now nine, and she's never, over the last three years, had a chance to see one of my plays put on properly in London. And she hasn't got escape routes. And I know that that sort of theater would give them to her.

Q   *Do you think children know what they want?*

A   No—they've got to be told. The child is a savage until it's taught things. If you put a bunch of children on a desert island and there wasn't anybody to teach them things, and you went back twenty years later they'd all be living in trees. They wouldn't really know anything. I know I'm very gentle with animals, but when I was a very small boy I blew a frog up with a bicycle pump, and watched it swell. An older boy saved the frog and told me off. It never occurred to me I might be hurting it. Someone's got to teach one those things.

Q   *You have a lot of confidence in traditional culture?*

A   Well, it's the only thing we've got really, isn't it? The only thing that has made us different from any other animal is that we can pass on information. This great long line of culture—I don't think it should be taken for granted, but I do think it should be passed on. Otherwise something is in danger of getting lost that might be important. One never says, "this is it"—the ultimate—but one passes it on, saying, "take it or leave it." I've taken the bits I want, and left the rest. I think everybody must do that.

Hampstead, 1973

Nicholas Stuart Gray's plays include: The Tinder Box (1951); Beauty and the Beast (1951); The Princess and the Swineherd (1952); The Marvelous Story of Puss in Boots (1955); The Imperial Nightingale (1957); New Clothes for the Emperor (1957); The Other Cinderella (1958); *and* New Lamps for Old (1968). Gawain and the Green Knight (1969) *is a play for older children, and Mr. Gray has also dramatized two of his novels for older children, namely* The Seventh Swan (1962) *and* The Stone Cage (1969). *His other books for young readers include:* Over The Hills To Fabylon (1954); Down In The Cellar (1961); Grimbold's Other World (1963); The Apple Stone (1965); *and* The Further Adventures of Puss in Boots (1971). The Boys (1970) *is a biography of two cats.*

11 Joan Aiken

Interviewed by Emma Fisher

Rather than exploring traditional fairy tales, Joan Aiken makes up her own improbable but humorous magic. She prefers near-reality: history not too long ago, and the laws of physics bent, not broken. Most of her full-length children's novels are set in an imaginary, though possible, England. James III is on the throne, and wolves have crossed the Channel Tunnel and terrorize Yorkshire. Her Cockney heroine, Dido Twite, appears in three of the books (*Black Hearts*, *Night Birds* and *The Cuckoo Tree*). In the third, she foils a Hanoverian plot to put St. Paul's Cathedral on rollers and slide it into the Thames during the coronation. The situation is saved magnificently at the last moment, with the Cathedral already teetering under the movement of the crowds.

Example is the only way to give any idea of Joan Aiken's dramatic historical imagination. Yet it cannot illustrate the breathtaking pace and vigorous plotting of her children's books, which is combined in her adult thrillers with a deadly sense of the ghoulish. Critics have sometimes categorized her as merely entertaining, perhaps because she is so compulsively readable. But her latest children's novel, *Midnight is a Place*, a sombre Dickensian story with some frightening scenes in a carpet factory, was acclaimed as deeper and more thoughtful than any of her previous books. She has also written many funny, magical or serious short stories, some of which she considers her best work.

Joan Aiken was born in 1924, and is the daughter of Conrad Aiken, the American poet. Her parents were divorced when she was five, and she was brought up in the household of her stepfather, Martin Armstrong, also a writer. She did not go to school until she was twelve, but was educated by her mother. She married in 1945 and had two children; in 1955 her husband died, and she took a job on *Argosy*, the short story magazine. In 1961 she moved to J. Walter Thompson as a copywriter, then left to write full-time. Success came when *The Wolves of Willoughby Chase* began to sell well in America, and since then she has kept herself by her writing. She lives in Petworth, the small Sussex town which figures in *The Cuckoo Tree*.

Joan Aiken

Q *With a writing father, and sister and brother (John Aiken and Jane Aiken Hodge), did you always know you were going to write?*

A Yes, I always knew I was going to. There was always writing going on somewhere, and I just always intended to myself. My stepfather used to give me his cast-off typed sheets to draw on, so it was natural to start putting down my own poems and stories. I kept a book—I can remember when I was five going along to the post office and buying a book that cost two shillings, which lasted for years. I wrote poems, and ghost stories that never got finished, and so on—not novels, though there was one quite long story called *Her Husband was a Demon*, divided into chapters. Mostly poems; I didn't really get to writing stories till I was in my teens. I used to tell stories to my younger brother on walks. We both had imaginary countries, about which we swapped details. One of the stories that got told to him, "The Parrot Pirate Princess," was the first story I sold, when I was seventeen. The BBC Children's Hour did it and the sale of that encouraged me to write more of them down. I hadn't intended to be a children's writer; I'd intended to write serious novels. The thrillers sort of dovetailed in and now I write about half and half.

Q *Do you remember any books or writers which particularly influenced you when you were a child?*

A Walter de la Mare was a very strong early influence, and various nineteenth-century books like *The Wide Wide World*—it's by Elizabeth Wetherell, who wrote quite a lot of children's books. My sister gave it to me when I was about seven, and it's a sort of harrowing prototype orphan book: the poor little heroine's parents die off almost at once, and she goes to live with a very harsh aunt on a farm in New England, and has a terrible time—the agony is absolutely piled on; it's a very long book, and she's in floods of tears on almost every page. It's full of marvelous detail, which I really loved—descriptions of food and places and clothes and houses, and austerities; how they killed a pig, and how they dried apples and hung them on strings, and so on. And then my mother was a great reader aloud, so from five on I was getting Dickens and Scott and a lot of Dumas, *The Three Musketeers* and all the sequels of that. And I read a great deal of Kipling to myself, all those Indian stories—and *Just So Stories* were read to me when I was about three. And I ploughed right through all the collections of short stories which my elder brother and sister had. I loved Dickens and go back to him a lot. Masefield, two lovely books, *The Box of Delights* and *The Midnight Folk*; a lot of his adult novels are rather middle-grade, but those two are absolutely marvelous. Our house was stuffed full of books, adult books and children's just mixed up. *Little Women* of course—things like that; and George Macdonald, *The Princess and the Goblin* and *The Princess and Curdie.*

Q   The Wolves of Willoughby Chase *was the book which made you famous as a children's writer. Was it your first full-length story for children?*

A   No, the first full-length book for children was written when I was about seventeen, reading it aloud serially to my brother; but then it wasn't published for ages. I entered it for a literary competition, and it never got sent back, and I'd only typed out one copy, so it stayed in various school exercise books in ink for years. Then when I was very hard up in 1955 I fished it out and typed it all out again, and it was published by Abelard Schumann as *The Kingdom and the Cave.* But it wasn't the first one I'd got published; by then I was doing other things. From 1955 to 1960, when I had a job on *Argosy*, which was run in conjunction with a magazine called *Woman's Journal,* I got to writing serial-length thriller stories for them. Several of those I subsequently enlarged and they were published as ordinary thrillers.

Q   *The plot of* The Wolves of Willoughby Chase *is almost exactly that of* Uncle Silas, *by Sheridan Le Fanu: the two girl cousins, one tomboyish and one shyer; the wicked governess, the will. Were you trying to take him off?*

A   It's quite true I had read *Uncle Silas*; I was trying to take him off in a way. It was supposed to be a sort of pastiche of all the Victorian tales about poor little orphans who were in the power of frightful villains. It's perfectly true, now you come to mention it—the wicked governess outside the window—it wasn't consciously based on that, but it was consciously based on the whole genre. I suppose *Uncle Silas* is really one of the original Gothics on which the whole current Gothic market is built up now. It's a great book. There's one episode where she writes a letter for help to her aunt, or receives a letter from her aunt, and Uncle Silas intercepts the letter and opens it in front of her. I think I did definitely make use of that as a model scene in *The Wolves.*

Q   *The scene where they send a letter for help, which gets intercepted and a blank sheet put in instead. So as a parody, it was written to amuse?*

A   Oh yes. It was meant to be funny, with all the exaggerations. I didn't expect it would get taken as seriously as it was, by children I mean, who tend to read things for the excitement, not the jokes.

Q   *Do children understand parody?*

A   I don't think they do, or not the ten to twelve age-group. Maybe the older ones would, but then they probably wouldn't be reading a book like that.

Q   *Was that the age you intended it for?*

A   I didn't think about that at all actually; I just wrote it for pleasure. Probably children vary as much as adult readers, don't you suppose, in their reactions? This is a thing I feel very strongly about. It's no use a writer worrying about how people are going to take what he writes; he simply has to write the way he wants to. I've discovered by trial and error it's no use trying—someone makes a suggestion, and I used to think: "Yes yes, I'll have a try at that," but it never worked very well. I produced second-rate stuff.

Q   *It has to be something that germinates of its own accord.*

A   Yes, definitely. I keep a notebook and put down ideas as they come, and then it's rather a case of fitting them into the available time.

Q   *How did the other historical romances develop from* The Wolves?

A   Growing out of *The Wolves*, the pastiche on Victorian moral horror tales—full of exaggeration, a Channel Tunnel with wolves coming through it—then it struck me that if I had a different dynasty on the throne, it could be liberating, because then I could invent my own details where I wanted to.

Q   *And it gives you a convincing set of baddies, the Hanoverians.*

A   Yes, you've got your whole framework set up really.

Q   *It polarizes vice and virtue conveniently. You said, I think on television, that you didn't mean your books to be moral. But they are to a certain extent, aren't they?*

A   It was the moral *message*—I said that deliberately setting out with the intention of putting in a moral message was the way to write terribly bad stuff.

Q   *One can write with a moral intention without consciously saying, "I am going to make this the moral point of my story."*

A   Yes; also when writing for children I don't consciously think, "now I'm writing for children," but a sort of subconscious monitor must take over; and there certainly is the feeling that children do have a terrifically strong sense of right and wrong and of fair play, and I think this just automatically makes a part of what one is writing.

Q   *Part of the tradition is that virtue should triumph at the end.*

A   Yes—though mine tend to slide nearer and nearer to a more gloomy ending.

Q   *In* Midnight is a Place, *a character is killed in a duel near the end of the book; you more or less say that he needn't have died but he did die—as if it's stupid to gloss over death and make it all come out right just because that's the way it's always been done.*

A   There was an aspect of that in it. When I started writing, I felt strongly that things like death weren't mentioned enough in children's books—the real sad facts of life. But of course since I began there's been a great revolution in writing for children, and death is now quite O.K. Sex too. There isn't any in mine, but people like Leon Garfield have put it in.

Q   *Why is there none in yours?*

A   I wouldn't deliberately put it in, because I think children in the twelve to thirteen age-group would find it boring—it's just not in their terms of reference. Emotional relationships aren't primarily what they're interested in at that age—they want things to happen. Of course there are plenty of exceptions, I'm sure. You *can* have emotional relationships—certainly friendships in children's books are very important—it's the analysis of them which children, I think, tend to find rather unnecessary, and want to skip. There are an awful lot of children's books written in America now about divorced parents and orphans and racial problems, situation books, all absolutely planked down with the message as the main function—and I think that's terribly dull, I must say.

Q   *It's the school of thought that children want to read about what they know about. I think that might be the argument of a teacher whose children don't really want to read, trying to attract them to reading.*

A   Again I don't think one can generalize. Very possibly this is true of some children, but I'm not sure it's true of all. People go on *behaving* just as much in fantasies, after all, as in any other sort of book. The C. S. Lewis books, for instance, are full of morality.

Q   *What do you think of those?*

A   I can't stand them, actually. My daughter was very addicted to them, she loved them all, but I prefer his books for adults— *Perelandra* and *Out of the Silent Planet*. The children's books are good adventure stories—but there's something slightly prissy, and slightly talking down; and the Christian message drummed home. And I just don't like that great big golden lion.

Q   *That sort of fantasy is the opposite of yours, where magic is something down-to-earth and funny, which happens on one day of the week while the other days are perfectly normal. In Alan Garner's books, for instance, magic is much more frightening and powerful and heroic battles between good and evil take place. Have you ever wanted to write about that sort of magic?*

A   I like and respect his books, but I wouldn't want ever to write a long fantasy like *Elidor*, because I think it takes much more self-confidence than I've got. I don't really like reading a very long fantasy—it's like listening to somebody's terribly long dream—you can listen to a short dream, but a whole book of fantasy I find too much. The reason that I read Alan Garner's books of course was that I read them aloud to my children; they enjoyed them, at least my daughter did. I think girls tend to like fantasy more than boys; my son wasn't so keen. What about Tolkien? He does write awfully well—I've read right through them once and I don't think I ever would again, though I do remember enjoying a lot of them. But if I'm going to read something as long as that, I'd rather read *War and Peace*, you know.

Q   *Because there's more truth in it?*

A   And more reality. That's why my full-length books don't have any magical element in them—even if they're set in a non-existent period, there's nothing actually supernatural.

Q   *Have you ever got the response from a child that "that could never happen"—that of course Nantucket would not recoil against the coast of America if you fired a big gun on it, as the characters all take for granted in* Night Birds on Nantucket?

Joan Aiken

A   There are probably children who feel like this, but they're not the ones who write letters. The ones who write letters either believe in it or they go along with the pretense.

Q   *The characters in the full-length stories speak a very colorful language, not the dialect of any particular historical period. Where did it come from? I'm thinking of phrases like "Right, left and rat's ramble."*

A   That's Sussex. A lot of my words are real ones. I've got a very nice dictionary of Sussex dialect.

Q   *I thought I recognized a bit of thieves' cant.*

A   There's a lot of that, I've got a beautiful book called *The Elizabethan Underworld,* which gives Elizabethan broadsheets, and I got a lot of language out of them. In fact, I got a lot from Shakespeare too. Words like "frampold," meaning "awkward, cussed," are out of Shakespeare; it comes in *The Merry Wives of Windsor.* Just occasionally, if I can't find a word which expresses what I want, I make one up, but most of it is real. And a lot is nineteenth-century slang. It began when I used to read my books aloud to my children as I was writing them, and I wanted to be able to read aloud and not need to put in "he said" and "she said" all the time. I tried to make the idiom of each character fairly distinct, so when one read it aloud it was instantly plain who was speaking. A lot of Dido's Cockney is real, I got it out of Mayhew; some of her swearwords I made up.

Q   *In* Midnight is a Place *the characters have a rather serious conversation about tools; they can be used for bad ends, as in the carpet factory, yet without them there would be no violin-playing and so on. It's a bit more philosophical than anything in your previous books, isn't it?*

A   True, there hasn't been anything like it before. It seemed relevant because this was a book about a factory and it was a more serious theme altogether. Perhaps addressed to a slightly older age group too.

Q   *Is that something you mean to go on doing?*

A   Well, I do plan ahead; I would like to write another couple of children's plays, that's the next project, and then I've got a commission for an adult thriller, a story which I've already written which I'm going to expand; that'll probably take about a year altogether, and I'd also like to do another in the Jackanory series about Arabel and her raven; so I've got quite a lot on hand. In fact I'm pondering about whether I've written enough children's books really, and I might stop. At least books of that kind.

Q   *When you've been developing something and it gets more complex, it must be difficult after a certain point to know what to do next with it. K. M. Peyton wrote simple books to begin with, which developed and became more complicated, and then she wrote a rather introspective book called* A Pattern of Roses; *and having written that, and everyone having said how good it was, she told me that she doesn't know if she can do the same thing again, and she feels that if she does something less ambitious, people will say she's falling off.*

A   I feel a lot of sympathy with that; I started writing my books for fun, I enjoyed it; and then several people said "this is a lightweight writer, and why doesn't she write something more serious," and *Midnight is a Place* was an attempt to write something more serious. And that was all right, but really what I want to do is either write adult books or go back to more frivolous children's books, I think; I don't want to write serious children's books just because everyone says I ought.

Q   *When you say adult books, do you mean thrillers or novels?*

A   Novels more. The thrillers I have been writing have tended more towards novels, and the last one I've done is really more of a novel than a thriller. It's not out yet; I finished it last week. It's called *Voices in an Empty House.*

Q   *Do the thrillers have any relationship with the children's books?*

A   They really have the same framework, in that there's a strong contrast between right and wrong, and right triumphs in the end. The difference is that in a thriller you can pull all the stops out. I like to alternate, just because of the difference in feel when one is writing. One is conscious of reservations when writing for children, so it's quite pleasant to be able to let rip. Technical things, like not too much introspection, and no flash-backs because I think children find those boring and difficult, and not too much description, because again I think children prefer the action to keep moving. When one wants to write in a more ruminative vein, an adult book is more comfortable.

Q   *What does it mean to write a novel rather than a thriller?*

A   I'm not really quite sure. I suppose a thriller has to have a murder in it for a start. There's the distinction between crime novels, which start with the crime and then there's a lot of detection, and suspense novels, which tend to end with the crime.

Q   *Could it be that in crime novels different people stand for the good and the bad, though sometimes you get conflict within a murderer's mind; but in an ordinary novel . . .*

A   *Everyone's* fairly bad. I find I'm interested in violence, so that there's always likely to be something of this kind in my books; what produces the sudden throwing aside of the restraint in people. When we were at a friend's for lunch the other day, someone was describing how they share a big house that they bought jointly with a pair of friends about ten years ago, and all was well for quite a long time, because both lots had children and all the children were there; but then one lot of children went off to boarding school, and this has thrown the whole balance out, because the parents who now haven't got children at home find the noise of the other children very tiresome indeed. Because they aren't making any noise in their part of the house. And from that, bad relations are building up by slow and steady degrees. Terrible complaints about piano playing, and rather paranoiac behavior on the part of a woman who keeps ringing up whenever they play the piano and then ringing off without speaking—and so on. I find that sort of thing very interesting; one can seen the germ of a plot there.

Q   *Why does one kill characters off?*

A   I think it's just a matter of feeling. It's rather hard to assign an intellectual reason for it. One sometimes feels that a character has just got to die; in one of my thrillers, *Embroidered Sunset*, the heroine has a bad heart, and drops dead on the last page. I had some bitter complaints about that from old ladies. But I thought that I had laid the foundations for it quite visibly. I had a terribly brisk review in the *Times Literary Supplement* which said this was a most unjustifiable end, and one can see that for that kind of book, that was a point.

Q   *Do you feel you're typecast, either as a children's writer or as a thriller writer?*

A   That's the trouble—one longs for a change. Like Mary Stewart: she had a terrific success, her books sold in millions, always set in Greece or somewhere, and always with a heroine in a predicament; and suddenly she got totally fed up with it and told her publishers she couldn't bear ever to do another. So she started writing about King Arthur instead. This is one of the problems—if something does rather well, people want you to repeat it over and over. I don't think I shall write a sequel to *Midnight is a Place;* I get letters quite a lot from children saying can't you write another book about so-and-so—but if everyone's happy at the end of a book there's nothing interesting to write about. And if you're going to invent a new situation, you might as well have new characters; after all, the situation develops from the characters. I did go on with Dido, mainly because of the letters, though I'd intended her to die in *Black Hearts in Battersea*, because I thought the death of a child was something everyone ought to face; and then I had a really heart-rending letter from a child in America saying why did she have to die, she was so good; so—at that time I was interested in whaling ships, and I couldn't resist combining the whaling ship with having her rescued from the sea. I don't think I will write about her any more, because she's now grown quite enough.

Q   *Do you read children's books now, as a practitioner? To see what other people are doing?*

A   Not very much, partly because I want to avoid any possible plagiarism—I don't want to pick up other people's ideas. I do from time to time—sometimes Kay Webb says, "you must read this," but there's so little time for reading if you're writing all the time. I don't read as much fiction as I used to at all. I admire Leon Garfield and Philippa Pearce; *Tom's Midnight Garden* is a marvelous book, a classic; and Rosemary Sutcliff. Gillian Avery I like; and I like the sound of Penelope Lively. I used to review children's books for my brother-in-law's magazine—he edits *History Today*—but I've given it up now. It took much longer than I could afford because I'm always so behind with my work; it just wasn't worth it.

Petworth, 1974

Joan Aiken's children's books include: All You've Ever Wanted (1953), *short stories;* More Than You Bargained For (1955), *short stories. These two books were reissued in England as an omnibus volume,* All The More, *in 1971.* The Kingdom and the Cave (1957); The Wolves of Willoughby Chase (1962); Black Hearts in Battersea (1964); Night Birds on Nantucket (1966); The Whispering Mountain (1968); A Necklace of Raindrops (1968); The Cuckoo Tree (1971); A Harp of Fishbones (1972), *short stories;* Winterthing (1972) *and* The Mooncusser's Daughter (1973), *both plays;* Midnight is a Place (1974); Arabel's Raven (1974).

12 Scott O'Dell

Interviewed by Justin Wintle

Another author who turns to the past for subjects is Scott O'Dell; but unlike Joan Aiken he deals in history realistically, as a way of exploring social equations that are still present in his own society on the West Coast of the United States. Many of his themes are well established in the annals of American literature. *The King's Fifth* is a full-blooded tale about a corrupting and divisive lust for gold among a band of early Spanish settlers. *Sing Down The Moon* tells of the suffering of an Indian tribe pushed forever westward by the European conquest. *Island Of The Blue Dolphins*, winner of the 1961 Newberry Award and later made into a film of the same title, is about an Indian girl left alone on an island off the coast of California, an American equivalent of *Robinson Crusoe*.

O'Dell's preoccupations are probably best explained by his long and eventful life. Officially, he was born in Los Angeles just after the turn of the century; unofficially in 1899. His father was a railroad man, and the family moved around what was then the frontier land of Southern California. After leaving high school O'Dell attended the University of Wisconsin, where, already determined to become a writer, he quickly became disillusioned with his academic courses. He abandoned the idea of graduation and concentrated simply on those subjects that appealed to him—psychology, philosophy, English and history. This, he claims, has given him "a sense of comradeship with the students of today."

Having left Wisconsin, Scott O'Dell went into films, and, among other productions, worked as a second cameraman on the original version of *Ben Hur*. He spent a year with the Air Force in Texas during World War Two, and subsequently became the book editor of a Los Angeles newspaper. He wrote a number of books for adults during the fifties, and in the sixties his books for children. In 1972 he was awarded the Hans Christian Andersen Author's Medal.

Scott O'Dell lives near San Diego, within striking distance of the Mexican border, with his second wife, who edits the popular journal *Psychology Today*.

Scott O'Dell

Q   *Your recent children's books have been written for what is referred to as the Young Adult market. Why is that?*

A   For one thing, we've found that here in the States children read more advanced books than parents and educators thought they could or would. Furthermore, there's a dearth of books for young adults, because they're not nearly as profitable for publisher or author. But there's an important need, so the last two books I've done have been in this field. One has just come out, called *Child of Fire*. The background is the Mexican border, just south of here. The story concerns five Chicano gangs and presents a problem that the ancestors of these boys met 400 years ago. Young Spaniards of the sixteenth-century, yearning for adventure, came to the Americas in search of gold. Their descendants, living in modern America, have the same desire for adventure, but no place to find it except in the world of drugs and pointless warfare. The Chicano, for all his proud heritage, is a prisoner of the *barrio*, a second-class citizen. *Child of Fire* deals with his problem, both realistically and symbolically and, I hope, with some understanding.

Q   *Many of your books (one is tempted to say all your books) are concerned with traditional American themes, particularly themes of the frontier—conquest of new lands, what it's like to be midway between having laws made for you and making them for yourself, the conflict of interests between the old tribes and the new settlers, and the sense of opportunity given to youth. Is this because of the life you've led?*

A   I've been asked that question before, and I've never given what I thought was an adequate answer. I've led a very full life, gone to many schools, done a lot of things, lived abroad extensively, been in a couple of wars. A mixed up sort of life, perhaps. I think the fact that I've written about the past has to do with this. It's not necessarily an escape (though I think there's part of that in it), or an attempt to look back at calmer times; rather I have the feeling that the present is the past and the past is the present. The fundamental human is about the same as he was a couple of thousand years ago. The basic changes have not been vast. Human needs for love, affection, understanding, a chance to succeed at something, are about the same. Although I may write about a Navajo girl (*Sing Down The Moon*), I feel that she is a contemporary. I just wanted to pay a tribute to the human spirit, and the fact that this spirit happened to be in an Indian girl is really incidental. I'm not interested in the Navajos particularly—they're not my favorite tribe even. They were marauders—they rode in and took the crops of other

Indians, after the harvest sometimes. But there was this thing that happened at the Canyon de Chelly. Carson and the government rounded up the Indians and drove them to Fort Sumner. The important thing was the story. If the story is a good story children will read it for the suspense, and you can use suspense to do things. In *Sing Down The Moon* I wanted to call children's attention to the fact that there are such things as endurance, as loyalty to your family, loyalty to the place where you live. Nowadays people are dispersed, can live anywhere they want to. That's the trouble here in California—we're just a bunch of uprooted people. You don't know your neighbor and he never speaks to you. But this Navajo girl—she did want to go back to where her family had lived and have a child and live in a cave on the side of the Canyon. Even though she knows her people were driven out, she still goes back and starts over again. I hope there's a lesson in this, an inspiration for children. It's very strong in me, this didactic, inspirational thing. I had a lot of circuit writers and educators in my family, going back for 150, 200 years. While I'm not formally religious, I think this messianic thing has rubbed off on me. I want to teach and say something to people. Adults have pretty well established their lives, but you can say something to children. If you can get their attention and their affection, then there is something that can really be done with children. You can tell a story and add something that might be of interest and importance in their lives. It is messianic. As I said I've had a particularly full life, which I've lived and don't want to talk about; and for the most part, with the possible exception of *The Child Of Fire* (which has some of my life in it) I have written about times before I was born. Perhaps leaving the present and going back furnishes sustenance of an emotional kind. But things haven't changed very much, so it doesn't matter what period you write about.

Q *Your books are full of respect for that human quality of endurance you referred to; but I can't see that there would be as much opportunity for children or young people to demonstrate such a quality here in California as there was perhaps when you were young, when the State was still opening up.*

A That's part of it. There are things like the SLA (Symbionese Liberation Army), but all they want to do is shoot off their guns. Like these kids who held up a bank for a million dollars just to prove they could get it. There's a need. They had nothing to do. They didn't have a job and they didn't have transportation. You can't walk in California, so it's bad if you don't have transportation. But there are things to do. Not necessarily here, but if they went to Africa they could do a lot. There are millions of kids starving over there. There are challenges all over the world, but nobody's bothered to point them out to the young. Their horizons are so narrow that they don't know anybody ever existed. They don't know that Caesar existed, or Alexander the Great, or Einstein, or anybody else. They're alone. They haven't got transportation. Maybe their old man's out of a job. They've gone hungry a couple of times, and they're all mixed up. There's this Hearst girl backing the SLA. It's so stupid, even the liberals are antagonized.

Q *Even so, she'll probably go down as a folk-hero among some people.*

A Oh sure, particularly if they don't analyze the escapade. For instance, that four million dollars' worth of food. It's just people cramming their stomachs for a couple of meals; instead they could have set up a center where really poor people could benefit—people who are poor materially and mentally and physically. A center like that, if properly funded, might have taken care of 500 people a day with a modest meal for a long time. Instead of this they bought a lot of groceries and threw them around. They were only interested in making a display and showing their guns. I've written against the gun. *The Island Of The Blue Dolphins* was a direct protest against the gun, and the killing of animals and the killing of people.

Q *That's another book that has an Indian girl as its heroine. Why is it that you write so sympathetically about the Indians?*

A I think it is accidental, in the sense that I've lived in a country of Indians. The story of an Indian girl who lives eighteen years on an island alone is a dramatic idea, so I used it as a vehicle for what I wanted to say. If she had been a girl from Iowa or the Mayflower I still would have done it, because of the situation. The same with the Navajo girl in *Sing Down The Moon*, a ready-made situation about a people who were persecuted, uprooted and driven from their homes. Again, *The Black Pearl* is based on a legend current down there below San Diego. Steinbeck also used it. Our stories are quite alike up to the time when the pearl is sold: then they diverge. I think of all this as just an accident, that I was born out here. If I'd been born in the Middle West and stayed in the Middle West, I would come into contact with different legends, probably about early French voyages and so forth. In *Child of Fire* it's a young Spaniard. They are people I've grown up with, people I do know. I have Indian friends, just as I have Spanish and Mexican friends. There's quite a difference between the Spanish and the Mexicans, who are really Indians, or who have Indian blood in them. There are also a lot of different tribes in Mexico. For instance I lived a summer in Patzcuaro, where the Tarascan Indians live, about 9,000 feet above the sea. They were never conquered by any Indian tribe, not even by the Aztecs. They lived in a beautiful little city called Zinzunzan, "the place of the hummingbirds." Then Guzman, a Spaniard looking for gold, came with his five men. He talked with the King, and told him "We come for gold." The King had never seen gold. Instead he gave Guzman beautiful garments made of hummingbird feathers which he promptly threw away. Guzman was sure the King was lying, so he tied him to the tail of a horse, dragged him round the square and threw him on a bonfire. Immediately all the Tarascans, who had never been conquered before, disappeared into the high mountains, and they're still there today. That's a long story. But there was a girl in Patzcuaro, one of eleven Tarascan children, and we took her on as our cook. I modeled my Indian girl on her. This illustrates the mechanism. If I had been in the Middle West it would have been somebody else.

Q *Your books are all told in the first person, through the eyes of the protagonist. Is that because many of them are based on stories you've heard word of mouth?*

A I think it's the easiest way to write, though some of my adult books have been written in the third person. Though I don't think you'd find any evidence of it in my present writing, I have been influenced by Conrad. I was a great admirer of his for many years. What he did was more complex than I am able to handle. Sometimes he would have three narrators—the author, Marlow and Lord Jim, for example—each telling different parts of the same story as they saw it. I think writing in the first person is easier because you don't have to work so hard for suspension of disbelief. When you read that "I did it" there's a tendency to believe what you're being told. You get an almost automatic identification which I think is so important in a story. In *Child of Fire* I have a device which goes back to the Marlow situation in Conrad. I use a parole officer, in charge of fifty children, who tells the story of one particular boy. It has drawbacks of course, because you can only report what you have seen. I have a situation in which the boy leaves San Diego and goes on a tuna clipper to Ecuador, where there's a mutiny and where he's thrown in prison. In the end he escapes and gets back to San Diego. Well, he has to tell this story; there's no other way of getting it. It's not as dramatic as it would have been if the parole officer had gone with him, and so had been able to tell the story himself, like an omnipotent

175

observer. But that was obviously impossible. So there are penalties.

Q *I understand you are now working on a novel about William Tyndale, the first Englishman to do a creditable version of the Bible. Although this is obviously set in the past, it doesn't seem to have much else to do with your other children's books. Are you doing this as an extension of your own messianic tendencies?*

A I'm terribly interested in his story. He wanted every ploughboy to read the Bible as it came from the original Greek and Hebrew, not as it came from the Vulgate, and not as the priest read it in the pulpit. This is what Tyndale wanted to do, and this is what Tyndale did—and he did it so beautifully that when the King James version came along they used 70 to 75 per cent of Tyndale in it. Today we speak Tyndale. It's extraordinary if you compare the passages he translated from the Greek with the same passages in the Latin. If you are really concerned with something it gets into the fabric of the story and is transmitted to the reader. That was D. H. Lawrence's feeling, and it's certainly one I share. I have only done things that I've been really enthusiastic about, stories that have stirred me. With Tyndale, and with this messianic quirk of mine, I feel that I am performing a mission; it may be a little grandiloquent to call it that, yet that is my feeling. Children speak the language, but they don't know where the hell it came from. They don't know whom to credit for it, and they certainly don't know Tyndale's story, how the man lived in attics and burrows and was pursued by spies all over Germany, Holland and Belgium, attempting to seize him and take him back to England. His Bible was smuggled into England. It had to be, because it was against the law to own it or read it. He very calmly gave up his life for this purpose. He was a hero. Today children don't feel there are important things to do. They take it out on sports—the football players and the baseball players are heroes, so that at any given time we've got 5,000 heroes. But this is a very empty thing; it's heroism delegated. Nobody enjoys sports more than I do, but I don't enjoy them for that reason. I don't think they should be used as a substitute for the meaningful things in life that never occur to children brought up by fathers who are crazy about sports in houses where there aren't any books. And our divorce statistics and our crime statistics are frightening. In this county alone, San Diego, there are 23,000 parolees. In other words, sometime this afternoon you have been in contact with two or three parolees in this area. You can't miss them. And what do you do with them? I'm on a board of directors for one of these crash programs. We run a tranquillity house where we have twenty or so very young girls and boys who have drug problems. They live in this house and police themselves under certain restrictions and rules. What we're trying to do is put them back in the mainstream. We've been most successful when they've gotten jobs or something to do, and don't have to sit round the house all day, which is lethal.

Q   *But one can see why they get like that in an overdeveloped urban society.*

A   Young people are terribly restricted on the basis of what we consider important. The country is poisoned by money, so that anybody who doesn't get rich and make a lot of it is considered a failure. There's none of the old idea, still around in some places of the world, that you do your work because you enjoy doing it. Well, the unions have taken over now. If you're a checker at a Safeway store, you get five dollars ninety-five cents an hour, and benefits, so you don't have to worry about a lot of things, the quality of your work for one thing. It's very easy of course to sit here having something quite different to do and talk in general terms. I think it's partly the way schools are run today. Think of the past, when children weren't children but a real part of the family. If the father was a stonemason then the son was a stonemason; and if the mother worked at a loom making tapestries, then the daughter learned to make tapestries. The family was monolithic, as the Tarascans are in Mexico today. The family was very strong, and the children learned trades and were proud of them. By the age of ten or so they were adults. I think children should be given adult responsibilities as soon as possible. Of course, child labor has been abused, as it was in the Industrial Revolution. What we're doing though is extending childhood to infinity, protecting our children from what, for Christ's sake? They're much smarter than we are, much smarter than their parents, certainly in worldly ways. We need to change the fabric of the family so there are books in the home and mothers and fathers reading to their children, instead of this generation gap, children wanting to get out of the house as fast as they can because of restrictions. How this is to be done I don't know. It probably isn't possible. There's some element that is missing. In the Orient the father is honored, and the grandfather and the grandmother are honored. There is honor. But here in America, when you get to be over forty you might as well be dead.

Q   *In* The King's Fifth *it certainly suprised me that a boy of fifteen was entrusted with the post of cartographer on a large exploring vessel.*

177

A   It's an example of what I'm talking about. For instance, our captains and your captains who sailed to the Far East usually retired at the age of thirty.

Q   *There is real evidence that a skill like that could be acquired by the time you were fifteen in the Spanish Empire?*

A   They learned these skills when they were very young. Coronado was *only* twenty-nine when he led his great expedition. In this story I've just published, *Child of Fire*, the boy was inspired by Coronado. But are there any Coronados around today! There aren't, but there are still things to do. We shouldn't try to make adults out of children too quickly; but we can still give them a sense of responsibility. We can give girls the knowledge that marriage won't solve all their problems, either when they're at junior high, or preferably before. They must realize that, though it's a wonderful idea, there will be more problems, more responsibilities after than before they're married. They have to learn that in marriage you're in trouble if you expect to find in your mate all the men in the world or all the women in the world. I don't think children are prepared for marriage at all. I think the statistics prove it, particularly here in America. California is the worst of all—something like one divorce in every two and one-half marriages. But if you tried to teach sex in the schools, the parents wouldn't stand for it. So the kids educate themselves, without good examples or good sexual relationships. They just bat their heads around until hopefully they find something workable. I'm all for divorce as an escape from horrors, but I still think it's a frightening indication.

Q   *Have you had any children yourself?*

A   No. My wife (we're both previously divorced) has two children—a girl who's twenty-four and married twice, and a boy still at school.

Q   *One can see how this society is bad for marriage. But on the other hand one might say that marriage is bad for this society. To you, obviously, marriage is important.*

A   I think it's terribly important. It's an anchor. I don't think you can have much without it, except chaos. There are so many things involved. Children first of all. You can say that children would be better off herded, as Shaw suggested, and taken away from their parents. It's an interesting theory, but it doesn't work. The human psyche is a very fragile thing. Children demand, must have, love. Most children don't have it, and that's one of our troubles. Children need to feel they have a place, that they're not some object, and that they have a designated and honorable role in a family where everybody contributes. American children don't contribute. They do what they want to do, or what they can get away with. And that's what they're brought up to do. It's difficult to argue with them, so parents don't argue with them. They are afraid to attack the problem because if they talk too much then the children will leave the house. The family is certainly fragmented. I would like to have it all go back to the farm, where children grew up knowing how to use a hoe and milk a cow. To live out in the country and raise a lot of the things that you use—that to me is the ideal life. It may be impossible, but it's still ideal. The last thing that ninety-nine out of a hundred people want to do is get up at four in the morning and milk a cow. But it's a wonderful life because once again the family can become monolithic, one depending upon the other. In the past there have been disadvantages to this—little schooling and a lot of isolation. But now with television it's quite different. This is what I'd like to see. How you get it in an overpopulated industrial society I don't know. Anyway people don't want it. They want what they've got now—a lot of sports and TV.

Q   *You're obviously a man of faith. Perhaps the most powerful moment in all your books occurs at the end of* The Black Pearl, *when despite the fact that the pearl has wrought such misfortune to the community, the boy still takes it back to the church where it is enshrined. Where did that come from?*

A   I think it's just a logical working out of the plot. At present *The Black Pearl* is being made into a motion picture. I've read the script—not that I have any say in it. What the producer does is to have the boy sell the pearl and buy food and clothing for the town. It's the SLA idea again.

Q   *And exactly what you avoided.*

A   Yes. I said to him, Well, it's dramatic, but I don't like it because, and I'm not a Catholic, you're criticizing the Catholic Church. In essence this pearl could buy twenty or twenty-five thousand dollars' worth of groceries, but in my version the pearl exists and everybody can come and look at it and feel that it belongs to them. That's the theory in the Catholic Church, that the Cathedral and the Virgin are yours. I've seen Indians who have come hundreds of miles to Mexico City to see the Guadalupe Virgin. These Indians come with a vision of the Virgin in their eyes and nothing else. They'd walk over you and never notice.

179

Adoration, excitement! So the way I closed *The Black Pearl* seemed the logical way.

Q   *How much research goes into your books?*

A   Certainly a lot for *The King's Fifth*. That was an overly ambitious book when I first started it. All the cities were allegorical cities. I woke up one morning and found that I was competing with Dante. So I quit that and started over.

Q   *Are your books intended as a way through the barriers between children and their parents, the problem we have discussed?*

A   Yes—I think the written word is one of the few great resources we have. I don't think our television, with its violence and over-display of firearms and bosoms and everything, is helpful at all. I have a dedication to the idea of trying to reach this young group that hasn't been abandoned yet, to reach them with a few simple comments about life. I get a lot of letters from children, particularly on *Island of the Blue Dolphins*. They like the idea of fighting for survival; they are challenged by it and they would like to try it themselves.

Q   *Do you have any opinions about the commune movement which has been going on for ten years or so now? It seems a variation on the idea of the return to the farm and a closer family existence.*

A   In the beginning I was critical about it because I didn't understand what they were trying to do. Then it became associated with marijuana, which, incidentally, I don't think is as bad as cigarettes. It has been degraded by the word "hippy" and by long hair. People don't realize of course that for thousands of years young men wore their hair long. What disappoints me about this youth revolution though, is that very little has come out of it artistically. The best is from the Beatles—they've made a contribution. But in poetry and prose and art there has been very little. They attend Woodstock by the thousands, but that's not productive. The same group with the same excitement 500 years ago would have built cathedrals beautiful to look at.

Q   *Perhaps it's a lack of independence among the gatherers at Woodstock that you find hard to take?*

A   I do think independence is a very important thing if you can combine it with the family. My father was an autocrat who couldn't care less about his children. I never had a good relationship with him, so I can't speak too much from experience about the family. But I still think we should try to restore it.

Scott O'Dell

Q *Would that help to solve the other problems in America—the racial problem, for instance?*

A It would help. I don't think you can solve the Black problem by any one approach. It's a tremendous task and all acts of good will help.

Q *Do you still have stories you want to write?*

A I have a lot more—three or four at the moment. But it's difficult to get to them because when I quit smoking four years ago I found that I could no longer write at the typewriter. Now I write with a pen. It takes longer to get myself together, using a pen, and I work more slowly.

California, 1974

Among the many books Scott O'Dell has written are: Island of the Blue Dolphins (1960, Newberry Award Winner); The King's Fifth (1966, a Newberry Honor Book); The Black Pearl (1967, also a Newberry Honor Book); The Dark Canoe (1968); Journey to Jericho (1969); Sing Down the Moon (1970); The Treasure of Top-el-Bampo (1972) *and* The Cruise of the Arctic Star (1973).

13 *Rosemary Sutcliff*

Interviewed by Emma Fisher

Although Rosemary Sutcliff's books relive history with passionate feeling, they are not escapist romances, and their appeal for many children lies in the fact that they are totally real. Sutcliff manages to keep a fine balance between the historical outlook—the fatalistic portrayal of events pushing her characters, the clash of civilizations or the ruinous consequences of war—and the novelist's viewpoint. She allows the characters to work out their own destinies. The emotions grow naturally from the background, with such intensity that she has sometimes been under-valued as a sentimental writer. She won the Carnegie Medal in 1959 for *The Lantern Bearers*.

Rosemary Sutcliff was born in Surrey in 1920, and lived in various ports with her mother, as her father was a naval officer. Since early childhood she has suffered from a form of arthritis, making it difficult for her to move about, but this did not prevent her from training hard as an artist and becoming a professional miniaturist. A patriotic miniature, *The Spirit of England*, which she painted in the year of Dunkirk (1940), hung in the Royal Academy and was much talked about. She now lives and writes in a country cottage near Arundel in Sussex.

Q   *I think you had a rather strange childhood, in that you didn't have a formal education, did you?*

A   No, I didn't. Partly because my father was a sailor, and we traipsed round the world after him, and partly because I was very ill when I was a small child, and didn't go to school; but my mother read aloud to me a great deal, and she would only read books that *she* enjoyed. So that wiped out all the "tripe" of the day, and I only got the best of everything from Beatrix Potter to Dickens, all at the same time.

Q   *Was that when you acquired your sense of history?*

A   Yes. She was very very fond of historical novels, and historical stories in general, and I was brought up on Kipling—*Puck of Pook's Hill* particularly—and various Victorian novels such as Whyte-Melville's *The Gladiators*, and things of this sort, and I think this was really my start, particularly my fondness for Roman Britain, and Roman times in general. I learnt about Beowulf and Middle English literature at the same early age—I was brought up on a book called *Myths and Legends of the British Race.*

Q   *So as a child you didn't read children's books?*

A   Not really. I read the odd Angela Brazil. But of course I didn't learn to read until I was nine, I was read to, and when you can be read to, the books you can read for yourself are not so advanced and you get rather bored with them. Actually Kipling was the same—he couldn't read until he was nine either—so I'm in good company. I don't remember whether he had anybody to read to him, but I know his sister could read at the age of about four, and he said "that's because you don't understand what it's all about, how difficult it is." We had Beatrix Potter, and I loved *The Wind in the Willows*; and all Kipling's so-called children's books, and *Treasure Island*; but on the whole not very many children's books, because I was so late coming to reading myself that I went straight into the adult ones. I came back to the children's ones later, when I started writing.

Q   *How much later was that?*

A   I was into my—I suppose—early twenties. I started off as an artist, I was art-school trained, and I've got all my City and Guilds certificates to prove it; I became a member of the Royal Society of Miniature Painters. And then I started scribbling, and gradually got something published, and as I started to write more and more I had less and less to give to the painting. The writing was the important one, the writing went deepest in me. So little by little I left off the painting. The books just took over; I hadn't got enough creative fire for both. This little desk that is now my writing desk was specially made as a painting desk.

Q   *You started writing children's books. Do you object to the classifi-*
     cation, or do you think it is a necessary one?

A   I have got the four adult ones to my credit, but they're no easier to write than the children's ones—in some ways they're harder. My sort have as big a canvas as the adult ones, but you have to write them to a certain extent with one hand tied behind your back. There are still certain things you musn't mention in a children's book, and certain complexities of relationship and motivation, this kind of thing; and you have to get your effects in a slightly simpler way, whereas if you're writing for an adult there's nothing you can't say or do.

Q   *Can you give me an example?*

A   After I'd written *Sword at Sunset*, I did an edited version for children, and they made me cut certain things—details of the battles, because they were too violent; and the fact that two of the soldiers were homosexuals, which was in fact a most natural thing to happen, and part of being a warrior. I discovered later that lots of children had been reading the adult version and loving it!

Q   *There is quite a lot of homosexual feeling in your books, or at*
     least very passionate friendship between people of the same sex.
     Is this part of the historical background (more plausible in the
     kind of society you write about than friendships between the
     sexes)? Or is this way of writing about love particularly suited
     to children's (older children's) books?

A   I would, I think, agree with you in all these suggestions, but add that I write mostly about men in a man's world, fighting men; and the homosexual relationship, or at any rate very deep friendship between men, tends very much to occur in this type of society. I imagine that the warrior "blood brother" relationship was often far nearer to the homosexual than to any kind of brotherhood, though possibly the men themselves were not fully aware of this.

184

Q   *The sort of cuts you made in* Sword at Sunset *wouldn't be necessary now, would they?*

A   I think perhaps not. And if the child is caught by your book, his imagination is caught, even if the relationship is complicated; they don't mind being stretched, they sort of hop along in your wake, and understand what they can. They can understand kind of through the pores of their skin; things that are beyond them mentally they can very often take in intuitively. But one can't count on that.

Q   *The soldierly or heroic virtues, courage and friendship, seem to mean a great deal to you.*

A   They do. I had a very Spartan mother, and was brought up rather like a boy, and I do appreciate the heroic virtues.

Q   *Do you look for them in your material?*

A   This is one of the reasons that I like writing historical novels, whereas I don't think I could write modern ones.

Q   *Doesn't one find those virtues in the present?*

A   Not in quite the same undiluted form.

Q   *How late in history can you still find them?*

A   The latest period I've ever written about is the English Civil War (the seventeenth century). There are certain periods I can't write: I can't write later than the Civil War, that goes kind of "cloak and dagger" on me. And I can't write Mediaeval England.

Q   Knight's Fee *manages all right, in the 1000's and 1100's.*

A   I can manage that, but I can't cope with—say from 1200 to 1500.

Q   *I wonder why?*

A   I don't know—I think I can't accept a world which is quite so absolutely impregnated with religion; the terrific hold that the Church had in every facet of life. I can't understand it. In the period of *Knight's Fee*, it hadn't really got this terrific hold that it got later. After the late Norman times, I just don't understand the people.

Q   *Yet you can put yourself in the place of people who followed the old religions—the people in, say,* Warrior Scarlet.

A   I think I have a very strong feeling for the old and primitive religions. I read Frazer's *The Golden Bough* in all its—is it eight volumes? I couldn't afford it, so I read it in a bookshop, where the keeper was a great friend of mine; I used to go back every week and hurriedly skim through a little bit more. I treated myself eventually to the abridged edition, and then of course went much deeper into it. *The Golden Bough* is I suppose a bit dated now, but it's still the basic book on the primitive faiths. I'm much more at home with the Bronze Age things, the fertility cult, witchcraft, than with mediaeval Catholicism.

Q   *Do you count as Church of England?*

A   I always put C of E on documents, but I'm such an unorthodox Christian that I rather doubt if I can claim to *be* a Christian. I don't even really believe that Christ was different in kind from other people—only in degree.

Q   *This is the Arian heresy—that Christ is not consubstantial with God. Do you think Christ was a particularly gifted and influential human being, rather than the son of God?*

A   I think that Christ was one of the great masters and leaders who appear from time to time—Buddha was another—men who are a kind of special flowering of humanity. If one believes in reincarnation, and I think I do, one might say that he was a complete soul who had finished with incarnation, but made the supreme sacrifice of coming back once more, to live that particular life and die that particular death, because it was needed.

Q   *There often appears to be a kind of pagan fatalism in your books. The country, and certain artifacts, live on while the people suffer and die according to their destinies. Do the objects which appear in more than one of your books symbolize this? I mean the flint axe in* Knight's Fee *and* Warrior Scarlet, *and the flawed emerald ring in the Roman books.*

A   No, they're not symbols; it's just continuity. I've got this terrific thing about continuity; they're the same hills in *Knight's Fee* as in *Warrior Scarlet,* and it suddenly came to me when writing *Knight's Fee* that I'd use the flint axe to show the continuity.

Q   *Do you see men as relatively small compared with the background against which they are set?*

A   No. I always feel very involved with the people, and very unable
to see the wood for the trees, when I'm writing about them.
But I am able to get involved with either side.

Q   *There are two "sides" you often make a distinction between—the
people who know about civilization, and the people who know
about life, say the Romans and the Britons, or Saxons and Celts.
The people of the day and the people of the night. Do you feel
something is lost in civilizing?*

A   I think the distinctions are much more blurred than they were,
but I think this one still exists to a certain extent. The same
things are lost now in civilizing—I won't say uncivilized people,
but people who have a different civilization from one's own.
You lose spontaneity, you lose contact with the life force. That's
something one can't correct; it's a dichotomy which just exists.

Q   *In* Knight's Fee *the central character is a blend of two races,
Breton and Saxon. When one race overtakes another, do you think
they should mingle into one? Is that what the book is about?*

A   I think it *is* a good idea; I think it always happens. Possibly
not a good idea in the first generation in certain cases. I think
the old prejudices against interracial marriages—between black
and white for instance—can be pretty difficult in the first generation or two, because they are a very different racial type.
But there's no real reason why it shouldn't eventually happen.
When you get a combination like say Celt and Saxon, probably
it's a very good blend—the perhaps rather more solid Saxon
side and the fire of the Celtic side come together and make
a good mixture.

Q   *The Celtic side provides the leaven.*

A   I think the Saxon side is more stolid. Mind you I'm absolutely
pure Saxon myself, we're from the North country and as far
as we know haven't a trace of Celt in us. But I always feel
in a way more at home with the Celt than with the Saxon.
I feel I know the way their minds work—this thinking in circles
that a Celt can do. The Saxon is a bit like the Roman; he
thinks in a straight line.

Q   *What's your attitude to the present, the time from which you look
back at these happenings?*

Randal holds the dying Bevis; illustration by Charles Keeping for Rosemary Sutcliff's *Knight's Fee*.

A   As I said, I'm never at all certain that I don't believe in reincarnation. I rather think I do. In which case one does know the other times, and one can go back. I think the present—1973—is a very exciting time to be living in, but I don't think it is altogether to my taste.

Q   *You've lived another life in Roman Britain?*

A   Yes. This is possibly the reason that a lot of writers have this thing, as I was saying just now, about not being able to write about certain periods. Whereas other periods and places one feels completely at home in. This could be explained if they were the places and periods you hadn't experienced yourself, in an earlier life.

Q   *So you don't find it too hard to think yourself into the period you're writing about?*

A   I mug up the history I need, and then I forget and mug up the next piece. I think I've got the trick of catching the feeling of a period.

Q   *Is it difficult to make people talk in a convincing way?*

A   I find it very difficult. I think I've evolved a style now which has a faintly archaic sound without being pish-tushery, but at the same time isn't quite modern English. I think the thing to remember is that people use the speech of their day, which sounds completely modern and normal to them, and if you get something too archaic, it sounds unreal, and comes between them and the reality of the story. There was a time when 1066 was *now* for people just as real as us.

Q   *There are certain similarities between your books and those of Mary Renault; are you an admirer of hers?*

A   Oh yes. I get completely carried away by her books. At the end of *The Last of the Wine*—when Alexis sees Lysis on the bier and the broken sandal strap—I couldn't believe it, it was like coming up to a car accident and seeing it is somebody you know. I turned back three pages and read it again, expecting it to be different this time—I couldn't bear it. I was slightly afraid when I produced *Flowers for Adonis*—about Alcibiades— that I might be trespassing on her territory.

Q   *What do you think of the strong elements of fantasy in children's writing nowadays—the classic example being Tolkien?*

A   I think he's a very difficult writer. Very difficult to understand, and perhaps not really appropriate for children. I think he's an adult writer masquerading to a certain extent. Adults tend to think that something which is on the surface a fairy story isn't meant for them, but I think in this case it is.

Q   *Do you prefer a more realistic writer like William Mayne?*

A   I think he writes beautifully, his books are poet's books, but I never get very involved with the people. They have a slight sameness. And he's utterly unaware of the nuances of different kinds of backgrounds. His children's fathers, whether they are lawyers or lorry-drivers, all have exactly the same sense of humor, which people don't, straight through society; and their children all call them Daddy, which again people don't, straight through society. This kind of thing. And therefore to a certain extent his books lack reality.

Q   *Have you ever been tempted to write about magic, an unreal world impinging on a real one?*

A   No, I've always been very well rooted on the ground. There's just an occasional touch of the supernatural here and there in the earlier ones. I think I'm very circumstantial in my books: I get terribly bothered by things like loose ends in the plot. And in other people's plots—I get frightfully bothered when it doesn't tie up.

Q   *You seem to have a favorite plot line—people who have a goal or achievement ahead of them, getting their Warrior Scarlet or becoming a Knight. They almost fail, but succeed in the end in spite of great obstacles.*

A   Some people do say that writers have only one plot, and I think really I've only got one plot; a boy growing up and finding himself, and finding his own soul in the process, and achieving the aim he sets out to achieve; or not achieving it, and finding his own soul in the process of not achieving it. And becoming part of society.

Q   *It is a sad process in a way.*

A   Yes, it is a sad process. Quite often I get involved in unhappy endings to my books; in *The Mark of the Horse Lord* I had actually to make my hero kill himself. I tried and tried to find a way out for him, but the shape of the story demanded it, and that was that. I get terribly involved with my own people, and very moved by them myself, so it's always good to hear that other people have been moved.

Q   *Is it a good thing—something to aim for?*

A   Oh yes. It stretches their emotions and I'm sure this is good. I think with children it helps them to grow and develop. It's educational in a way, education in living.

Q   *You've lately done your telling of* Tristan and Iseult, *and* The Witch's Brat *for younger children—what else is on the way?*

A   There's this little book, *The Capricorn Bracelet*, which is being published in two days' time. It's set in Roman Scotland. I feel terribly at home in Roman Britain—I feel here I am again in my own stamping ground. I'm slightly ashamed of feeling so at home among the Romans, because they were an awful bourgeois lot, but there we are.

Q   *Do your readers like the Romans as much as you do?*

A   Well, I get a lot of fan letters, generally saying: How did you come to be a writer, how long does it take you, how can I become one; sometimes they inquire anxiously about particular characters—did so-and-so find a nice wife, and this kind of thing, which I find really rather touching, because one feels they have become really involved, and the people are real to them. One fan letter I had once, years and years ago, said, broadly speaking: Dear Miss Sutcliff, I enjoy your books very much, and I hope that when you are dead you will go on writing books and I can go on reading them.

Sussex, 1973

Rosemary Sutcliff's children's books include: The Chronicles of Robin Hood (1950); The Queen Elizabeth Story (1950); The Armourer's House (1951); Brother Dusty Feet (1952); Simon (1953); The Eagle of the Ninth (1954); Outcast (1955); The Shield Ring (1956); The Silver Branch (1957); Warrior Scarlet (1958); The Lantern Bearers (1959); Knight's Fee (1960); Bodley Head Monograph on Kipling (1960); Beowulf (1961) *(reprinted in 1966 as* Dragon Slayer*);* Dawn Wind (1961); The Hound of Ulster (1963); The Mark of the Horse Lord (1965); A Circlet of Oak Leaves (1965); The Chief's Daughter (1966); The High Deeds of Fin MacCool (1967); The Witche's Brat (1970); Tristan and Iseult (1971); The Truce of the Games (1971); The Capricorn Bracelet (1973); The Changeling (1974).

14 Leon Garfield

Interviewed by Justin Wintle

Leon Garfield's chosen stamping ground is eighteenth-century England, although recently he has wandered further and further away from that era. His early books are remarkable chiefly as exceedingly good adventures, but even *Jack Holborn*, Garfield's first novel, suggests that he is something more than a talented story-teller. A young orphaned boy smuggles himself on board a merchantman on an outward-bound voyage from Bristol. From this moment he is whisked along on a stream of improbable but well-flighted coincidences, which include, inevitably, a pirate attack, a shipwreck, any number of near-misses with death, and at least one pseudo-resurrection. All this may sound familiar, but there is no lack of original energy in the narrative. At one point the survivors of the shipwreck are faced with a long march through subtropical forest: "So the forest it was to be: the dark and dangerous forest. That was the way for four rich men." Already there is a hint of the elemental imagery which so enriches the later books.

Collaborating with Edward Blishen, Garfield has also produced two retellings of the Greek Myths—*The God Beneath the Sea* (which won the Carnegie Medal in 1970) and *The Golden Shadow*. Each book takes about twenty of the original myths and weaves them together in new combinations, striking fresh nuances and rediscovering universal human truths. The effect is little short of shattering. Both books are illustrated uninhibitedly by Charles Keeping.

Leon Garfield was born in Brighton in 1921. His studies in art after school were cut short by the war, which sent him on service to Belgium and Germany. Later he worked in a hospital as a biochemist, and began writing in his spare time. He is now a full-time writer, living in Highgate, London, with his wife and adopted daughter.

Leon Garfield

Q   *Your work falls into two seemingly distinct parts. On the one hand are the novels of historical adventure, and on the other your highly organic remolding of the ancient Greek Myths. Perhaps we could begin with the historical books, since that is where you started. Up until* The Strange Affair of Adelaide Harris *they are all situated somewhere in the eighteenth century, or at least a version of that period. Why is that?*

A   That's something I find very difficult to explain. Someone once attempted to explain it to me—that my childhood was spent in a very eighteenth-century town, Brighton, just before the war, and the architecture had an influence, although I don't think it's a very strong reason. The first book I published, *Jack Holborn*, was set in the eighteenth-century because I'd been very influenced by a book I'd just read, namely R. L. Stevenson's *Master of Ballantrae*, which, of course, is set in the eighteenth century. But I don't think that in itself is sufficient for one to continue in it. Obviously I like the way I can use language for that time, language that wouldn't be so suitable for contemporary narrative. It effected some sort of release in writing. When I first started that book I was aware of a distinct difference in my writing, as though one were aware, for the first time, of being able to make some sort of contact. Certain inhibitions that everyone has about expressing themselves seemed to be removed. It's finding a remove, a better way to express oneself decisively. Whether or not my affection for writers like Fielding and Jane Austen existed before that I don't know—it's difficult to remember. Since then though I've had an enormous affection for them, Jane Austen particularly. My reading of Dickens came quite a lot later.

Q   *Was* Jack Holborn *your first attempt at publication?*

A   No—I'd written many things before that, as one does in imitation of every writer one's admired in turn—Dostoevsky, Tolstoy, Lewis Carroll, Hans Andersen, the lot!

Q   *How long had that been going on for?*

A   Since I was about twelve, but never quite making that sort of contact with the paper. Probably it's an inevitable process of experimenting with writing of the most florid type, as one does when one's very young. But unlike most writers I never turned to poetry—or at least not since I was about eleven, when one wrote elaborate narrative verse. But after that my interest was essentially in narrative prose, but in the most high-flown manner possible. One was trying to draw the line between prose

193

and poetry, when of course there is no such line that really exists.

Q *Certainly I thought* Jack Holborn *suffered from too much descriptive flair—the facility for atmosphere—at the cost of shape in the plot. There's an abrupt change of gear at the end, so that the last chapter has less than nothing to do with most of what preceded it.*

A There's a very mundane reason for that. The book was cut drastically. Originally it was nearly twice as long, and the plot probably worked rather better at the fuller length. There are great sections missing because when the publishers accepted it they said it was too long for a juvenile book. Would I cut it? Of course I was only too happy to do that, even though I'd spent five years writing it, which meant that I lost control of the plot in that time. For a novel that length one needs a lot more experience than I then had. I just continually invented to keep it going. It was splendid practice for writing.

Q *You say it was reduced according to the publisher's specifications of a juvenile book. Is that what it was intended to be?*

A No. It may have been when I first started the book—I mean in the very first paragraph. But after that I really became involved in the writing, and the idea of an audience didn't really occur to me. I sent it to an agent, to whom I had been recommended, and she submitted it as an adult book, because that's what she thought it was. It was turned down by Heinemann after three or four agonizing months, when they said they couldn't quite decide whether it was adult or junior. It was at a time when there was no such thing as the young or teenage novel—1964, when it was scarcely beginning. It was then sent to Grace Hogarth at Constable, where they were in fact just beginning a large juvenile list. She suggested that, if I would be willing to cut it, then she'd publish it as a juvenile book. And of course, though I'd vowed I'd never alter a word, once the possibility of its being published became real, I cut it in about a week.

Q *After the success of* Jack Holborn, *did you see the eighteenth century as a line that could be profitably pursued?*

A My first reactions after *Jack Holborn* was finished were—What the hell am I going to write next? I seemed to have exhausted all the possibilities for the adventure story. My agent asked me to write an adult novel as she had delusions of grandeur.

But I don't think alternating ever works really.

Q   *Why's that do you think?*

A   I don't know. Because one just writes as well as one can? I think if one were to write books that were only suitable for adults, this would simply mean that the other books possess a sort of holding back, a deliberate aiming.

Q   *So what happened?*

A   Well in fact I did try to write an adult novel, based upon episodes in the Newgate Calendar, sticking to the same period I'd done so much research into over the previous five years. I found that this, rightly rejected by every publisher, was in a curious way written down: it was very artificial, as though I'd lost all contact with the paper. Then Grace Hogarth, having seen that *Jack Holborn* had done well, actually gave me a contract for another juvenile novel before I'd written a word of it, which was about the most sensible and generous thing any publisher could ever do. This really made me feel I must write another book—*Devil-In-The-Fog*, which fortunately did even better than *Jack Holborn*.

Q   *You say that you've spent five years at least researching the eighteenth century. What kind of relationship is there between your writing and the process of research?*

A   Very close. It's either an advantage or a hindrance, but I find it impossible to invent without a very strong basis of fact, and also a very strong basis of memory.

Q   *What would be an example of the basis of fact in, say,* Jack Holborn?

A   Oh—all the maritime details were absolutely accurate, even to the time it took to cover certain distances by boat in those days. I worked from sixteenth-century maps of that part of Africa —such maps as would have been available. Things like the value of money. The social detail of the time was accurate. This was all necessary because I couldn't believe in what I wrote unless I could believe in the solidity of the research.

Q   *And what of the second basis, memory?*

A   That's obvious. One cannot really invent outside one's own memory. And it was in *Jack Holborn* that I discovered that really one can use one's own experience. For sheer physical sensation it's essential.

Q   *And how did the plot itself originate—the young apprentice who becomes a stowaway on a pirate ship?*

A   That was quite mechanical really. The original idea for the plot was the idea of contrasting two identical brothers, one good and one evil, and posing the question, how does one tell the difference between them at any given moment? And, is there any difference? It probably derived from *The Master of Ballantrae*, which also has two brothers, though not in the same way. The rest of the plot—the secret, etcetera—was just mechanical devices to explore this idea.

Q   *Is there a particular reason for the recurrence of identity as a motif in the adventure novels?*

A   Not that I know of. These are stories that just occur to me. I suppose the question of identity is very basic. I'm always aware of the fact that halfway through a book one is echoing one's other books, so one tries to explore their ideas differently. In *Jack Holborn* the question of identity is there very strongly as a dramatic device. Also in *Devil-In-The-Fog*, which may have something to do with that, at that time, we adopted our daughter. The question of identity then is obviously one that fascinates, because one attempts to understand the child's development and the problems it faces. This must influence one's subconscious creative thinking.

Q   *I thought perhaps it might have been you who was adopted.*

A   No, not as far as I know—though with my haphazard parents I wouldn't be surprised. I had a rather Dickensian background, with the constant warfare between mother and father that occurs in most families. My father was particularly flamboyant; he was alternatively wildly successful and plunged into abject disgrace.

Q   *As . . ?*

A   As a businessman. He was probably an actor manqué.

Q   *Perhaps it explains some of the theatricality in your writing, the air of Grand Guignol.*

A   My father was very like Mr. Treet in *Devil-In-The-Fog*, a very flamboyant man who always created an enormous impression, although one always had the sneaking suspicion that there was very little behind it. It was a gift for being enormously liked by everyone except my mother, who became rather tired of it. She went to the other extreme—excessively careful and neurotic, being driven to it by a most erratic and irresponsible husband, who at the same time presented a façade of enormous solidity.

Q   *Most of your books eschew the idea of home.*

A   That may be because my own was fairly unsettled. There again, there are other reasons. My stories are usually a movement away from home. It's very difficult to construct a fast or fairly fast-moving story in one locality.

Q   *Why do your books have to move so fast?*

A   Basic insecurity I suppose, and a fear of boring my audience. I'm a very impatient reader myself. They are slowing down now, though whether that's age or experience I don't know. But I find it difficult to slow down. The thing I'm writing now is presenting enormous difficulties because it is set in a home and I'm having to find movement in quite other ways than I've found it before—in sheer description and the interrelation of the characters. One never ceases to marvel at the construction of something like *Pride and Prejudice*—the absolute miracle that the story can be so utterly absorbing, can move with apparent rapidity when in point of fact very little happens.

Q   *In a contribution you made to J. R. Townsend's* A Sense of Story, *you said that the kind of writing you liked has "something of the character of morality" as well as excitement and adventure. And yet in so much of what you've written there never seems time for any of the characters to consider the consequences of their behavior. Jack Holborn for example: his virtue is innate, so there's never really any question of him doing something seriously amiss. That seems to me a concession to the character of morality, rather than an understanding.*

A   I cut out an enormous amount of introspection in that book—those were the parts that went. Otherwise the story wouldn't have worked at all, though I think it was a much better book at the full length. In subsequent books I have tried to explore a bit more, each time learning more about how to develop the characters and illustrate them changing.

Q   *Yes, you do change your handling of morality, though I think the tendency has been toward symbolism. In* Black Jack *for instance, there is a series of extraordinary transformations, in which insanity becomes sanity and evil is turned to altruism, but all in a slightly superhuman way.*

A   Yes, it was completely different because I had intended Black Jack himself to represent a force of nature, neither good nor bad; a force, a vital force, but capable of being influenced either way, and being influenced by the boy, who is a very middle-class version of Jack Holborn, with many faults and restrictions. There was a very complicated series of themes in *Black Jack* in which insanity was peculiarly important. The girl was based upon an actual case I came across when I was doing some part-time work in a mental laboratory—a type of encephalitis that leaves the patient with about a fifteen-second memory. I chose that as an actual case because of a certain verisimilitude, and also because it's not understood now and so it certainly wouldn't have been understood then. And—nobody knows why—such cases can have a spontaneous cure. In *Black Jack* I postulated this cure by the fall from the coach, because the neurologist I was talking to said it would be quite possible.

Q   *I gained the impression that the girl's cure had more to do with her relationship with the boy.*

A   This would help, but the cure really begins when she falls from the coach. After that her memory gradually becomes consecutive. But it would take her a year at least to recover completely.

Q   *Again in* A Sense of Story, *John Rowe Townsend has criticized the structure of* Black Jack, *chiefly it seems because Black Jack himself more or less disappears for roughly a third of the book. But the story isn't really about him, is it?*

A   No—Black Jack is a catalyst really. The story becomes central without him, between the boy and the girl and their deepening relationship, so that the boy is brought to a point of natural desperation that would have been impossible for him at the beginning of the book.

Q   *And it all winds up, most convincingly, in the millenarian panic of prophetic earthquakes.*

A   Again, there's a very practical reason for that. Longmans (the publishers) asked if I would use an actual historical fact for a change. The earthquakes which happened in 1749 are obscure, but they seemed to fit this upheaval of nature and the other theme, that expectation comes to nothing and realization at what the actual miracle is—that the world doesn't collapse. And I arranged all the images in the book to lead toward that: most of them are concerned with an upheaval in nature which reflects *Black Jack* as well.

Q   *Were you attempting to delineate a confusion between badness and madness?*

A   Yes, very much so; and again between ignorance and innocence —the sheer horror of a fourteen-year-old in a madhouse.

Q   *A modern theme.*

A   Certainly conditions in mental hospitals haven't changed very much. The attitude of the matron (in *Black Jack*) is very much the attitude of the older nursing sisters you find today, who literally confuse ignorance and innocence.

Q   *Do you think you would be able to treat a similar story in a modern setting yourself?*

A   I find it impossible to say. The most modern story I've done was in late Victorian London—*The Ghost Downstairs*. This one I'm doing now is set in 1789 because I'm trying to show the IRA or Black September sort of violence through a young man filled with Tom Paine's ideals, the ideals of revolution—a bored young man who eventually becomes a fairly mindless and brutal criminal, because what has attracted him is the licence to violence: and when he can no longer support the idea, he is quite happy to go on supporting the violence.

Q   *All your adventure novels have pretty desperate environments— pirate ships, the empty highroad, madhouses and the criminal East End of old London. Would it be possible for you, do you think, to write about people in circumstances which didn't immediately pinpoint their moral hue?*

A   Oh yes. This one I'm engaged on now has a very accurate and happy setting in it. *The Strange Affair of Adelaide Harris* had one I think.

Q   *What have you learnt from writing the eighteenth-century novels?*

A   Much greater fluency, much more ability to control plots, and to discover that there is time, even in a fast-moving narrative, to develop character. I've become much more interested in people. I'm always struggling to continue the use of atmosphere, but relating it much more strongly to character. I don't think the age-range of my books has materially altered. I am tending to write longer books.

Q *You've said elsewhere that it's one of your ambitions to attempt the resurrection of the family novel, as well as writing for young adolescents.*

A I haven't entirely succeeded but I think I am getting closer to it than at first, when I was very much influenced by discussions with publishers. Obviously the more successful one becomes the more freedom one has in what one writes. Certainly the last book I wrote (*The Sound of Coaches*)* is very much more of a family book than any of the others. In the United States it's been chosen as Book-of-the-Month both for adult and young adult readers. One wonders under what imprint something like *Wuthering Heights* would have been published now—probably on the young adult list, which is ridiculous, but nevertheless it would be.

Q *Perhaps we could turn to your refashionings of the Greek Myths—*The God Beneath The Sea *and* The Golden Shadow—*books which I think you could throw at anyone regardless of their age and expect to score a hit. How did you come to do these?*

A They date back a long time to when I was about twelve. I had a very ambitious and idiotic but characteristic project of transcribing *Genesis* into rhymed couplets. In the same way I've always been fascinated in attempting to impose a narrative order on the Greek Myths, linking apparently disparate events. The actual origin was when Kathleen Long was compiling an anthology and asked me to do the creation myths. I became quite absorbed in that and found various linking passages—principally the two falls of Hephaestos and the Broach of Thetis —and constructed a long short story. But it didn't quite work out. I asked Longmans if they would be interested, and then asked Edward Blishen if he would like to help, as it was rather a large undertaking.

Q *Why Edward Blishen?*

A He's well up on Greek myths, well-read and easy to work

*Published in March, 1974

with, and an admirable editor who errs, if anything, on the side of enthusiasm. Also, he is a friend.

Q   *So what did his contribution involve?*

A   Nearly all the research; discussion as to which myths we would use—and how they would be used; and approving ideas on what they meant in largely contemporary terms—because it seemed to both of us pointless to do them unless they had a very strong application.

Q   *Something which other versions for children conspicuously lack; I'm thinking, for instance, of Roger Lancelyn Green's* Tales of the Greek Heroes, *which strike me as coy, fragmented, and at a loss for purpose.*

A   Yes—that sort of thing I find incredibly difficult to read. The myths really need to be colored enormously, because surely they were when they were first told. And surely when they *were* first told they were given very local application, as hinted in the second book (*The Golden Shadow*). I really can't see people sitting listening to them otherwise.

Q   *Were these two books in any sense a personal application for you?*

A   Oh—the absolute fascination with them since childhood—a rather Proustian desire to recreate that childhood. Memories of one's own imagination.

Q   *There must have been a lot of temptations that needed avoiding.*

A   There are so many myths that one wanted to use—Echo and Io and Pygmalion, thousands of them—but they had to be rejected because they didn't fit the particular scheme that had set them off.

Q   *What made you choose Heracles as the human hero for* The Golden Shadow *instead of Oedipus, the obvious choice given the tenor of your personal involvement?*

A   It was literary considerations that made us avoid Oedipus—he has been rather overdone. It would have been impossible, like trying to rewrite Hamlet.

Q   *So why Heracles?*

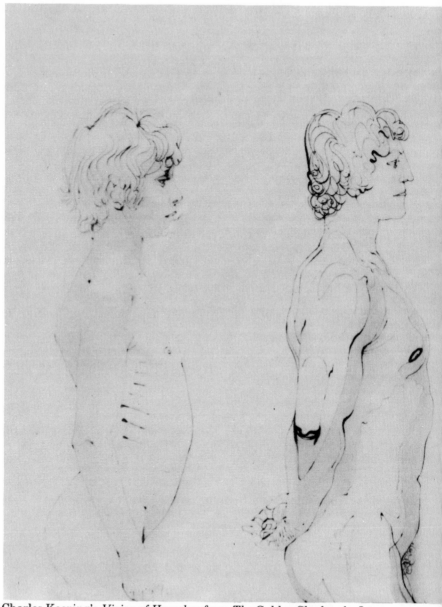

Charles Keeping's *Vision of Heracles*; from *The Golden Shadow*, by Leon Garfield and Edward Blishen.

A   Again for practical reasons. The adventures of Heracles touched so many other aspects of the Greek Myths. He's a hero, a wandering figure. One's first impression of him is of a mindless brute possessed of incredible strength—until one reads the early Labors rather more closely, when he suddenly seemed to me a rather Dostoevskian figure. He's haunted by guilt and a desire to expiate. This had an emotional and literary fascination. Then there were problems in choosing Heracles, because one couldn't possibly do all the Labors, because they simply do repeat themselves.

Q   *Is there anything that links the Greek myths with the subjects of your adventure novels?*

A   They're both held up by a very strong moral framework. I am aware when constructing a story of parallels in mythology, and one tends almost to follow the same patterns. In both I've wanted to apply the principle of as much visual imagination as possible to events that ordinarily are not treated as visual. So that when something falls from the sky one should actually see what it was like.

Q   *Would a leaning toward symbolism be a link?*

A   I like symbolism very much—I do tend to use it more and more. I suppose I am trying to bring together a clearer symbolism and a more realistic narrative. It's a question of relating everything more closely to the substance of the story and being much more careful with the images. To be fertile with images can be a disadvantage. In *Jack Holborn* they were used fairly indiscriminately.

Q   *If anything was needed to complete the effectiveness of the symbolism in your versions of the Greek Myths, then it was surely Charles Keeping's illustrations. Who selected him to do them?*

A   That was my idea. I'd seen very little of his work, but I'd met him several times and had been impressed by his views and by the fact that he was so dynamic a person. Neither of us wanted a traditional illustrator—it needed somebody who was going to be as free with my narrative as I had been with the original material.

Q   *I suppose it's ironic that you won the Carnegie Medal for* The God Beneath The Sea *and not for one of your other novels.*

A   Aggravating rather than ironic.

Leon Garfield

Q   *Now that you're back to writing historical adventures, can you say whether the experience of retelling the Greek Myths has had any effect on them?*

A   *The Sound of Coaches*, which I wrote immediately after *The Golden Shadow*, is very related to that book. I found myself using symbolism on a much larger scale. The whole of the last part is a gloss on *The Tempest*, and the relationship of a Prospero to an Ariel. Again, in *The Golden Shadow* I learnt a great deal ahout using narrative—holding very diverse things together—and that was useful in *The Sound of Coaches*.

Q   *Many novelists have inside them one book, which they keep rewriting. Would you say that's true of yourself?*

A   I think it's true of anybody who is creative. One is exploring oneself the whole time, which is only a single subject at different periods.

Q   *The reason I ask is that I see a complication, or a possible complication, peculiar to children's writers. The novelist begins with his first book, and elaborates from there. That's fine with adult literature because one can drag one's audience through any amount of introspection (if introspection is the measure of the individual novelist's development), so long as they're not bored. But as a children's writer I'd have thought one sooner or later reaches a point where one loses their comprehension. This seems to have happened with Alan Garner, for example, in his last book,* Red Shift.

A   Yes—this point is absolutely inevitable. The only thing one tries to do is retain the first links. Whether or not this is possible I don't know. Probably one will eventually shift, although one usually has a hangover from the previous book.

Q   *When did you first become aware of a possible tension between continuing to develop as a writer, and continuing to satisfy a particular stratum of the children's market?*

A   Probably with *Black Jack* I think, when so many people complained that it wasn't really a young person's book—which I could understand to a certain extent, although as far as I am concerned it was in just about the same area as the previous book, *Smith*: it was merely exploring a different aspect. The writing was no more difficult.

Q   *Do you think a writer's first responsibility is toward his*

Leon Garfield

established readership or toward himself? Is he committed, or does he have a licence to retreat into his own consciousness?

A   Obviously one feels one has a licence to tackle these problems, but at the same time craftsmanship must remain preeminent. When one is alone in one's room one is only aware of one's licence. When one receives letters from one's readers, one is conscious of being a supplier, and feels a certain guilt about not supplying what they want. Of course, though, it's hopeless, because the supply becomes before the demand. I think what it amounts to is that one does write first and foremost for oneself, and the consideration for the reader only takes place after.

Q   *It seems an oddly contemporary problem. One doesn't imagine E. Nesbit, for example, being confronted by it.*

A   It's an utterly different readership now. There's far greater literacy than there was then, and the coziness has gone. But we are progressing backwards from one point of view, in that childhood, as many people have said, was almost entirely a Victorian invention. In some ways it's ceasing to exist. It's no longer seen as a separate area of one's life, but as the beginning of something. And there's no reason at all why certain vistas shouldn't be presented—from an intelligible standpoint.

Q   *So what exactly has been happening to children's literature in the immediate past, in your view?*

A   I think for the first time there are professional writers for the young, which there weren't before. There's a new breed.

Q   *In the light of what we've just been saying that sounds paradoxical.*

A   I meant that before the children's book was a freak—not necessarily of a writer but of an individual: books like *Alice in Wonderland* or *The Wind in the Willows*, they're freak books, they're games to themselves. No one can go on from those, no one can write a series of books developing from that nature. Lewis Carroll's own attempts were nowhere near as good. I think a book like *Watership Down* is the same thing, a freak book by somebody who is not naturally a writer.

Q   *So what do you think will happen to the children's novel in the immediate future? Could it save itself by becoming political—something which up to now it has been notoriously slow to do?*

Leon Garfield

A   I can't see it going the way of *Animal Farm*. I think there's a great danger of its burying its head in the sand and becoming very coy. I think it will split. I think there will be very realistic and social books, and there will be the *Watership Down* sort, an attempt to impose an improbable childhood. I personally think it *might* become much more political, as I find myself becoming much more interested, and appalled, by revolutionary action and terrorism.

Highgate, 1974

Leon Garfield's novels include: Jack Holborn (1964); Devil-in-the-Fog (1966); Smith (1967); Black Jack (1968); The Boy and the Monkey (1969); The Drummer Boy (1970); The Strange Affair of Adelaide Harris (1971). Mister Corbett's Ghost (1969) *and* The Restless Ghost (1969) *are collections of short stories. With Edward Blishen he has written* The God Beneath the Sea (1970) *and* The Golden Shadow (1973); The Sound of Coaches (1974).

15 Lloyd Alexander

Interviewed by Justin Wintle

Lloyd Alexander is a practitioner of high fantasy, imagination taken to its limits in fiction for serious philosophical or moral purposes. His *Prydain Chronicles*, five long books inspired by the ancient Arthurian legends, are one of the monuments of contemporary American children's literature. Many of the characters, themes and subplots are borrowed from the *Mabinogion* (the word means "instructions for young bards"), a collection of Welsh myths and legends recorded in the early Middle Ages. The central figure, Taran, and his immediate companions, are Lloyd Alexander's own creations. These figures serve to provide a common focus both for the disparate scraps of his Celtic source, and for the ideas he develops.

The *Prydain Chronicles* may not be as learned or weighty as Tolkien's *The Lord of the Rings,* an obvious comparison which draws on many of the same legends; but they are almost certainly better suited to younger readers, children from the age of eight or nine upwards. Each of the five books can be read individually, although there is enough lateral continuity and development to reward anybody who reads them all. As one would expect in a work of this length, the field of action is dominated by a contest between the powers of good and evil, but there is an abundance of humor that makes Alexander's imaginary kingdom altogether inhabitable.

Alexander was born in 1924 in Philadelphia, where he still lives scarcely two blocks from his first home. He is mainly a mental traveler, and claims he is accident prone if he tries it any other way. One of the few trips in his life that brought him more benefit than hazard took him to Wales during the war, where he was posted by a military intelligence center in Maryland. He moved on to counter-intelligence in Paris, where he later enrolled at the Sorbonne to study literature, and where he met his French wife, Janine.

Lloyd Alexander

Q   *I often begin these interviews by asking some biographical questions. But let me put it to you more directly. Do you think that
a knowledge of an author's life helps one understand his work?*

A   That's a hard question. How can I answer both yes and no
to that? I suppose it depends on what level you want to go
at it. Let's say in principle that the work of art must stand
by itself, and that it doesn't make the slightest bit of difference
what the artist was or who he was; that the work of art is
what speaks for him; that his moral character and his habits
have no bearing on his work. All that's true in a sense. And
yet, speaking for myself, I've always found it illuminating to
know something of the man who did it. But it's two different
things somehow.

Q   *One is wondering perhaps whether a work of art can be properly
understood in isolation from its culture. Your own work, at least
the* Prydain Chronicles, *is based on ancient Welsh mythology—
legends that seem a far cry from America today. It's easier to
understand why Tolkien, for instance, was interested in those
legends, being English and a teacher of Old English at Oxford.*

A   Yes, he was a linguist primarily. There are a couple of things
I'm trying to figure out here. First, my own attraction to this
particular area, which I've always had. Without being too heavy
about it, it seems to me that any type of mythology can speak
to anybody in any culture. I don't think you have to be brought
up in or near a given culture to get something from its
mythology; and for some reason I got an awful lot of sustenance
and insight from mythologies as a born and raised American.
There's not a question of nationalism involved somehow. It
would be very convenient (but I would lie if I said it was the
case) to say that I absorbed all this at my mother's knee. But
that's not true at all. In my family we made very little of it.
It was only after I was a grown boy that I began to be interested
in mythologies. I think if anything it's an artistic connection
or some response that has nothing to do with my family upbringing; the same way any person in any country can love Bach
or Mozart. And yet I suppose that it was almost presumptuous
for an American to undertake a work based on Celtic mythology
and any number of other mythologies. What business had I,
for heaven's sake, to undertake something which indeed Tolkien
and others have done so superbly well? I suppose I finally said,
I don't care: this is what I want to do. Good, bad or indifferent,
that was where my head was at that particular moment. I've
tried to rationalize why it was there, but I don't have a rational
answer.

Lloyd Alexander

Q   *One talks about, say, the universal qualities of the Greek myths;*
    but it seems possible that if one had been alive then, they would
    have meant something entirely different from what they mean to
    us today. Do you think myths carry universals?

A   That depends on whom you read. If you read Jung, there is
    a world myth—what James Joyce, I think, called the monomyth.
    If you read Jung there's the archetypal racial memory common
    to all people at all times. It's a lovely idea, a very poetic idea,
    but whether it's true or not I don't know. I'm convinced that
    we today can read mythologies and draw meanings from them
    that may or may not have any resemblance to what was
    originally meant. For example, I don't believe we have any idea
    what function the fairy tale served. From what I've read I believe
    it may have served a ritual religious function—but this is long
    gone. We can never put ourselves back in a time when we could
    understand what these fairy tales were doing in a cultural sense.
    The same for 8,000 years hence: they could never understand
    our religious beliefs, but I believe they would nevertheless find
    elements that would speak to them. Whatever one's condition
    at the time, it does seem that the great myths strike a responsive
    chord somewhere, that we do live on them.

Q   *I've read that you always wanted to be a writer, at least from*
    a very early age. Could this be a reason, do you think, that the
    initial inspiration for the Prydain Chronicles *was literary rather*
    than anything else?

A   There may be two answers to that. It would be very convenient
    to say yes. I'm looking for a somewhat harder answer though.
    Although the sources may be literary, an awful lot of it, even
    most of it, comes from my younger adult experiences. To give
    you a silly, ridiculous example: many of the things which hap-
    pened to me in World War Il show up in those books on a
    symbolic level. When Taran and his companions are sleeping
    out on the ground and get caught out in a winter storm, I have
    a direct personal reference to the way they feel. I know
    what it feels like. Certainly some of the decisions and moral
    binds facing Taran have happened to me in disguised terms.
    And they're still happening. Life is not a few basic decisions
    and that's it. I swear that sometimes the most heroic thing we
    can do is get up in the morning. Everyday living is a hard
    piece of business, and I sometimes think that Hobbes was right
    when he said that life is short, brutal and nasty.

Q   *Though he also talked of sudden glory.*

A   That's true. There's that as well.

Q   *If it's possible that we interpret myths for our own use, do you think we sometimes do the same to childhood—that we look for meanings we can't have any certain idea are there or not?*

A   Yes. I was reading a book by John Holt not so long ago in which he refers to the "cuteness syndrome." With all the best intentions in the world many adults have a very peculiar view of childhood. It's strange, because we were all children at some point, though we've forgotten that. We sentimentalize childhood. We look on it very often as a happy golden age. We impose certain notions we have as adults on children and make them almost sacred objects, which I don't believe they are. And then we tend to see them as cute or funny. It's "funny" that the child speaks in a "funny" way. Or he falls down the stairs and stubs his toe: isn't that "cute," we say. But he's crying his head off. He's hurt and he's scared. Children, it seems to me, have the same emotions, generally speaking, as adults. They may not be as complex, or as overlaid with certain years of experience and subtleties; but as primary colors, fear is fear, happiness is happiness, and love is the same sense for a child as it is for any other. We laugh, but the child is suffering just as much as any adult ever did from the pangs of unrequited love or whatever. Without pushing it too far, I might also say the same thing about animals. I look at my cats. I think it's a mistake to turn them or any other animals into miniature human beings, to anthropomorphize them; but where we have a common ground is on the emotional level. I have no idea in the world what a cat is thinking about. I can amuse myself by imagining, but I don't really know what the real nature of his life is. Yet there are certain moments when I know that he is frightened, or that he is affectionate. Then I'm convinced that the feeling tone, the affect, the basic emotion, is identical with mine. On that deep level I can say: Yes, we are one of a kind. One of my theories is that there is basically one life process, whatever form it may take. There are certain deep points of identity that we can all recognize, I hope. We're all part of the same thing, all at one with nature, to use the cliché.

Q   *What are the other ingredients to the "life process," apart from the emotions?*

A   We're getting into deep philosophical waters here. This is a recent idea, a scary idea in a way. Without minimizing the work of Darwin, or Freud, or Jung, I'm beginning to have this funny feeling that all our art, our creative impulses, our thoughts, our civilization, if you want to call it that, are desperate attempts to console ourselves in the knowledge that we are going to die, that ultimately we are born alone, that we die alone; that all the things we do are, in the deepest sense, games. We may play them consciously or unconsciously, but they are games of solace and consolation in our occasional intimations that we are going to cease to exist. This is an idea that has come out of a very hard winter.

Q   *Nevertheless, something of this seems latent at the end of* The High King, *the last of the* Prydain *narratives, when Taran relinquishes the chance of immortality by choosing not to go with the others to the Summer Country.*

A   It's a kind of commitment to the human condition, that there are no easy outs. There was an easy out for Taran and his companions in a fictional sense. Yet it would have been false, certainly on the basis of my beliefs, to have had him take this out. I think I was trying to say we are human beings and must therefore live as human beings. Taran had a choice, fictionally; we don't have that choice.

Q   *And fictionally, in* The High King, *that was the moment of real heroism. But fiction aside, is there anything particularly heroic in accepting a situation to which there are no real alternatives?*

A   I don't know. You raise a subtle point, because in a way it may depend on one's attitude. I think perhaps it may be more heroic to say: This is how things are, and I must see them as they are, rather than give myself any kind of happy illusion, or escape into a saccharine dream of any kind.

Q   *But isn't there a degree of illusion in all fantasy, particularly the sort you wove around* Prydain?

A   It seems to me on the contrary. Using the device of an imaginary world allowed me in some strange way to go to the central issues. In other words I used the imaginary kingdom not as a sentimentalized fairyland, but as an opening wedge to express what I hoped would be some very hard truths. I never saw fairy tales as an escape or a cop out. I think Tolkien would have borne me out on this. I don't think he or anybody else working in the high fantasy medium would see it as an escape from reality. On the contrary, speaking for myself, it is the way to understand reality. In the *Chronicles* there are questions about the nature and use of power, of self-aggrandizement at the expense of others, of kindness and of other humane qualities. If you set up a conflict between good and evil, how can you define the two camps? I suppose one rule of thumb is that the evil thing dehumanizes people, that evil has an absorption with death rather than an absorption with life. In the *Prydain Chronicles* the Lord of Death lives in a kind of static, unchanging world.

Q   *Emphasized by his hoarding, but not using, all the tools and implements of trade and agriculture?*

A   That's right—a question of deprivation. It's not that through his own greed he wants to use them for his own benefit. He simply wants to deprive anybody else of using them. A key example is the nature of the Black Cauldron. The Cauldron-born, who emerge from it, have forgotten what it is like to be human beings: they've forgotten themselves as men. They can't weep, they can't laugh, they can't even speak. The worst cruelty is that they have no memory; they don't even remember they ever had any human emotions, which is perhaps the ultimate evil that can be worked on anybody.

Q   *Looking at the whole five books of* Prydain, *one is struck by the gradual process of growing up that Taran, the central character, undergoes. He begins as a very pig-headed Assistant Pig-Keeper, and ends up as an established, almost Promethean, hero. Is this one explanation of the books' great fascination for young people, because the readers themselves are aware and interested in the process of growing up?*

A   I think so, and I most certainly hope so. I never intended to write down to children. I would much rather speak to the growing adult in the child than speak to the child where he is at a given moment. I hope they sense that, because I believe growing up is what it's all about. The more I look back, not only on the books I've written for children, but on those I've written for adults too, it seems to me that this is the deepest underlying theme. It's certainly one that has preoccupied me constantly. There are a great many writers for children, and splendid writers for children, who are perhaps more interested in recapturing their own childhood; whereas I am trying to come to terms with my adulthood. I have a funny kind of impression that the kids sense this too, that I speak to the child as a growing person.

Q   *I think that's why it appealed to me.*

A   I am amazed and delighted by how many adults read the *Prydain*

213

Chronicles. I don't think adults stop growing, or at least they shouldn't. If you stop growing you're dead. At any rate, I've never tried to pull any punches with the kids. There are a great number of hard situations in those books, and I've tried to go at them head-on. For example, the scene in *The Black Cauldron* where Taran must trade his magical brooch, which is the greatest thing that has ever happened to him, for a cauldron that is going to be destroyed: it's a terrible decision. The feeling tone is most anguishing, at least from my point of view. And I'm sure that every adult and every child has gone through that in one way or another. It's one of the deeper levels of the emotions that we share in common, whatever our age or nationality.

Q   *The structure of the first book,* The Book of Three, *is a curious reflection of the overall structure. In the middle of it there's a soft interlude, when Taran visits Medwyn's valley. Similarly,* The Castle of Llyr, *the third of the five chronicles, is, in contrast to the others, a romance. How much idea of where you were going did you have when you first started out?*

A   I didn't have any idea in the world I was going to write five books. It's a funny thing, but I thought at the beginning that I was going to do something quite easy. I had become very fond of mythology, and I was fascinated by the *Mabinogion.* If you know the original text you will know that it's a very difficult book: there are so many things mixed up in it—courtly romance combined with Stone Age mythology, a mixture which can never be sorted out. Unlike the Irish and Scandinavian mythologies, which are pretty much of a piece, I don't think the Welsh mythology has been lucky. As far as I knew, with the possible exception of Gwyn Jones, nobody had tried to make much sense out of the *Mabinogion.* That's what I wanted to do; and I thought it would be a pleasant and simple thing to do. All I needed to do was retell the magnificent mythology, and being bone lazy this appealed to me. I tried this at first, but strange things happened to me. I found I had been kidding myself: I didn't want simply to retell anybody's mythology. What I really wanted to do was invent my own, or at least use my own in some way. So originally I did not foresee a work of that length involving that amount of time. I thought at the very most it might be three books. I began on that basis, not quite knowing where I was going. But the more I worked on *The Book of Three* the more I realized the personal importance it was taking on. As regards the *Mabinogion,* I found that what I liked I could use, but I no longer felt obliged to do a scholarly work. It was a tremendously liberating decision. I found myself, to my amazement, tapping into various areas of my personality that I never even knew existed. So the work that began as external became internal. I still had no idea how things were going to work out. I realized pretty early on that I was accumulating debts that had to be paid; that there were situations, objects and characters that had to be accounted for. I knew that there would be a day of reckoning when I would have to pull together all the promises I had made and all the hints I had dropped. Interestingly enough, the same way Taran changed and grew in unforeseen ways, the same happened to me. I had to engage ideas and attitudes and really examine my own feelings and beliefs in ways I had never done before. I didn't do this in my adult books—not that I hadn't wanted to, but it never became an issue somehow. All of a sudden I found myself immersed in a work that was becoming larger and larger and more and more personal. I'd bitten off more than I could chew. As I said before, there was the presumption of an American daring to work in a tradition he knew nothing about. This was insanity. After I finished *The Castle of Llyr* I thought I was nearing the end when a funny thing happened. I was walking down a street in Philadelphia past a construction site; when I went home that evening I saw in the papers that a gigantic steel girder had fallen down on the pavement where I had just passed. I thought to myself, what a disaster to end my life before finishing the *Prydain Chronicles*. It scared me. Seriously. So I got down to it and wrote the last volume, *The High King*. I sent it to my editor, who made one small criticism: she said that I needed another book to precede it. Evidently, without realizing it, I had implied certain things in *The High King*—characters and situations—which had never existed in the previous books, and which needed some kind of introduction. This rather took me by surprise. I had to put aside the semi-finished manuscript I'd just done and spend another year or so writing *Taran Wanderer*, the book which bridges *The Castle of Llyr* and *The High King*. I realized that my editor was right, that *Taran Wanderer* was an essential step I hadn't seen.

Q *Because it sets out a major episode in the development of Taran's personality?*

A That's right.

Q *You've said how you identified with Taran while writing the books. Did you also, as the maker of the Tales, identify with Dallben, the wise enchanter who never changes?*

A I don't know. Offhand I would say not. It seems to me that I could never reach the area of the mythological characters,

215

which would include Gwydion, the other heroic figures, the enchanters—all the "nonhuman" characters. In other words I'm only a human being, and as much as I would like to be as wise as Dallben, or as brave as Gwydion, I have to accept the idea that I can't be. These are people you can love, admire, try to imitate even, but I don't believe you can ever become one of them. On the contrary, I identified with the nonheroic figures, the fallible humans: Fflewddur Fflam, for instance. I think we have many personalities—an infinite number perhaps; and all these characters, Gwystyl, Fflewddur Fflam, Gurgi—are refractions of myself. I've been as scared of things as Gurgi, stretched the truth as much as Fflewddur and whined as much as Gwystyl. I think this is why it may go down so well with kids and adults—because they are able to sense some of these characters in themselves. I don't believe that they identify with the mythological figures. They're much more of the common earth.

Q   *Why is it that, in terms of human capabilities, the most identifiable characters are the most comic, and the least identifiable the most heroic?*

A   I would use different words—accessible and inaccessible. Let me try this: given our various personalities, some we can grasp more easily than others—the ones close to the surface perhaps. These can be the comic types—the typical blunderers—because most of us, God knows, are terrible incompetents. That's accessible. But I wonder, as we grow and try to come to terms with ourselves, if we don't find some of the more inaccessible areas, and perhaps darker areas as well. As we begin to push a little deeper we find a set of personae we didn't know were there: we can be braver than we ever thought we were, bigger rascals than we ever thought we were, worse scoundrels, and more selfish than we would ever like to think.

Q   *But there's still the question of the comic nature of the accessible personae, and the not-so-comic nature of what might be called our dream personae.*

A   I'm a little stuck on the word "comic." Don't forget that in most of the myths there is a duality, a hero and his mirror image, his sidekick, his partner, who is usually a clown. The sky hero and the earth clown, two aspects of the same personality. Don Quixote and Sancho Panza, Mr. Pickwick and Sam Weller—these are the archetypes. It almost seems that every hero has his comic companion.

Lloyd Alexander

Q   *Taran and Gurgi, yes. But why?*

A   Isn't it just the simplest reflection of the most basic duality
    in ourselves? One part is striving for wisdom and exaltation,
    something beyond ourselves; the other part gets hungry, gets
    sick, gets scared. Is not this the most simple and obvious paradox
    of the human personality? On the one hand we can be philoso-
    phers and artists; and on the other we get drunk out of our
    minds.

Q   *Distinguishing tragedy from comedy, you once wrote, in a contri-
    bution to the* Horn Book *Magazine: "The differences lie not so
    much in vision as in method." What did you mean by this?*

A   In a very general sense the difference is that in tragedy the
    hero sees the truth and dies from it; in comedy the hero sees
    the truth and is forced to live with it. It's not just a question
    of a happy ending as opposed to a sad ending. Then there are
    the differences in comedic modes, between high comedy and
    low comedy. Low comedy tells us what a ridiculous place the
    physical world is—a place where a man with the highest aspi-
    rations can be defeated by a shirt button, where people become
    the butts of life's joke. High comedy is a play of ideas—certain
    ideas of ours about ourselves and the world are deflated and
    shown to be preposterous.

Q   *Confusing the sublime and the ridiculous?*

A   That's right. In low comedy the sublime is reduced by the physi-
    cal world; in high comedy it is reduced by ideas.

Q   *Books that are obviously not comedies, high or low, are the early
    novels of Alan Garner, which, like your own, draw heavily on
    the* Mabinogion. *Have you read them?*

A   Yes—and I think he has written masterpieces. Garner is one
    of the great writers.

Q   *How do you see the differences in your individual approaches
    to the Welsh legends?*

A   I don't think I am as much, if I dare use the term, of a mystic.
    As far as my own temperament is concerned—and this may seem
    paradoxical in a person who tries to write fantasy—it seems
    to me that I am a very hard-headed realist; and by virtue of
    that particular turn of mind I tend not to rely on mysticism

as any kind of resolution. Possibly one of the driving ideas in all the *Prydain Chronicles* is the uselessness of magic—the books end with the end of magic in the world. Magic can't help us. It's very nice to imagine that it might have been like that at one point, but if it ever existed it's gone. We are stuck with our own human resources. From my point of view this is the crux of those books. It's a question of my own personality, and has nothing to do with whether the work is good or bad. You can write superb masterpieces as a thoroughgoing mystic. If I'm not mistaken Tolkien was a deeply religious man. So was C. S. Lewis: the *Chronicles of Narnia* are a work of theology.

Q *The* Prydain Chronicles *apart, perhaps the most interesting of your work is* The Marvelous Misadventures of Sebastian. *What was that about?*

A In one sense it is my homage to Mozart. It's a Mozartian book in background and atmosphere, and there are some little secret Mozart references that a Mozart fan is going to pick up. Essentially it is a very personal book indeed. As you know, I've tried to play the violin. Even though I've failed, it has meant I've been able to hear music in ways that I never heard before in all my life. It was the most insightful thing that happened to me. And I make a direct analogy between that and writing for children. For years I wrote for adults. I was perfectly happy with it, having a certain modest success, and that's how I thought I would continue. But what happened to me when I began writing for children was the same thing in literary terms as had happened to me in musical terms in trying to play the violin: I discovered things about writing and the creative process that I never knew were there. Essentially this is what *Sebastian* is all about. He begins, as you know, as a fairly competent fiddler and a fairly light-hearted young man. He has facility, but he has never scratched below the surface. In the course of the story he comes into possession of a fiddle that allows him to play and hear music as he has never done before. It changes his life. The fiddle, of course, is a mixed blessing because it also drains his life away the more he understands his magnificent discovery. Without being pretentious about it, I suppose *Sebastian* attempts to say something about what it feels like to be an artist. The Gallimaufry Theatricus involves the idea of art as illusion—the interchange between reality and illusion runs through the book. As far as I can remember, in nearly every chapter there's a flip in which what seemed make-believe or illusory turns out to be real, and vice versa. The concept of the theater becomes an analogue for the concept of art in general. Quicksilver, the proprietor of the theater, says this:

that his theater provides people with a balloon they can go up in, in the belief they are going to the moon, at least for a moment. And to an extent that's real in a way.

Q   *Why do you admire Mozart so much? Because nothing in his music is accidental?*

A   Taking Mozart, we have the conscious use of form to contain all kinds of strange and nonrational things. If you take a little pile of gunpowder and set a match to it, it goes off with a flare and doesn't do anything. If you put that same gunpowder in a sealed metal container, you'll get the biggest explosion you can imagine. The formal elements in Mozart I would compare to this container; oddly, your formal limits provide a source of strength rather than a restriction.

Q   *Finally, let me ask you about your work in hand, if there is any?*

A   Within the last few days I have finished the final version of a new manuscript. I'm so muddled about it at this point that I don't know if I dare make any comments. If anything it's a vaguely Dickensian fantasy. The central character is a heroine, a young girl—something I've never done before. There is no handsome young swain in the background to help her out of her difficulties or provide any kind of hopeful romance. She's utterly alone and there's very little going for her. It doesn't end very happily—it's rather a dark sort of book.

Q   *Where is it set?*

A   It's a fantasy, but the historical reference would be a small village of the industrial revolution in late eighteenth- or early nineteenth-century England. It's at that point where the money you had in your pocket became worth more than the skill you had in your hands. There's a fine villain—a great nefarious, foul, sanctimonious, Pecksniffian, hypocritical, rotten local squire whom the girl runs foul of. One of the things that happens is that the no-good squire has decided to mine for coal to run a textile mill, cutting through the local forest to make a road to transport cheap manufactured goods from the capital into the local village. In so doing he destroys an ancient oak tree. The girl comes across an enchanter who had been trapped in that tree for ages and ages, and who should have disappeared long before. All he wants to do is to escape—he's not interested in humans or their problems. The two of them, the girl and the ancient wizard, are forced into a kind of working relationship

219

by their respective interests. They become very fond of each other, but you can see how it's going to work out. Eventually they will have to go their separate ways. Their relationship is not sentimentalized at all. At the beginning the girl believed literally in fairy tales, but the enchanter explains to her that the world in which enchanters and magicians lived alongside human beings was nothing like what she imagined it to be; that the humans were just as greedy and selfish, wretched and destructive then as they are now. There were no spells to make anybody kinder or nobler or wiser. People couldn't be saved from themselves, and so the magicians left. He explains that real magic takes place internally, and not on the outside. And he says: "I create illusions. I don't indulge myself in them." In the end he leaves and the girl is left on her own. Again, it's about growing up I suppose. To give a ridiculous example, I can well imagine a child having a crush on a teacher; but it can't work, nothing can come of it. At a certain point the teacher is going to go away, and the child is going to go away. While it's going on it's as agonizing as any love affair. And one of the hardest things, for a child or for an adult, is to come to terms with a situation in which it must be faced up to that a love affair isn't going to work out.

Philadelphia, 1974

Lloyd Alexander's Prydain Chronicles *consist of:* The Book of Three (1964); The Black Cauldron (1965, a Newbery Honor Book); The Castle of Llyr (1966); Taran Wanderer (1967) *and* The High King (1968, awarded the Newbery Medal).

Lloyd Alexander's other books include: Time Cat (1963); Coll and His White Pig (1965); The Truthful Harp (1967); The Marvelous Misadventures of Sebastian (1970); The Four Donkeys (1972); The Foundling and Other Tales of Prydain (1973) *and* The Cat Who Wished To Be A Man (1973).

16 Alan Garner

Interviewed by Justin Wintle

Another author who has mined the *Mabinogian*, though more intuitively than either Tolkien or Alexander, is Alan Garner, undoubtedly the most gifted but perhaps the most problematical author writing for children in England today. Two early books, *The Weirdstone of Brisingamen* and *The Moon of Gomrath*, are accessible to readers of most ages, and are widely believed to be his best work. However, while they are good yarns, they have none of the obscure fascination of *Elidor* or *The Owl Service* to make up for the flat portrayal of characters which afflicts all four books. *Elidor*, the story of four children, and in particular one boy, who accidentally slip into an alternative world only to discover that they cannot really return to it any more than to the one they have left, is probably best described as an essay in metaphorical autobiography. *The Owl Service* is a tight, and on a mystical level evocative, recreation of an ancient Welsh legend about a curse which revisits the members of a modern family. Like Garner's other books, it dwells on the premise that there is a dark magic in the world which can sleep but never expire.

Both these later books, *Elidor* and *The Owl Service*, which enjoy a cultish reputation among many adults, make it abundantly clear that Garner is not naturally a children's author. He is now styled a young adult novelist, but only by default. He has yet to write a properly adult novel. His most recent book, *Red Shift*, published since this interview took place, received a tortuously mixed press. The criticism that it is beyond the comprehension of any young person is neither here nor there: an author has the right to write for whom he pleases. But the criticism that *Red Shift* is also beyond the wits of most adults is altogether more relevant. One would suggest that, somewhere between Garner's professed admiration for William Golding (whose originality is too idiosyncratic for borrowing) and his own self-absorption, a major talent is energetically destroying itself; or that, more hopefully, it is remarshalling its resources.

Alan Garner was born in 1935. He spent nearly all his childhood near Alderly Edge, the vicinity in which his early books are set. After an education in exile he returned to Cheshire, where he now lives in two houses that stand beside each other on the flat top of a neolithic tumulus. One of these dwellings is a medieval apothecary's which he first found on the verge of demolition some twenty miles from its present site. Garner moved the entire structure himself, timber by timber, without damage to any of the fabric. The other house, equally old, is called Toad Hall. He is married, with three children. He lives entirely by his writing.

Alan Garner

Q   *Your childhood: You lived near Alderly Edge, the setting for the first two books and a center for the supernatural. Obviously there were things happening in your childhood that perhaps have affected you?*

A   That's an enormous matter—I could hardly get through it in two hours. Where does one begin?

Q   *I can't believe that you had a "normal" childhood. . .*

A   No. God no. First of all I was saved from an education by being too ill to go to school. It was very dramatic—spinal and cerebral meningitis at the same time, diphtheria, pleurisy and pneumonia—there seemed to be a difference. I hardly went to school before I was eleven. It was largely—and I think I'm being charitable—that my mother functions best in a crisis; and now I understand a lot more I see that she precipitated situations by which I became ill. Quite unconsciously, of course. A lot of the illnesses were caused initially by severe periods of emotional tension. My mother was a superb nurse. It sounds rather sick to say that she made me sick in order to function, but I've seen her do it to other people since. She's a very good nurse and tends to become rather destructive in other situations.

Q   *Did she have any special methods?*

A   She doesn't believe in doctors, which is why I was written off three times. She nursed me just by looking after me. Childhood memory is difficult. I seem to have spent about six years alone in a room looking at a wall. And that seems a common denominator among writers for children—that (*a*) they were deprived of a conventional primary schooling, and (*b*) that they were ill, thrown in on themselves.

Q   *Who else was like that?*

A   Of the people I know, William Mayne, Rosemary Sutcliff, Roger Lancelin Green and a couple of others. Though I don't know how statistically true that is—how many people who weren't ill became writers, and how many people who were ill didn't become writers.

Q   *What did you do in that room all day?*

A   Well, I was lucky. I lived in a room where the walls were lumpy—there were landscapes on those walls. When I was fifteen we moved fifty yards into a respectable house where all the walls were straight. I got out of there pretty quickly. That's why I am here [Toad Hall, his fourteenth-century house] because it happens to be something with texture and fabric. I do know that's true, because it's something I wanted. I didn't want to go back to that house, the respectable house.

Q *When did your enthusiasm for archaeology become conscious?*

A Soon after I left Oxford.

Q *Not until then?*

A Oh no. At Oxford I specialized in Homeric archaeology, but I didn't enjoy that at all. Right up till then British archaeology had not seemed at all important. This was because I was brought up as "first generation educated." I went to Manchester Grammar School, and there, at that time, although it's not true now, there was a feeling among the members of the arts faculty that if you weren't good enough to read literature in a foreign language, then, and only then, were you allowed to read English. So again I was saved—I didn't read any English until after I left Oxford. I was a classical specialist. I remember in my last year there, being in the library and a mathematician coming in and saying that he had been told to read a novel: did I know any? And the shocking thing is I didn't. I hadn't read anything in English since I was aged about eight—apart from comics. When I had meningitis, and I was in an isolation ward, I remember reading a comic and knowing that the little marks in the balloons related to the action, and that I could in fact understand it. I could read.

Q *How old were you then?*

A Six. And I came back to convalesce; and my grandmother, who had been a Victorian pupil-teacher, had a whole wall of Nelson's Illustrated Classics, with seedy illustrations—*Children of the New Forest*, that sort of thing, "definitely to be used in schools." And because I was at that stage when a child just wants to read—mechanically—I got through the whole of the nineteenth-century novels. Went straight through them like a termite. And the beneficial side of that is, although I can't remember any of it, I don't feel guilty about not having read it. Again, I was lucky in first reading Shakespeare because I was acting.

Q *When was that?*

A That was at Oxford. Straight in at the deep end. I was hanging around and somebody said they were short of a part. I had done a lot of acting at school, so I did it. And that was *Everyman*. The next thing I knew I was doing Antony in *Antony and Cleopatra*, which led to a crisis because the director and I didn't exactly agree. He sacked me as Antony and I took over the part of Caesar. A week after, whether I was bad or good, he realized he had nobody who could play Antony at a moment's notice. So I did Antony and somebody else was found to do Caesar. But I'd learnt the words for both parts, which cured me of any lurking wish to be a professional actor.

Q   *So, having read classics at Oxford, and having hated Homer, what suddenly prompted you to explore British mythology, particularly of the area where you had been brought up?*

A   It was the fact that possibly in some way I was unbalanced, which is a very healthy, a very productive state to be in. It is a situation—and I don't want to make a sob story of it—that is eternally with us. It is the situation of first generation education, the dilemma of it. The pattern was, and still is, pride in the child getting to a grammar school, and inability to accept the effect that grammar school will have on the child. So, as a successful child, you go through a period of being thought extremely precious and mannered and snobbish. And in fact that may be true. But the fact is that the parent cannot encompass the effect of his child being taught three or four languages and mathematics and history: of becoming educated. And so two things can happen. One is that the child folds in some way—you get the dropout who can't make the break, who thinks that the price is too great. And you get the other situation: a traumatization within the family resulting in a total failure of communication, absolute social breakdown, collapse.

Q   *Where the child gets taken in by the languages he's learning?*

A   Yes. And there is still a great inability on my part to communicate with my parents. Although they live just seven miles away we don't meet. There's been no row—it's simply that it is so disastrous every time when we do meet. So I avoid it. That results, in England, from a period in adolescence when everybody is a bit adrift. There is a double sense of loss. There is a loss of roots, and there is a loss of the ability to use the education. It's a kind of aborted period of life. With me it was a totally instinctive process which I can only rationalize with hindsight. What happened was that I was educated to understand what it was I had lost. Whereas the rest of my family and my cousins of the same age, who were not educated, do not have a feeling for their roots and do not feel strongly about the place where they live, and are talking about emigrating all the time. The difference is we all grew up on Alderly Edge, but only I came to know what Triassic and keuper and bunter sand-stones are. And so there is a very dangerous reaction, or there was in me, of rejecting living people and going to the dead—that is, those who are safe in parish records, the Garners who were saved, who didn't change. And I was trained to talk to them, to communicate with them. Through my higher education I knew how to go about researching into parish records, how to read different types of hand, how to think through academic problems. That's why the first two books have no people. They are a kind of scream about landscape. The only thing that is good in them is a sense of landscape and an almost Jungian sense of personality. All the characters that have any vitality in them are archetypes. They are all me too, even in a very crude sense. And at the age of thirty-eight I'm still writing about myself twenty-three years ago.

Q *Emotionally and psychologically?*

A I don't like social realism. I don't like the documentary form of writing a novel. It's subjective, and I don't feel that's realism. I think that when someone gets really hung up on social issues and doesn't put them through the filter of his own personality, but just goes out with a banner, then the form of the novel suffers. For instance, in *The Owl Service* I didn't set out to write "about" the problems of first generation grammar school and illegitimacy. Rather I asked myself, What is the best way to present this boy? What is it that would really make him incapable of coping with the epic quality of the situation? Illegitimacy. Given illegitimacy, you musn't climb back from that. It's just a different way of looking at social issues. Not to look for the social issue and then find the story; but to find the story, and whatever social issue arises from that you must not flinch from. I can't be dogmatic about that—it's just the way I work.

Q *Going back, what happened when you left Oxford University?*

A I knew where I wanted to live, because, although I loved Oxford, it was dangerously cloud cuckoo land. It was dangerous because I have a very arrogant personality: there was no point in my staying since there was no possibility of my working hard enough to get a double First.* I could have got a good second, and carried on acting, standing on my head. But that would have been some kind of failure. That has been a weakness in me all my life: I will not fail.

Q   *I have read that you were a remarkable athlete; which, given your early illnesses, really is remarkable. Are you so highly motivated in everything?*

A   Absolutely. The true inferiority complex. And I was unpopular at my school as an athlete because I had no team spirit. I wasn't doing it for anybody else. And what they didn't know was that if I had ever been beaten I would have retired.

Q   *Were you ever?*

A   I was never beaten.

Q   *So you came back to Alderly Edge.*

A   Yes—I knew that whatever it was that I could do, I could do it here, in this area of Cheshire. By going away I knew what roots were, and I knew that they were important for me at that time. I just quite coldly and quite analytically set about working out what I didn't want to do.

Q   *Perhaps something of Ulysses rubbed off on you unawares?*

A   [Laughs] Yes, yes. But there was no literary ambition. I am a great illiterate in most fields. I don't read novels. My writing is a totally selfish process that other people seem to find it worth spending money on. Although I do know that I came to it by a conscious elimination of the things I couldn't stand to do. I was left with a very narrow arc in which to operate. The only thing I was trained for was the arts, and therefore I had to be an artist. And the only art form I had any proficiency in was language. Therefore I had to write a book. It was as crude as that. But I do know that if I hadn't been whatever a writer is, that would not have been enough to get me through the fourteen years before I was ever earning more than five hundred pounds a year.

Q   *What has being on the breadline meant to you?*

A   Nothing at the time. I look back and think: Heavens, not only was it thin ice, there wasn't any ice! It was just water. But at the time, nothing. There was also that defence of the crude, conscious reason for doing something. And that was simply—"I'm too lazy to work. Why should I?" I was summoned before what was then the National Assistance Board to sign on. There wasn't much call for a classical specialist round here, so they had to take me. Because I was a student—had been a student—I couldn't qualify for unemployment benefit. So it was straight off to the National Assistance. For which I am very grateful—four years of it. They hauled me up and told me to have a sense of responsibility. It wasn't until the chairman, a solicitor, started to get wise that things slackened off a bit. There were hilarious scenes when you had honest self-made men saying: "Come come, don't you think it's about time you got a respectable job?" And the chairman would come in at a very high level of language. For instance, one man said: "What's it coming to when you go to university and you can't even get yourself a decent education?" And I said "What do you mean by education?": and the chairman said "This is hardly the time to be discussing semantics." From which I straight away got the message—"Shut up, leave it to me, and don't make them cross." You know, I was the least angry of young men. The Welfare State has been very good to me.

But at school and university I saw people examining the works of men who had written, and they were examining these works purely to get a good start on the right rung of a good ladder in Unilever. Then I found out that certain people on the staff at University were being paid retainers to point out bright young students to firms like Unilever, and that was one of the reasons I left.

Q   *What finally decided you?*

A   The actual breaking point came for another reason: when a man had been lecturing for two months on Aristophanes and hadn't smiled once. And then we started the *Agamemnon*. Right in at the beginning, the thirty-sixth line, there are some words that just riveted me. One of the characters says, "A great ox has come upon my tongue." We spent an hour and a half comparing manuscripts in Zurich and manuscripts in Rome and variants on the readings and textual analysis. Finally the lecturer asked if there were any questions. So I stuck my hand up and asked, "What does it mean?" He looked at me and said: "That hardly comes in the terms of reference." I got up, walked down the road, saw my tutor and said: "I'm sorry. I'm going. Now. This afternoon." He asked why. I said, "I'm going to write." He said "Good luck."

The point of all this that I was highly educated, highly able; and it was this very education that enabled me to reject it. I have a reputation for integrity which fifteen years ago was called "scyvving." And I don't know which is the better description. It's the same phenomenon, but the difference is the scyvving succeeded and therefore became integrity. The funny thing is that on national assistance the government was giving me £150 a year less than if I had remained a student. But I am a writer, whatever that is; and that must be so, because you cannot put up with fourteen years of that without some enormous compensatory factor which takes the sting away.

Q   *Is your love for the various mythologies—English, Scandinavian, Teutonic, etcetera—simple so great that you have to use them personally? Or do you use them because they provide ready-made plots and patterns?*

A   No. It's a recycling of energy. Myth is a very condensed form of experience—it is very highly worked material. It has passed through unknown individual subconsciouses, until it has become almost pure energy. It is a way for me to tap that energy—energy which, until after *The Owl Service*, I couldn't tap any other way. Now I can because, although I have no specific religious belief, working it out is a religious experience, almost an act of forgiveness—forgiving those people who attacked me when I was a child: I have to forgive them not for their sake but for mine, so I can release that energy, free it from keeping them at bay and get on with something else. About three years ago several levers all bore down on the same point, and I suppose for about three months I was technically mad (but not certifiable). Certainly I was mentally very very sick. The result of fighting that one and seeing things clearly again was that I wrote two operas within six months. And I can't read music. Then I wrote a proper one—the first two were very much apprentice pieces. Until that energy was freed for other things I hadn't realized just how much of my personality was being used in holding at bay the eternal present tense of childhood. We are layers of onions, and there is still the seven-year-old in you as in me. And if you get all the holes in the computer card coming down, if something is precipitated, you are suddenly in the present tense. It's all wham, now. Seven years old.

Q   *There's a passage in* The Moon of Gomrath *when you take battle, through the wizard Cadellin, with the age of reason, which is pictured as a great divide, virtually cutting people off from the forces of nature. You apparently have very definite feelings about the age of reason.*

A   That was part of coming to formulate what was damaging about my education. There was no connection between the heart and the head, the emotion and the intellect—they just did not meet. That is why I walked out of the lecture, because the man was

229

performing one exercise and I was asking questions about
another function. Tom Stoppard, who is very very good on this,
said quite recently that academic analysis is a perfectly respectable occupation for people who find it worthwhile; but it has
nothing to do in his case with the playwright, the actor, the
director or the audience. After all, you don't expect a postman
to be a philatelist. Quite often I am expected to be a compendium
of English literature. And one of my biggest safeguards is that
I am not. The English graduates I have met tend to be journalists.
When pressed they admit that they wanted to write, but they
admit that because they were aware of the course behind them
they daren't: there was nothing else to say. Of course everything
has been said.

Q   *Even so, there are many passages in your books, especially in*
The Moon of Gomrath *and* The Weirdstone of Brisingamen, *that
reflect a scholarly knowledge of the language and literature of
the Anglo-Saxons and their contemporaries.*

A   Yes—I was a highly skilled and well-trained linguist. Therefore
I can comprehend the essence of a language very very quickly.
For *The Owl Service* I learnt Welsh in about three months.
A Celtic language is essentially a spoken language—it's almost
impossible to learn it academically. The real way I learnt it
was by getting the confidence of an old Welshman.

    In fact, of course I was very ill-educated. I had to find out
for myself what it was about sitting on Alderly Edge at night
that was quintessential to me. How was I to get at it? It occurred
to me that it was something very English; so I thought let's
have a look at *Beowulf* and Anglo-Saxon.

Q   *So your experience on Alderly Edge informed your subsequent
reading, and not the other way around?*

A   Yes. What I always feel is, Where is the nearest linguistic equivalent to start from?

    After the first two books, when critically I was recognized,
it was possible to do radio and television interviewing about
once every six weeks. This often meant having to condense what
somebody spent an hour saying into three minutes—without
cheating!—preserving the root of what they were trying to say.
The pressure of this programing meant having to listen very
very carefully to what was being said. And this is why in *Elidor*
there is very sudden switch from the first two books, which
were mainly narrative, to dialogue. *The Owl Service* is almost
completely dialogue. That's why I learnt Welsh, because it's
my training, it's the way I comprehend things. Somebody from

another discipline would do something different. The research is often more interesting than the writing.

Q   *I was going to ask if that was ever the case.*

A   The attraction is that, unlike the academic career I'd been schooled for, where I could see myself becoming the world authority on the fourth line of the tenth book of the *Iliad*, I have to go out and grasp subjects that I know little about, such as physics, and find the point where physics and harmonics and megalithic archaeology actually overlap. That's originality, that's creativity. It's seeing or making a point of overlap that nobody has seen before. The same is true of working with people. Largely as a result of what happened three years ago I finally had to face up to the fact that you can't shut away childhood traumatization; and I found I could do the things I had always wanted to do. I was never a recluse by nature, only by pressure. I found that I could talk to people and get on with people; and strange things started to happen. There were certain people I had observed from a distance who were very passionate about the theater. There was one man in particular who seemed to be in an area of overlap with me—we overlapped in some part of our personalities. And if ever I worked in the theater I would want to work with that man. And the same thing with a composer. And then the composer Gordon Cross wrote to me and said I was a natural librettist: would I consider working with him? He came to see me and for three days it was incandescent. Then he took me to Manchester to the theater, where the director was Michael Elliott, the man I just mentioned. So the three of us met in a hotel in the middle of Manchester. For tea. For five or six years we had been part of a mutual admiration society, and none of us daring to approach the others.

Q   *Moving on—Why do you write for children?*

A   I don't. That is it—I just don't.

Q   *You certainly write about children.*

A   They're me. The danger about the autobiographical question—which one is you?—is asking the question the wrong way round. Every one of them is autobiographical, some more than others of course: But I don't think I've ever written about anyone else. In *The Owl Service* some of the minor characters are very much the me I don't always want to see.

Q   *It seems to me that as your novels have appeared you have progres-*

sively refined the area of overlap, to borrow a term, between your modern children and the world of myth and legend. How has this come about?

A   Through trusting myself. I can't answer your question analytically at all—I can't give you a detailed answer. All I know is I started off thinking and writing, and the result was for me an enormous gap between what I saw and what I achieved, and therefore for me that is bad. When I say something is good I mean that gap is quite small; when something is bad, that gap is enormous.

    Now what I find bad may be much better for you than what I find good. The whole process of writing is in coming to terms with language, which I am now very deeply concerned with—the nature of language. At the same time I can't yet abandon my background. I analyze. I think. I read. The book which I have just finished (*Red Shift*) after nearly seven years of unbroken work has involved a bibliography of something like 200 books. I got that out of the way in the first two years. It's like reading for a degree—that intensity. And now I have come to trust what I used to call the Oh-my-god-period. All the work has been done. The original conceptual spark which directed the reading has burnt up, there is nothing left, all the intellect is spent, there is no more excuse. The only thing to do is to write the story—and there is no story. That's the Oh-my-god, when the nights are very long and the days are cleaving. And then the computer starts to print out the relevant information as original ideas. And now I am trusting myself to fly. I am finding that the facility of controlling language has reached the stage where to a certain extent I can rely on the thing I was taught to beware of: that is, sloppy intuition. And that is where all the best stuff that I have ever written has come from—the apparent mistake, looking for one thing and finding another, observing things for the first time. In writing this present book, which was seven years' work, the typescript was 335 pages: the first hundred pages took me a year, the second hundred took four months, and the rest just under four weeks. Like a Saturn rocket—the slow lift-off, the sudden acceleration. The first year was a messy year in which I was disengaging the thought process. Then the intensive middle period, and finally the white-hot end period, where I just wasn't stopping to think what I was writing. And it's certainly the best thing, in the way I would define it, that I've ever done. No doubt about it. And it's a new form of writing. Whether it's a good form of writing or not I'll never be able to tell.

Q   *I was thinking how in your first two books the children are sub-*

jected to a welter of events that willy-nilly go on round them; but how in The Owl Service, *and to a slightly lesser degree in* Elidor, *the sequence of events is much more dependent upon them using such powers of logic as they have, upon them consciously doing things. I suppose the immediate instance of this is Alison, when she discovers that the pattern on the dinner service can be rearranged to make an owl. Has this anything to do with the closing of the gaps you have mentioned—the gap between intent and performance, and the gap between your background and the present?*

A   Well, take *Elidor* instead, which is very much a watershed piece of writing. In fact it's the only nihilistic thing I've ever written. If the book had gone on another page Roland would have gone mad. When it ends he is about to go mad. It is the destruction of his personality. He has always wanted to shun reality, and when he sees Elidor, that's it. At the end you realize that Elidor is just a parallel and not a superior world; and the cost of achieving Elidor is the death of the reality. When he watches the dying Findhorn (based heavily on Platonic philosophy), it's not the back of the cave he sees when he looks into the creature's eyes, but rather he is in the cave himself: and he sees that in order to achieve another shadow he has killed the reality.

Q   *Why didn't you go on to that last page?*

A   I didn't want to. I think it is explicit enough as it stands. It says "He saw the morning. It was not enough. He cried his pain." I'm the only person I know to whom that has really happened. There are all sorts of internal connections between that boy and myself. Roland was just somebody who didn't stop to think properly. He thought. But not properly.

Q   *The endings of your books are often the hardest parts of them. The final paragraphs of* The Owl Service, *for example, I find almost impenetrable, except on what can only be described as a mystical level. Is there any reason for this?*

A   I don't know. I suppose so. The only thing that is consistent about my method of writing is that the end, the last paragraph, has always presented itself before the story. Writing a book is always a case of walking, or ploughing, toward that last paragraph, hoping that on the last day one won't miss it.

Q   *What regard do you have for Japanese mythology, another source of energy I would have thought?*

Alan Garner

A   I have a strong affinity for it. I am fascinated by Japanese legends. They have the real touch of fear in them. You find this in Celtic and in some English writing too. Perhaps this is because Britain and Japan are both islands—because eventually you can't run away from them. You soon reach the sea. Certainly that is one of the factors that make British fantasy so strong. It's the sense of the shadow behind the shadow. And that abounds in Japanese mythology. They have a very good sense of the macabre, and a very good sense of the demonic. An example of that is *Hoichi the Earless*. It is strangely Celtic. Whereas an awareness of Chinese literature just makes me feel —Yes, well, it's a very big country. But I'm influenced even more by Japanese films. You could play an amusing game by seeing how many times in each book I milk *Seven Samurai*. And in *Red Shift*, for instance, the death of Magoo is the climax of *Throne of Blood*. I don't do it consciously.

Q   *Are your books allegorical?*

A   Only if you find them allegorical.

Q   *Is it possible to write allegorically for children and be aware that that is what you are doing?*

A   Yes. But dangerous. Take C. S. Lewis's allegories. They are some of the vilest ever written. They are fascist in style and in method. If you want to see what I mean, read the first page of *The Voyage of the Dawn Treader*. Although I may happen to agree with the opinions, Lewis sneers at people. People who behave in the way he describes I *may* find objectionable. But he says they *are*. Also I think his books are very badly written and morally repugnant.

    The one thing that I am dogmatic about is that my job is to show people, not to tell people. I think education should be on that level too. A lot of didactic writing is didactic because it has been shoved out too early. The writer is not necessarily didactic toward his readers. More often he is being didactic toward himself. He should write another draft before publishing.

Q   *Is this attitude nourished by the knowledge that you have a young readership?*

A   I don't know. But why are children treated as if they are a different kind of species, a different kind of vehicle? It's my experience that adolescents read with greater application, intelligence and understanding than anyone else. Why this is I don't know. But certainly I have never been asked a stupid question by a child reader. I have seldom been asked a sensible one by an adult.

Q   *Why is it, do you think, that you are published on the children's list?*

A   In the United States I'm not—not, at least, in paperback. Over there my work is published as science fiction. The reason they are published over here as children's books is that they are the kind of stories that are only children's stories. In fact most of the people who read my books are adults—whatever their age.

Cheshire, 1973

Alan Garner's novels are: The Weirdstone of Brisingamen (1960); The Moon of Gomrath (1963); Elidor (1965); The Owl Service (1967) *and* Red Shift (1973).

*Degrees at Oxford are ranked in order of descending merit: Firsts, Seconds, Thirds and "Passes." Generally the number of entrants who gain Firsts is never more than 8 per cent.

17 John Rowe Townsend

Interviewed by Justin Wintle

John Rowe Townsend comes from Leeds, a city in the heart of England's industrial north. He was born there in 1922, four years before the post-war depression culminated in the General Strike. Although Townsend did not begin writing fiction until 1960, when it seemed that affluence had come to stay, there is a sense of hard times in all his work. His career as a journalist is probably responsible for his lively awareness of social imbalance and distress. His novels are relentlessly realistic, without indulging in the shock images of the realism of some contemporary cinema. Townsend is also perhaps the first children's writer of genuine stature to concern himself with those class barriers and differences that have become so intolerable in post-war Britain. *Hell's Edge* portrays a romance between a middle-class girl and a working-class boy. There is no question that love alone will necessarily conquer their mutual social embarrassment. What is rewarding about Townsend's approach to this kind of situation is that he refuses to be doctrinaire, to take sides. Social adjustment in the last decades of the twentieth century is likely to be arduous for both parties. What Townsend does is demonstrate that there is no need for the barriers to become barricades.

After reading English Literature at Cambridge University, Townsend returned home to work for the *Yorkshire Post* before eventually joining the staff of the *Manchester Guardian* in 1949. Subsequently he was appointed editor of the *Guardian's* weekly international edition—a post he relinquished four years ago to give himself more time for writing fiction. He keeps a connection with the *Guardian* however as children's book Editor. His interest and love of children's literature is cast wide. He is the founding figure of a movement to create a National Center for Children's Literature, an attempt to establish a national collection of books and works of reference and to promote public awareness of the benefits of better facilities for young readers. Apart from his novels, Townsend has written a study of English literature, *Written For Children*, and he has published a collection of essays on many leading contemporary authors, *A Sense of Story*. Both these books can claim a credit for the improved critical standards that in recent years are gradually being brought to bear on juvenile literature.

John Rowe Townsend is married, and lives in Cheshire.

John Rowe Townsend

Q   *Why do you write for children?*

A   I don't know. When I was working on *A Sense of Story* I talked or wrote to about twenty people who were regarded as children's writers. I didn't find a single one of them who would admit outright that he or she wrote specially *for* children. I think insofar as one has any of the instincts of the artist—or if you prefer a less pompous word, of the craftsman—one must write first of all for oneself with the aim of making something. I think that the book comes first and the audience comes afterwards.

Q   *Yet it does seem that your books are tailored for a particular age-group, children in their early adolescence. Take* The Intruder, *for example. To appreciate the book, it is necessary to understand that Arnold, the hero if you like, is illegitimate, a bastard in the technical sense. So obviously it isn't for the very young. On the other hand, when people reach the age of sixteen or seventeen these days they have started reading adult novels about apparently adult people—James Bond, or the work of Micky Spillane, Philip Roth, that sort of writer. Your books are usually about early adolescence.*

A   Yes. I think the answer to the question "For whom?" is always "For whom it may concern." All the same I think I ought to try and improve on my previous answer. There are two converging viewpoints. On the one hand, one is a craftsman trying to make something; and if one doesn't please oneself one won't please anybody. On the other hand a book is a communication, and an act of communication has two ends. Just as a play is only completed by being performed in front of an audience, so a book is only completed by being read. Each reader completes the book for himself, and of course the book is different for each individual. A book that doesn't communicate fails. So if your book is going to appear on the children's list of a publisher, then somewhere at the back of your mind you must have a sense of audience, a subconscious sense that you are likely to have a particular kind of readership. Courtesy and common prudence are going to demand that you don't treat them too harshly.

Q   *So the fact that you are writing for particular people does play some part in the process of writing?*

A   Yes, it must. You are both craftsman and communicator, and you must carry out each function with proper respect for the other. But as soon as you start thinking in terms of *catering*—a word I particularly detest—for a special readership, then I think you are heading for disaster.

Q   *Does it please you to think that your books are read by a young audience? Or do you feel that children (or adolescents) are only second-best to a readership of adults?*

A   It delights me to have a young audience, and I don't feel there is anything second-best about it. Young people are the most exhilarating readership one could wish for. They are energetic, positive readers; they come to books with a marvelous ability to enter into things and "live the story." They are never world-weary. You can and must take up your theme as if it was something absolutely new. Your book has to be a voyage of discovery, not just another trudge along well-trodden paths. Of course there is another side to this. No child or adolescent will go on reading if the book begins to bore him. Adolescents, whom you mentioned particularly a few minutes ago, are busy people with plenty of other things to do, and if they feel you have nothing to say to them they won't waste valuable time reading your book. That can be both a stimulus and a discipline.

Q   *The reason I used the term adolescence is because you often write about children who have reached the point when they are becoming aware of what they are, of what they will do, of what they will become. Arnold, in* The Intruder, *realizes that he is going to stay in Skirlston, the run-down seaside village, for the rest of his life, and decides, even at the age of sixteen or seventeen, that he wants the village to remain as it is. Again, in* Hell's Edge, *Norman is determining what he is going to become. Is this selection of one area in people's lives deliberate?*

A   No, not really. I just write the books that I can write. I don't know what they're going to be before I start thinking about them. Curiously, my views have become modified in the last few years. I think that when I started writing I had more of a sense of needs not being met than I have now. This is partly because some of the needs that I saw as not being met have since been met more. It comes back to the two viewpoints again—the craftsman and the communicator. When I began my first book, *Gumble's Yard*, thirteen years ago, I thought among other things that I was setting out to fill something of a social void. It seemed to me at that time that children's books tended to be terribly harmless and hygienic.

Q   *Written by the middle classes for the middle classes?*

John Rowe Townsend

A   Yes, yes. . . carefully calculated never to give a child a nightmare or a complex, and therefore in many ways fundamentally frivolous. That is, they were not about anything that really mattered.

Q   *And is that still true?*

A   I'm not sure that it was as true even then as I thought it was. But I don't think it's at all true today. The back streets have become something of a bandwagon. Everybody is writing children's books set in back streets.

Q   *So your views have changed?*

A   Only in this—that I now think that some of what I saw as my intentions were possibly rationalizations. Perhaps the real reason I wrote *Gumble's Yard* was that it was inside me hollering to come out. And the real reason that I chose that particular setting and those particular kinds of people was that I knew them in my bones, and they interested me. They were what I had it in me to write about, and in a sense I had to find a cover for myself to do it.

Q   *What you had it in you to write about: as part of your background? What was your background? Was it working-class?*

A   Exceedingly poor, though not strictly working-class I suppose. Very down-start, lower-middle-class. My father was a permanent invalid. Although I was a bright boy, and won scholarships, and went to Leeds Grammar School and to Cambridge, it comes more naturally to me to identify with Arnold than with the other children in *The Intruder*, with Jane and Peter Ellison, who are middle-class. It was the same with the poor children in *Gumble's Yard*: I felt myself to be inside them, not looking at them from outside.

Q   *What were the origins of* Gumble's Yard?

A   There were several, I suppose. First, I was dropped on to review children's books for the *Guardian*, and I began to feel, as I said before, this sense of a terribly comfortable, bourgeois middle class full of children whose fathers were stockbrokers or doctors and lived in nice old houses in the country, and who had ponies and nannies and who went on holiday in Switzerland. I was very much aware that this country after all has poor fathers who are not stockbrokers and doctors—children who couldn't tell a pony from a nanny, and who certainly don't go on holiday in Switzerland. Next, I had also done a series of articles about the work of the NSPCC (National Society for the Prevention of Cruelty to Children). This had involved me on going round on the beat with some of the old NSPCC inspectors; rather a shaking experience because I thought I knew something of what it was to be poor. I realized that although I had grown up in a poor home financially, I had a very good home in everything that matters. I realized there are an awful lot of children in this country who are brought up in circumstances not so much of financial as of spiritual poverty—parents who never talk to them except to bawl them out. I met a little girl aged about nine who didn't know when her birthday was because nobody had ever bothered to tell her. That's a very tiny thing, but imagine—a child without a birthday.

Q   *What else?*

A   Another thing was our evening paper, the *Manchester Evening News,* which ran a story about a woman who had four children and whose husband had walked out on her. So she packed her bag and one day she went off with her kids to the bus-stop. She got on the bus, waved them goodbye, and off she went, intending never to see them again. The children went back home. The eldest, a boy of about twelve, was afraid that the family would be broken up and they would be sent into homes or something like that. He didn't want this because they were a very solid little family. So for about three or four days he looked after the younger children—sent them to bed, got them up, sent them to school, made meals of a sort for them. Mind you, the powers that be did catch up with them—obviously before long they had to. The story as far as I know had a happy ending though. The mother was found and a lot of people rallied round.

Q   *What inspired the particular setting, the open space around a disused canal?*

A   I used to go to work in Manchester on the train. The train used to stop, as trains will, on a viaduct outside the city's old central station. The viaduct ran beside the old headquarters of the Bridgewater Canal. It's a very strange and mysterious place: the water always seems to be a thick dark green, full of half-sunk barges, old wharves, piles of mysterious junk, warehouses, cindery towpaths where the horses used to go, and, in those days, sloping down to it used to be a grimy tangle, a tatty old slum district. This had a very strong appeal for me visually. At first you look, and you think, My God how ugly! Then, if you keep on looking, after a while you realize it's not ugly, but beautiful, in rather a strange, sad kind of way. I got

into the habit of wandering around there in my lunch hour—
trespassing I'm sure, but nobody ever threw me out. It remained
a mysterious place, quite a maze in fact; you never knew when
you were going to come on water, and the perspectives were
all very strange and intriguing. I found myself putting people
into this setting, in particular what I supposed to be the children
of this abandoned family (of course I didn't actually know any
of them). In my mind's eye I could see the eldest child—I thought
at the time it was a girl, not a boy—a rather thin straight-up-and-
down child, maybe eleven or twelve, long fair hair I think, not
too clean, and a thin, pinched, sharp, shrewd kind of face; a
child who was perhaps a bit old for her age, who would know
how to mend clothes or where to buy potatoes a penny a pound
cheaper than anywhere else; a salt of the earth child, a splendid,
sterling child. And I think the story of *Gumble's Yard* really
grew out of this. And because at the time I had been reviewing
children's books, it emerged as a children's book.

Q *Parentlessness, whether temporary or permanent, seems to play
an important part in your books. You said that your father was
an invalid—Did this provide you with a basic situation?*

A Not to my knowledge.

Q *Is parentlessness a connotation of the poverty you write about?*

A Yes, it is a connotation of poverty. But it's never been a conscious decision, to write about someone who is parentless. There
are books, especially in America, which are called situation
books. They provide a character with a certain situation, and
then the reader is supposed to identify and feel what it would
be like to be in that situation. You know—you write a book
about a girl whose parents are getting divorced, or who is starting at a new school and can't make friends, or who thinks she
is unattractive. This is probably constricting. In my last two
books, *The Summer People*, and *Good-night, Prof, Love*, each
of the two main characters has two parents, and very permanent
homes.

Q *Your books are full of social detail. You describe the history of
a place with loving care, and your characters always come from
somewhere, unlike many other children's writers' characters, who
seem to come from nowhere—*Alice in Wonderland *I suppose is
as good example as any. Your people have explicit backgrounds
and explicit status. Is this because you are interested in how
whole communities work, or because of your training as a
journalist, which has obviously made you aware of social attri-
butes?*

A I think it's more the former of these. I'm very much concerned with roots. I'm not a political person, but I have a very strong sense of what happens to communities and what happens to places—the loss of rootedness of communities, the loss of people's sense of belonging.

Q *I noticed at the end of* Hell's Edge *that everybody seems fairly pleased when the plans for a new town center are brought before a sympathetic Sam Thwaite—even Norman, who is brought round to seeing at least some advantages in a redevelopment that now seems likely to happen. Yet throughout* The Intruder *the bias is heavily against any kind of redevelopment at all.*

A That's not my bias, necessarily. People constantly identify one with the sentiments of the characters in one's books, particularly if they don't like the sentiment. *The Intruder* is not "against" anything.

Q *Is it "about" anything?*

A I think originally I intended it to be about identity. It has always seemed to me that the great adolescent problem is to do with identity—not sex, not drugs, not all the other fashionable things that come in and go out from time to time. The real adolescent question is, Who am I? What am I here for? What do I have it in me to be and to do? And I had in mind, particularly to begin with I think, the boy, Arnold, because I wanted to write about someone whose whole identity depended upon what he was and where he was. I wanted to write about a slow boy, in the sense of being slow to make the necessary marks on paper and cope with all the paraphernalia of our civilization. Which is not to say that he is slow for other, more fundamental purposes. So I had the character of Arnold. And I had this sense of rootedness as opposed to change. I had also in my mind the menace it could be to a person whose identity depended on a place and his role in that place if his identity were to be threatened, particularly by some rather malevolent influence coming in from outside. Sonny, the Stranger, is the other side of the coin from Arnold. He is all the things that Arnold isn't; and he is not all the things that Arnold is.

Q *And the Ellisons—Peter and Jane, together with their parents? What part did they have to play?*

A I wanted a clash between ancient and modern. Arnold is ancient because he is rooted to Skirlston, a village that is cut off from the motorway. The Ellisons are modern—mobile and middle-class. Also I did want to write about a boy/girl relationship which is dogged by social and sexual unease: two people who want to get onto each other's wavelengths, but who are prevented from doing so by all sorts of intangibles. But more than anything else I wanted to get across a feeling on the one hand of our frailty and impermanence in the face of the elements; and on the other hand that it is we, in the last analysis, who count, and that all the rest of the stuff is so much earth and water rolling about in the sky, and it is we who give meaning to it.

Q   *I thought that the Intruder himself, Sonny, was a new element in children's literature because unlike most children's villains, who are on the level of witches, he has what can only be described as a criminal mind—enough to disturb a reader of any age in fact. Was this deliberate?*

A   Yes—he's a dangerous psychopath. He is evil through ignorance and imbalance. He is the ordinary man driven by the intense and therefore malignant—almost cancerous—sense of not being ordinary. He is the man from nowhere—the only place he comes from is Gumble's Yard. And in the end of course Arnold survives because he is rooted and because he belongs to the place; and the stranger dies because he is not rooted and doesn't belong— because he doesn't know and he doesn't understand.

Q   *Arnold survives, but it is not a happy ending. It is stated explicitly that he will never see Jane again. It seems in fact that you have always resisted the big happy ending.* Gumble's Yard *ends where it began—the children return to their uncle, but there is no guarantee that they will be any the happier. And in* Hell's Edge *the relationship between Norman and Ril, the most hopeful thing in the whole book, is never more than tentative.*

A   I think a happy ending is only legitimate if it is the proper and, artistically speaking, inevitable sequel to the events that have become before; otherwise it's artificial and you can't really use it. I feel that a story can really only end the way it would have ended, just as I feel that characters can only do the things they would have done. This is one of the things that makes writing the books so hellishly difficult.

Q   *You are an optimist though?*

A   I suppose I am a kind of modified optimist.

Q   *You say that allowing your characters to develop according to*

John Rowe Townsend

their own natures makes writing difficult. Could you give an example of any exceptional difficulty you've had?

A   Yes, in *Goodnight, Prof, Love* I was presented with a forced choice. At a certain point the boy and the girl find themselves alone in an attic at night—in Gumble's Yard as it happens. Obviously the question arose—Do they or don't they make love? Now if the book is appearing on the children's list, an author is going to be in trouble—with teachers and librarians and reviewers—whichever way he plays it: if they do, you will be blamed for writing what is unsuitable for children; and if they don't, you will be accused of ducking the issue. So you just can't win.

Q   *What did you do?*

A   The only way of solving it I could find was to ask myself, in the circumstances would they? And it seemed to me that they would. So they did.

Q   *Television and the media have developed so that most children now encounter in very clear terms what was not even talked about —at least in front of them—ten or fifteen years ago. Do you find as a result of this there is pressure on you to be more explicit about sex and other subjects?*

A   I think an awful lot need not be explicit, although I don't think one ought to worry too much about corrupting children, so long as one's books are honest. It has always seemed to me (and this may sound unduly inspirational) that what is honestly intended, and done as truthfully as the author is able to do it, cannot intrinsically be regarded as harmful. On the whole I am inclined to think that children will pass unharmed over what they do not understand. The objection to the heavy sex novel is not that it is going to corrupt them, but that it is going to bore them stiff—by elaborating on experiences that are beyond meaning for them.

Q   *So when you are writing for children you prefer to concentrate on what is well within the scope of their experience?*

A   Yes, I suppose so. And within mine, of course.

Q   *Is that why places are so important in your novels?*

A   Perhaps. Places work very very strongly on me.

John Rowe Townsend

Q   *What about Hallersage in* Hell's Edge, *one of your most convincing portraits of an environment, and one that seemed to provide a key to the characterization and relationship of the book? Were you thinking of any particular northern town at the time?*

A   Halifax more than anywhere else, but there are a number of towns in the industrial Pennine country of the West Riding of Yorkshire that would do. They are ugly on the surface, but beautiful in the bone. The typical one is found in a basin. I always imagine them seen from above, looming up through a bit of haze—the chimney fingers. When I wrote *Hell's Edge* I used a theme that had been lying in my mind for as long as I could remember—the theme of North and South. The symbolism of North and South applies to Europe and North America as well, not just England. I don't know whether it applies to Japan.

Q   *What is that symbolism?*

A   North is hard, South is soft; North is industrial, South is pastoral; North is scientific, technological, South is artistic; North is tough, South is tender. One could go on with ten or a dozen of these contrasts. Above all North is masculine, South is feminine. North and South love, hate and need each other. It takes both North and South to make a world.

Q   *Like the oriental Ying and Yang?*

A   Right. North and South—a theme. When I wrote *Hell's Edge* I began with the theme, and created my characters to express that theme, the polarities of North and South. It is the only time I have allowed my characters to arise in this particular way. Rather deliberately I decided that I was going to have a boy who is tough, rough, gruff, Northern, good with his hands, anxious to leave school and earn some money. And the girl, who I knew from the start was to be a distant cousin, came from the South, a socially superior setting, on the whole of rather artistic impulses, a girl who would like history for example, while the boy wouldn't. And somehow I was going to work the North-South theme out between them. Naturally they went their own way anyway after about chapter one—as people, not symbols.

Q   *And you think of them—Norman and Ril—as people?*

A   Certainly. I know them very well as people—much better than lots of people I know in real life. I know a lot more about all my characters than ever appears in the books. What I mean is, I think the characters extend beyond the pages of the book; and if they didn't, they wouldn't be satisfactory characters.

Q *You always seem to take great care to use the right expression at the right time. That is to say, your novels are well culled. Is there any writer who has influenced you in this or any other way?*

A I quite honestly think I wouldn't like to name any writer who has had an influence on me. Obviously when one is writing out of one's whole experience, then that includes the experience of what one has read. It's not that I am reluctant to name influences, but simply that I can't. I have read and read and read, so there must be influences, but mostly unconsciously.

Q *How do you see your own writing in a general literary context?*

A It always seems a bit pompous or pretentious to put oneself on the map, but . . . I think that perhaps with *Gumble's Yard* and *Widdershins Crescent* (the sequel to *Gumble's Yard*) I was part of a trend to widen the social base and the area of real-life experience which was acceptable in writing books for children. I do not however think that realism is the only writing of value to children; I just think we were weaker when we didn't have these areas open. I'm all in favor of fantasies, historical novels, and all the rest of it.

Q *How do you respond to J. R. R. Tolkien and C. S. Lewis, in the light of what you have just said?*

A I am not the world's greatest admirer of either Tolkien or C. S. Lewis. That is a personal thing—I find there are other kinds of fantasy that work better on me. On the whole I think I like the kind of fantasies that arise from and are related to the life we know. That is, I would like fantasy still to be rooted in us.

Q *Do you think children's literature has changed since, say, 1960?*

A Yes, although I think the change came in the mid-fifties. Since then the most important change, I think, is that there has been more talent writing for children. The areas that are open for children's writing have widened as a consequence. I believe very much that children's literature should also be more of an international thing. I'm particularly sorry, for example, that whereas the Japanese get so many of our books, we get so few of theirs published over here.

John Rowe Townsend

Q   *Can children's literature be international?*

A   I would like to think that what is local in the manners and in the settings and customs in my and other people's books in England is not going to be off-putting for young people with different backgrounds, like the young people of Japan. It is a very very firmly held belief of mine that the basic truth of literature is truth not to the changing surface details, but truth to the underlying enduring realities of human nature. And this is the truth that I have always, according to my lights, aimed to attain.

Q   *And of the future?*

A   As long as there are books inside me wanting to be written, and as long as anybody I respect is willing to publish them, I shall go on writing. If there cease to be books wanting to be written and worth writing, I hope I shall have the sense to stop. I don't feel at the moment as if I was going to stop.

London, 1973

John Rowe Townsend's novels are: Gumble's Yard (1961—in America, Trouble in the Jungle); Hell's Edge (1963); Widdershins Crescent (1965—in America, Good-bye to the Jungle); The Hallersage Sound (1966); Pirate's Island (1968); The Intruder (1969); Good-night, Prof, Love (1970—in America, Good-night, Prof, Dear); *and* The Summer People (1972). *He has also edited* Modern Poetry (1971)—*a selection for young people.*

18 Madeleine L'Engle

Interviewed by Justin Wintle

One of the genres of modern literature which children share with adults is science fiction: there is no need for a separate corpus of juvenile SF. Madeleine L'Engle, in her most famous book, *A Wrinkle in Time*, avoids making it look as if there is a need; but what she does do is borrow some of the well-established techniques and stylistic devices of science fiction, and then employs them in the service of speculations which are non-scientific. Through a complicated trick of astrophysics a group of three children are transplanted to a planet whose population is mesmerized by a single naked brain. The question of liberating the inhabitants of Camazotz does not arise; the important thing is to save themselves: by achieving this they will rescue their own species (a pleasantly middle-class conceit), though just how is never made quite clear. In the end it is Love that triumphs, not a counterblow of superior technological intelligence. The conceptual elements of this extraordinary novel are diffuse and never completely synthesised. Homilies to Einstein exist crudely beside quotations from the Bible. One suspects that Madeleine L'Engle might have been a bluestocking novelist for adults had she been born in an earlier age.

Meet The Austins (1960) is a different sort of book altogether, at least on the surface: a completely realistic portrayal of the harmonies and discords in a family which is, for the most part, unruffled by whatever energies may roam the cosmos.

Madeleine L'Engle was born in 1918, the daughter of the journalist and playwright Charles Wadsworth Camp. Most of her schooling took place in Switzerland, although she returned to the United States to attend Smith College. For a brief period she worked and acted in the theater before settling down to write and bring up her children. She is married to Hugh Franklin, the actor, and lives on the upper West Side of Manhattan.

Madeleine L'Engle

Q   *You started out on the stage. What made you leave it?*

A   I only went into the theater because I thought it was a good
school for a writer. That was number one reason. Number two
reason was that I had been in female institutions since the age
of twelve. I was terribly shy, and I thought it would help me
get over being shy. Both reasons worked out. I was in a play
with Eva Le Gallienne and Joseph Schildkraut called *Uncle
Harry*. Then I went into Chekhov's *The Cherry Orchard* for
a year in New York, followed by a year on the road. As a
writer that was probably the best experience I ever had. I was
only doing bit parts and under-studying and assistant stage
managing, but it was like a new play every night. I also had
the benefit of meeting a young man whose name was Hugh
Franklin, which I hadn't expected. We met in *The Cherry
Orchard* and were married in *The Joyous Season*, which was
Ethel Barrymore's last legitimate show. I decided that if I was
going to be a wife and have babies and write, something would
have to go. In any case one actor in the family I think is enough.
So I left the stage.

Q   *What in particular had you learned from it?*

A   I think the most important thing I learned is that not every
word that drops from my pen is a precious pearl. Things can
be cut and things can be rewritten and changed.

Q   *Did your director cut* The Cherry Orchard*?*

A   Not *The Cherry Orchard*, but other plays, yes. One would see
that a thing didn't work. Then the author would go home and
stay up all night and come back with another scene next morning. I realized that sometimes you have to write something fifteen
or twenty times before it comes out right.

Q   *How did your parents respond to the idea of your going into
the theater? I should imagine it was still an "unladylike" profession in those days.*

A   Oh very definitely it was. However they had a sort of mixed
reaction. My father, who died when I was seventeen and who
had been a journalist and a foreign correspondent, also wrote
plays and scenarios. He was gassed in the First World War,
so I never really knew him. My mother had been in music before
she was married, so they were both used to artists. Nevertheless,
that their only child, who came late in their lives, should go
into life as an actress!—my mother was less than happy about

it, especially when I married an actor. Of course, she ended up adoring him.

Q *When did you first start to want to write?*

A I've always written, and I think that's because, being an only child of much older parents with all the focus on my father, and no libraries available then as they are now, and not being allowed out on my own, when I'd gone through what few books were available I just had to begin writing them. It became another world. When I was twelve it became apparent that my father couldn't live in London or Paris or New York or any other city. Since he was a writer and his work went with him it was cheaper for us to live in the Alps than anywhere here. I was put in an English boarding school. It was in Switzerland, but it was one of those schools where a lot of colonials sent their kids. I was the only American, a total minority. I had to learn to put on protective coloring very quickly, so I learned to concentrate, and to write stories when I should have been doing homework and things like that. We were never given an iota of privacy. Privacy was suspicious. If you wanted to be alone you were thought to be doing something nasty. I learned to put up a forcefield around myself in the midst of everything. Because of these lessons in concentration I was later able to write my first novel while I was on tour with a play. I wrote it in dressing rooms and railroad stations and hotel rooms.

Q *When you were still very young?*

A Yes. I'd written a lot of it when I was still in college.

Q *What happened to it?*

A It was published in the States, an adult novel. Two or three of my books which were originally issued as adult books have been reissued in this so-called boom of junior novels.

Q *What was your first real children's book, and how did it come about?*

A A book called *And Both Were Young*, a terrible title I did not choose. I was asked to write a book about my boarding school experiences. Again, it wasn't a children's children's book. My feeling is that if a children's book isn't equally or even more enjoyed by adults then it's not worth doing. I'm not interested in doing anything that doesn't interest me. I probed into some of my own particular problems at boarding school. I set it later in history, right after World War II, so you had some of those problems coming in too. I still get quite a lot of mail on it, so it's still selling. It's a good book. John McLoughlin says he feels it's about time that period had a revival.

Q *In the best known of your children's books there is always a feeling of protection within the families you describe. Each member is concerned with and cares for all the other members. Does this reflect your own experience of family life?*

A My own experience as a child was the complete opposite. Because my father was slowly dying there wasn't very much time for me. But I enjoyed being by myself, and I didn't bug anybody. I just sat and played the piano and wrote music and stories and did things like that. When I got married I think I probably had an ideal of what I hadn't had. We moved to the country to a little tiny village of well under five hundred people where there were about a dozen couples of us with kids of the same age who were all very very close. During that time tragedy kept striking the people around us. We acquired a seven-year-old child when her father dropped dead in November of a heart attack and her mother had a cerebral haemorrhage eleven months later—wham! wham! Things like that kept happening, so that the security of the family hearth and the feeling of an unrestricting, open-handed love became terribly important. My children and my husband were very tolerant of me, allowing me to be myself. Certainly at that point I was anything but a success. I was a total failure. If I made fifty dollars a year I was doing well. Nevertheless they were perfectly willing to help me. They gave me an example of a kind of love that doesn't clutch, but which was nevertheless comforting in the sense that it gave me a lot of strength. I was able to write *Meet The Austins*, which, as it was printed, I think is weak. I wrote it originally as a love letter for my husband. It was a much stronger book. But I was at the end of a decade of nothing but rejections, and I had lost confidence in my own work. I didn't know that what I was trying to get onto the paper was actually getting there. So when a publisher finally took it and said it would be better if we did this and we did that to it, I let them do it. I regret that now.

Q *What changes did you allow to be made?*

A One reason that it was rejected so often is that it begins with a death. The effects of that death had to be weakened—the effects on all of the relationships between all of the characters. It became a bit pious and a bit sweet, which I don't think was

in the original. After it had gone into galleys I realized that
I should have had more faith in it. When *A Wrinkle In Time*
began to be rejected and rejected and rejected I refused to water
it down.

Q   *That early death in* Meet The Austins *is provocative. To me it
confronted a problem that faces many children: that masochistic
desire for somebody close to them to die. It was weakened in
the sense that in your book it happens to someone outside the
Austin family proper.*

A   It's the way it happened to us, though Maggie is not like our
adopted daughter at all. Two people who had been very close
to us suddenly vanished.

Q   *I was really wondering why you didn't begin with the death
of one of the Austin parents?*

A   Again, because that's not what happened. Although the Austin
family is not my family, I nevertheless was writing from a framework of our experience. The things they did were very much
the things we did. As I said, it was originally written for my
husband, and much closer to what I think originally happened.
It kept getting much further away as it got sweeter.

Q   *The relationship between the parents is definitely "sweet" in your
usage. They aren't heard to argue much, and they never "stay
mad."*

A   Only in *Meet The Austins*. In *The Young Unicorns*, when they
move to New York, you do begin to get a dividedness between
the parents. Although the nine years we spent in the country
were intensely unhappy ones for me in most ways, there was
a kind of strange non-twentieth-century security to life in that
little village. Because we were intensely involved in making
the seven-year-old child feel secure I don't think we ever did
have the corrosive kind of fighting that goes on in many marriages. We fought, and that was in the original book, but not
like that. I remember one time when my mother was with us,
and she and my husband and I were having a violent argument
at the table. It was perfectly amicable, but we were arguing
like mad. Our adopted child, who hadn't been with us very long,
burst out with "Don't fight, don't fight, don't fight!" I realized
that she had come from a destructively fighting household. We
explained that this was not bad fighting, simply that we were
getting excited about something.

Madeleine L'Engle

Q *Two ingredients particularly seem to me to underly the basic family harmonies in your books. One is a sense of culture—the Austins all listen to Brahms, and* A Wrinkle In Time *contains a rather extraordinary roll call of the heroes of Western civilization. The other is a feeling of piety, Christian piety.*

A I wrote *A Wrinkle In Time* as a violent rebellion against Christian piety.

Q *Perhaps I should have said a feeling of religious spirit.*

A I guess there is that in it, but it wasn't what I was getting at. New England is Congregational. It's been Congregational ever since this country was born. Life in a little tiny village tends to revolve around the church. If there's any reading done the Minister does it. Not many others read books, so if you want to know something you have to consult the Minister. I got to know several Congregational Ministers when I lived in the country simply from the hunger of having somebody to talk to who didn't discount words. They were all very eager to convert me to Christianity and gave me many German theologians to read. I thought "If I ever have to read all this stuff I will never be a Christian." So I wrote *A Wrinkle In Time* as an heretical book, of what I thought was a possible universe. It turns out as not an heretical book at all. But for me at that time it was a fumbling toward something that wasn't an offence to my instincts and to my mind. The two have to work together. That's why the villain in *A Wrinkle In Time* is a naked brain. The brain tends to be vicious when it's not informed by the heart. I'm still not very happy about the Establishment, although I'm part of it. I have many close friends within the Anglican Establishment, but I still find myself unhappy about it.

Q *The book has whole sections of quotation directly from the Bible, and there is a message of Love which has its ultimate source in the Godhead, or at least a godhead.*

A The thing I was looking for at that point was something that would tumble over the world's idea of what is successful and what is powerful. Therefore Meg succeeds through all her weaknesses and all her faults. When I was in college I had a teacher who was very famous in this country, called Mary Allen Chase. She told me that anybody who was considering writing as a profession had to know the King James translation of the Bible. So I went back to it purely for literary reasons (I had been at Anglican boarding schools all my young life). I will always stay with it for literary reasons, whatever my state of enchantment or disenchantment with its theology might be. The Authorized Version, along with Shakespeare, is essential to me, just for my undergirding. It's a powerful repository of story-telling—the stories in it are brilliant. The thing that has come through to me is that nobody ever succeeds because they are virtuous or because they are pious or because they are good or because they are moral. It's not a moralistic or pietistic book at all. It's a book of enormous cosmic power. The human beings are all fallible, sometimes downright wicked. But they all have an enormous sense of their own limitations, and of the unlimited-ness of the universe.

Q   *Returning to that roll call of names—Jesus, Leonardo, Einstein, Shakespeare and so forth: what was the purpose of it in* A Wrinkle In Time? *Are they simply your cultural heroes?*

A   My household gods? Possibly. Back in college where I was read-ing English, I remember being asked in an exam "Why did Chaucer do this and that?" I didn't think Chaucer had any idea why he did these things, and that's what I wrote. I think that's true. I can tell you some things by hindsight or from what people have told me. But basically, when I'm writing a story it's like riding rather a wild horse, letting it go where it wants to go. The only thing I'm in control of is seeing the parts I can simplify and seeing that it remains a story.

Q   *You combine a lot of very disparate ideas in* A Wrinkle In Time—*there's metaphysics, science fiction, mathematics, a bit of political theory and many other ingredients.*

A   That's where I was at the time of writing it. I was trying to discover a theology by which I could live, because I *had* learned that I cannot live in a universe where there's no hope of any-thing, no hope of there being somebody to whom I could say, "Help!" I was finding my theology basically in Einstein, in the quantum theory, in Eddington. It's funny that my theologians are the mathematicians. I still find more theology in the great scientists than anyone else. Tycho Brahe always used to put on his court robes before going to his telescope. That kind of thing I find very exciting and stimulating. Probably I need to. We lost our five closest friends in our generation within three years. Statistically this was an awful lot of death.

Q   *The scientific observer is a priest?*

A   Yes, but I think it's only true of one in every hundred thousand scientists.

Q   *Are the rest misusing or abusing science?*

A   I suppose most of us think that we can rely upon a total do-it-yourself philosophy, that science can cope with it all. Just wait and we'll take care of cancer and we'll take care of death, we'll take care of everything! We've gotten into this idea that man is perfectible by his own effort. Finally that's a dead end. The great scientists have always been immensely awed by the mystery behind the universe. Einstein said that anybody who doesn't have a total awe and adoration of the mind behind the universe is as good as a burnt-out candle—and I'm quoting him almost exactly. He also talked about the necessity to ask questions of the sort a small child asks—Why am I here? Does my life have any meaning? Are we just an unfortunate skin disease on the face of the earth? Is there a validity in asking these questions? Einstein said yes, there is a validity.

Q   *Is there a connection between what you've been talking about and the much more down-to-earth expressions of family love which one also finds in* A Wrinkle In Time?

A   I think that any time you start talking about great cosmic things you get lost unless you particularize. It is incomprehensible to us unless it becomes what the theologians call the "scandal of the particular"—taking a small incident and finding in it an expression of something much more general. And that I do believe in.

Q   *Still, one of the problems I felt with* A Wrinkle In Time *is in equating the grand cosmic adventure that the family goes through with their return to normal life in Connecticut at the end. One feels they will get very bored unless they are thrown into another adventure of similar proportions.*

A   Of course I'm not entirely successful. I think that is why I was so shattered at the long time it took the book to sell, because I did feel I had moved beyond where I had been in my writing, that I was into a new area. But it was so new I had no idea whether I had got it out or not. I think I must have said at least some of what I wanted to say, judging by the response I get. My only hope is that as I learn more as a human being and as a writer, each time just a fraction more will join properly. And I *do* take the family on to further adventures—in *A Wind In The Door*.

Q   *Do you think children are equipped to grasp the large intellectual issues you write about?*

A   They are more able than most people had anticipated. I know the original idea was that maybe high school kids would get it, but no lower than that. Well, again just judging from the letters I get, sixth-graders do get an enormous amount out of it. But then they've had a lot more of that kind of science taught them at school than even someone as young as you has had. And they seem to get the other implications, the personal and the psychological ones.

Q   *Which came first in that book, the ideas or the characters?*

A   It got started when we decided to leave the village in the country and come back to New York. But first we took the kids out of school and went on a ten-week camping trip from the Atlantic to the Pacific. We were driving along one day when the names of Mrs Whatsit, Mrs Who and Mrs Which popped into my head out of the blue. I turned round in the car and said "Kids, I've just thought of these three marvelous names. I'll have to write a book about them." I was seeing my country which I didn't know at all, sitting out every night by the embers of a dying campfire, looking up at the stars which you never see in the city. I'd taken along a lot of books on physics and cosmology. My subconscious mind started turning all these things around. When we got back Hugh went off with a production of *Heartbreak House* on the road, and I got down to the book.

Q   *Have you read a lot of science fiction?*

A   I discovered H. G. Wells when I was twelve. Then of course Arthur C. Clarke. I like science fiction very much. I wouldn't say that science fiction writers' styles have influenced me very much. It was their way of thinking that attracted me, their way of saying "Yes, but what if?" An open, as opposed to a closed, universe.

Q   *Early on in* A Wrinkle In Time *the children are spun through space into the land of Camazotz, a Kafkaesque place where everybody literally conforms to a uniform pattern. What gave you the idea for that?*

A   I think it sprang mostly from seeing Camazotz round the country. When you leave New York tonight you'll be flying over Camazotz—house after house after house, the people in them all watching the same television programs, and all eating the same things for dinner, and the kids in their mandatory uniforms of blue jeans and satchels or whatever. I keep getting asked whether Camazotz is a protest against Communism. I suppose it is, but really it's against forced conformity of any kind.

Q *You think the United States is moving toward greater conformity despite the cultural upheavals of the last few years?*

A I hate to say yes, but I'm afraid I do. Not of course that I can speak for the majority of Americans, in that they live in suburbs and I never have. I've either lived in a very tiny village or in a great big city like New York. I don't know suburban life. I see it briefly if I go to speak at a suburban school, or visit a friend. It's a whole way of life, the typical way of American life I suppose, and I don't much like it. I think we have a more glamorous version of the word than you have in England. It means having enough money to get far enough outside the city so that you can have two big cars. It has to do with affluence and having to make a certain amount of money.

Q *Obviously one is seldom expected to take science fiction, or speculative fiction as most of it is more aptly described today, at its face value. On the other hand one would hesitate to describe a book like* A Wrinkle In Time *as allegory either. How would you explain the workings of that sort of fantasy?*

A Let me give you an analogue. In my first boarding school we were totally restricted and had to do everything by bells. We were also numbered. I was number ninety-seven. My napkin, my cubbyhole and my locker were also numbered ninety-seven. In the Spring we were given garden plots to cultivate with partners. My partner was ninety-six. We were allowed to bring the produce of our gardens in for tea, an important meal. Most people grew tomatoes and lettuce and watercress and radishes and cucumbers and things like that. Well, my garden partner and I planted poppies. It was permissible to be a great deal more naive way back then than it is now. Our illicit reading included *Fu Manchu*, so we knew that opium came from poppies and that it was supposed to give you beautiful dreams. We were eating poppy flower sandwiches and poppy leaf sandwiches and poppy seed sandwiches, and going to bed with our dream books and a flashlight under the pillow. Now what I think we were doing was instinctively rejecting the world of provable fact in which the adults were trying to cram us. The world was rushing down into the devastation of the Second World War. Hitler was already in Germany. My parents were very aware of what was going on, and yet we were still being taught "Try a little harder chaps and everything's going to be all right." And we knew it wasn't. So what we were doing was an unconscious rejection of the values we saw leading into hell and damnation, quite literally. There's a chasm between the conscious mind which we can control and manipulate and the subconscious creative intuitive mind. To become mature or to become religious in my sense of the word ought to be a journey into integration. Far too often it's a journey into disintegration. I think that in this kind of writing you integrate the two. Your mind and your instincts collaborate and go a great deal further than either could go alone. It's a way of bridging the gap between the part of us that sings songs and likes to dance and paint pictures and tell stories, and the part that is pragmatic and wants provable facts. The older I get the more I realize that you can prove almost anything. You can prove by mathematical equation that the world is the centre of the universe. Those old equations are still there. The reason Copernicus got upset about them was not that he didn't think the world was the center of the universe, but because they were clumsy equations. He didn't like the fact that mathematical equations which ought to be beautiful were ugly. So he set about trying to do something more aesthetic until he got himself a beautifully aesthetic equation which turned everything upside down. For me this kind of writing is a making of a more beautiful equation.

Q   *Do you think it's easier to bridge that gap between the mental and the intuitive when you're a child?*

A   Yes. I think I deal with ideas that are too difficult for adults. Grownups will just get uptight. Children still haven't closed all their doors and all their windows. They're not afraid to get upset, and they're not afraid of new ideas.

Q   *One wonders why adults read fiction at all. . .*

A   I think they're reading less and less. Check the lists of books published in the last fifteen years and I think you'll find fiction steadily going down. People read more and more nonfiction.

Q   *New ideas aren't always presented in fiction!*

A   On the whole when you get new ideas presented in a documentary form you get a frame round them. They're safe, and they're in a cage and they can't upset you. But in fiction there isn't any frame, any cage. I think that's what bothers me with most theological writing—they try to get God down, cremate Him or embalm Him or whatever and put Him in a coffin where He's safe, not wild. My whole feeling about any God worth believing in is that he is something totally free and totally wild and totally beyond human comprehension; and that therefore it isn't possible to believe in Him more than once a minute once a month. I think that in all fairness I could be anti-Church. I'm not sure why, and I know it's a contradiction. I still go to church.

Q   *In that your books imply that good and evil are coeval, you are a heretic, a Manichean heretic.*

A   No, I do not imply that good and evil are equal, and I am not a Manichean. But most of the really great theologians aren't restrictive either. Some of them got murdered or excommunicated. I do have the feeling that the earth has its own sentiency, that it is a thinking creature and that paradoxically some of our "natural" cataclysms are when it gets too irritated at what we are doing. That's a basic myth of the human being, and I believe in it. Another thing that has led up to things like Watergate is that we have lost our myths. We've tried to kill them off. When you lose your myth you lose your being. Jung said that modern man has lost a myth to live by, and now we suffer. But myth, you see, has been made into a bad word, something that isn't true. I think that to see something mythically is to try to see something that is not in the realm of probable fact, a way that is at least going to give you a glimmer of light and understanding. That's what all the great myths do. In some primitive tribes the old men and old women are valued because they are the keepers of the myths. I don't think it is a coincidence that as we are discarding our myths we are discarding our older people.

Q   *Is providing children with a notion of the possibilities of myth a reason why you write for them?*

A   No. I think that would be a truly noble purpose, but it's not why I write. I write whatever story has come to me at that moment to be told. I'm not a teacher and I'm not didactic. First and foremost I've got to be a storyteller. At the moment I'm getting into ecology, and it comes out in the book I'm writing. I didn't plan a book in which ecology was going to play a part. It's just happening.

Q   *Lloyd Alexander told me a similar thing is happening to him in a book he's writing at the moment. Do you think authors are motivated by the social issues around them?*

A   Yes I do, though I think it's largely unconscious. But unless you are sitting in an ivory tower—and the suburbs can be an ivory tower—you are bound to reflect the concerns of the world around you. If you are worried that there are millions of starving people, then that will come out, even if it isn't in an obvious way. Your own attitude toward everything is bound to be underneath what you write. I think for my age and for the kind of life I've led I am naive. I hope to outgrow it one of these days. But I also think there's a certain strength in my naiveté which helps me throw off some puerile stuff that I might get stuck with otherwise.

Q   *We haven't really talked about* The Young Unicorns, *a novel that in a way synthesises some of the things you were doing in* Meet The Austins *and* A Wrinkle In Time. *The science fiction is less cosmic, and the family, the Austins again, less together.*

A   Yes. The Austins move back to New York to the upper West Side, and they get involved in an attempt by a scientist to take over the city. I was studying the laser, and I was speculating what would happen if it were projected onto the pleasure center of the brain. This was really rather scary. We now actually have El-ads, electronic addicts who are addicted to having their pleasure centers tickled with electricity. Anyhow, the Austins get involved in this pretty horrendous situation. The father becomes withdrawn. The mother feels completely cut off and left out. They are there in the center of a cauldron with all their "small village" naiveté. All their relationships have got to respond to this. And because they're living in the middle of a big city there's not so much of that sweetness we talked about earlier. The father falls apart pretty thoroughly, at least for a while. It's not the adults with all their scientific knowledge who get to the bottom of the problem. It's the youngest child and a blind girl. Again I suppose it's a case of the weak being able to do what the strong in their arrogance cannot do. A child knows its dependency, how far it can go and how far it can't. But, in total contradiction to this, he also knows he can do more than he can do, and he does it. It seems to me that all the very great things that have happened in the world have been more than man can do. It is not possible to write *Hamlet* or the Bach *B minor Mass*, and yet they've been done. Each great work of art has its own life that is quite separate from the life of its artist. It comes to the artist and says "paint me" or "write me." In an age when the idea of servants isn't thought to be good I still think that the artist is a servant. I'm a pretty bad servant. I have yet to serve a work as it ought to be served. I find that when I'm writing I must listen—listen to the book. Often it will take me in directions I hadn't ever expected. It always knows more than I do. You can say it's

261

my subconscious mind releasing itself, but I think there's probably more to it than that.

Q *There's a ritual the Austins go through. When the going gets tough for them they go out as a family somewhere where they can be near the elements. Should that be a part of people's lives?*

A I don't know whether it *should*. I know that it's an important part of my life. When I'm stuck I have two ways of getting unstuck. In the city I take the dog out for a walk in Riverside Park. In the country I walk in the woods. The other way is to go to the piano and play Bach, which is an equivalent thereof.

Q *There's a lot of talk at the moment of a renaissance in children's literature, paralleled perhaps by a falling off or decadence in adult fiction. Is that a view you would subscribe to?*

A I admire a good deal of contemporary children's writers, and I think some of the best writing being done in this country at the moment is being done for children. Ideas are being explored which simply would not be allowed to be explored in adult fiction, which is doing the same thing as some contemporary painting—they are both looking at the world and seeing only chaos. So they are saying "Help! Chaos!" and reproducing it. In children's books one is not imposing the same restrictive pattern on the universe, and this makes for freedom. For instance, I was talking to a seminar of young theological students. One evening I went in and said "Tonight we are going to talk about structure," knowing that this was going to be very unpopular because at that time they were all discussing how they wanted to be free to make love and so on. Anyway I kept asking questions, particularly "What makes one free?" until one of them unwillingly said "My skeleton." An amoeba has very little structure and I doubt if it has very much fun. Similarly, if I want to climb up on the roof I need a ladder. There's a kind of despair in a lot of contemporary "adult" stuff that is just looking in the mirror and reflecting back worse than you see. A child is not going to settle for a total absence of meaning. A child is born with at least some sense of his own value, a sense that his life matters.

New York, 1974

Madeleine L'Engle has written: The Small Rain (1945); Meet the Austins (1960); A Wrinkle in Time (1962, winner of the Newbery Medal); The Moon by Night (1963); The Arm of the Starfish (1965); Journey With Jonah (1967); The Young Unicorns (1968); Dance in the Desert (1969); *and* A Wind in the Door (1973). A Circle of Quiet (1973) *is autobiographical.*

19 K.M. Peyton

Interviewed by Emma Fisher

Unlike Madeleine L'Engle, K. M. Peyton denies a specific moral intention in her books. She treats her adolescent characters with motherly
affection, allowing them tempestuous emotions and wayward behavior, but believing them to be nice people at heart. She trained
herself as a writer from an early age, publishing several pony books
and adventure stories under her maiden name. With *Windfall*, published in 1962 by Oxford University Press, she began a new career
as a more serious children's writer. This book, and the next two,
were runners-up for the Carnegie Medal. She finally won it in 1969
with *The Edge of the Cloud*, the middle book of her *Flambards* trilogy
about a headstrong girl growing up in the early years of this century.

She tends to be too humble about her own achievements. She
is in fact a marvelous storyteller, twanging the reader's emotions
and marshalling her climaxes with skill and verve. It is this ability
which makes her *Pennington* trilogy such a good read, although
the subject—the story of a rebellious working-class giant who
becomes a great concert pianist, overcoming several setbacks such
as a spell in prison and getting his girlfriend pregnant—might sound
unlikely. Children, especially girls, adore her books and they sell
well as Puffin paperbacks. She is also an artist, and has illustrated
several of her own books.

K. M. Peyton was born in Birmingham in 1929, and brought up
in Surbiton. She and her husband live on the Essex coast, where
they do a great deal of sailing. They have two daughters.

K.M.Peyton

Q   *How did you progress from pony books to your more ambitious later books? Tell me something about your early books.*

A   Well, I've always written, since I was nine years old; I had about seven books published before *Windfall*, which is the first one most people have heard of. The first one was published when I was still at school, so I did start young. I was very horsey, crazy about horses—and the first three books were about ponies and riding. Then I got married and needed the money desperately, so I wrote boys' adventure stories; *North to Adventure, The Hard Way Home, Storm Cock Meets Trouble*; Michael, my husband, thought up all the plots and I wrote them down. I didn't know what was going on half the time. Then there was *Brownsea Silver*, which was written for the centenary of the Scout movement; that was a commission. The Scouts were founded on Brownsea Island, and that was lovely. We went there before it was open to the public, and it was all very wild and belonged to this old lady. We went there in our boat, and anchored off it, and clambered all over it thinking up this plot.

Q   *What was your connection with the Scout movement?*

A   The *Scout Magazine* published all my early work, and they just said "How about writing a story that would do for the centenary?" They didn't say what, so I never thought of it as a commission so to speak.

Q   *What happened with* Windfall, *the first one which was more than a simple adventure story?*

A   We were making more money then and it wasn't so desperate, and I decided I'd like to write something to please myself, where I could ramble on; the first ones had all been written as serials— fourteen chapters, every chapter so many words, and each had to finish with a cliff-hanger; they were written very much to a pattern, and after they'd been published in the magazine Collins would publish them as a book. I got fed up with this and thought I'd like to write a proper book. And that was *Windfall*, which I sent to Collins, and they wouldn't have it. They said they would have it if I shortened it by at least a quarter and cut out all the "thinky" bits, the philosophical bits, which of course were what I thought were all the good bits. So I asked them if I could try it somewhere else; it was all done in a very amicable way and they said: yes, try it somewhere else, and if you can't get anyone to publish it we'll have another talk about it. So I made out this list of publishers which I thought were the best, and I put Oxford at the very top of the list, and pushed it off to Oxford, and to my amazement they kept it. So I stayed with them. They never interfere; I've had to change a few things, but I think they probably interfere or suggest or try to influence you less than anybody. I've got a very good working relationship with them.

Q   *You have an editor who keeps you at it?*

A   My editor, Mabel George, has got her own standards; you meet them, and you'll get on with her. Her standards are almost too high—she makes me feel I'm slacking if I don't produce a book that's up to standard. Some books you go into and you know it's going to be more difficult, more ambitious, and another book you'll start knowing it's going to be quite easy. I suppose you can always write the most difficult book, to your way of thinking, but I don't always; people don't. William Mayne, for example, whose books I love, has his big books and his smaller ones, for younger people.

Q   *Have you ever tried writing for a younger age-group?*

A   I can't. I've tried, and I just can't do it. I tried to do books for quite small children at one time, because I was asked to by a friend and I thought it would be a great lark, and fun, and I had masses of ideas; but when it came to writing them down, they were hopeless. I don't know what went wrong, but they didn't work.

Q   *Why do you think you feel so much more at home writing for the thirteen to seventeen age-group?*

A   I don't feel I'm a writer who wants to write adult books and has just missed off; I never have that feeling. I sometimes think perhaps I'm mentally retarded, in some way, because I haven't ever grown into wanting to write about truly adult people. I'm very interested in this age, this age where young people change so quickly, and are so difficult to understand, in all ways. I can remember those feelings so clearly. It is a fascinating age, and everything matters so much. With those last books, the three *Pennington* books, people were saying: "Are you going to write another one?" But no, it's finished, there's no question of it. His problems are ironed out all right; from now on I'm not really interested in him at all. I wouldn't find the interest to write any more. It happened the same with the *Flambards* books; I wouldn't want to write any more. In fact, I never intended with either of those two trilogies to write any more than one book; they weren't conceived in threes. At the end of the first *Flambards* book she goes off with Will, and I was prepared to leave it there, though as I was writing the book I realized that it could well go on from there. And because I had got so interested in them as I was writing, I wanted to go on, very badly, and the next one then carried on directly. But after that, there was a bit of a gap, before I wrote the third one; I knew it could carry on, and I could see how it would all work out, but it meant killing off Will, which I thought was such a bad thing to do that I couldn't do it. I discussed this with my editor before I started the book; I said I would quite like to do this book, and she wasn't all that sure that I ought to do it either. She didn't mind about killing Will, she thought that was all right. I thought it was all right authentically, it was correct, because I don't think a single pilot who joined up in 1914 survived until 1918, but I didn't want to do it just for the sake of writing another book.

Q   *Were you happy in the end with the way it turned out? I know some of the critics said the last one was the best of the three, though I like* The Edge of the Cloud *best myself.*

A   I thought the last one skated very close to being *Woman's Own*-ish, I think all my books do; I have to be very careful. I recognize this in myself, and always have done, you know.

Q   *Do you think it could be something to do with writing for that age-group, when you can't perhaps be all that subtle, and everything is much more black and white?*

A   I think I just am like that. I think that's the way my mind works. Any plot I touch, I—perhaps it's the wrong thing to say—I bring it down to my level.

Q   *What do you call* Woman's Own-*ish about it? Do you mean the romantic plots?*

A   Well, look, if anybody says to me, "This book you're writing now—what's it about?" If I begin to tell the outline of the story I just stop, I'm so covered in confusion; and all my books are like that to me. If you sum up the plot, it's been done so many times, they're so hackneyed, and they all sound so *unworthy*, if you just put them in a few words. They sound terrible. This happens time and time again. So I do have to be fairly careful. But I was aware of this long before it was actually pointed out; it's been pointed out a lot of times now, but I was just waiting for that to happen. Every time I started these books and I was well under way, I thought "I really am going to come a cropper. I really am." And so far I haven't. And I don't think it will happen now.

Q   *From the critics, you mean.*

A   Yes. I am going to go too far and they're going to laugh their heads off and say, "What a load of rubbish." And so far they haven't, which really does amaze me.

Q   *Almost any plot described like that is going to sound corny. Surely the intensity of the feelings you describe is the important thing.*

A   This is what I say. I write like this because this *is* me—it's very sincere, you see. This is how I do feel. Christina in *Flambards* is what I would like to be, strong and fearless. She's everything, isn't she? Not very subtle, as you say; I think my characterization is all right as far as it goes, but I don't think it goes very far. When I read other people's books, I often think "Gracious me! I wish I could write."

Q   *I find in reading your books that the hero/heroine is sometimes in a way too young for what's going on; they act out adult events while they're still underdeveloped characters—Ruth gets married when she's only seventeen and childish at that. Are you aware of this as a problem?*

A   I don't feel they're too young for what happens, but I think there is always a technical problem in children's books. If you want anything to happen, and problems to arise, to make a story, if they have understanding parents the problems are ironed out for them. This is why I—and not only I, ever so many people—tend either to have them as orphans, which is the easiest thing, as in *The Maplin Bird*—which was all right in Victorian times because that happened so often, but now it's pretty rare—or get rid of their parents abroad, or make them horrible parents like in the *Pennington* books. So that these children really have got problems. But there again, back to William Mayne, he writes beautiful books, and nearly always with very understanding parents. But perhaps I need this, I need to have in my books the sort of problems that parents might be able to solve.

Q   *What sort of problems?*

A   Don't you think, at the age they are, sixteen or seventeen, that parents can help a lot? Or perhaps they've broken away anyway, even from understanding parents, at that age, and they want to get on with their own things. I wouldn't expect my children to confide in me, I respect their privacy and I think you shouldn't ask them terrifically leading questions. I took my seventeen-year-old daughter to the doctor this morning and I was dying to ask her—I bet he asked her all sorts of questions I would love to have known the answers to, but I thought, well, it's not your place to ask. She wouldn't tell me. We're very close in understanding, but I would respect that sort of privacy, and she would expect me to, I think.

Q   *It can be dangerous. . . like Ruth in* Pennington's Heir, *who gets pregnant because she thinks if you only make love once it's all right. Her mother never told her.*

A   Well, she's a bit of a twit, Ruth. She's all right in the end, in the things that matter, but she's a bit humorless really. In our family we all laugh at her, and that's why I chose the name—I said what's a good name for a prissy girl? We were

Pennington's parents; drawings by K. M. Peyton from her *Pennington's Seventeenth Summer.*

all suggesting names for her sort of character, Ruth came up and I thought yes, that will do. I think she has some admirable qualities, though her poor lad, I think he might regret her later on.

Q   *Do you ever consciously try to influence your readers? Do you ever think you might be doing them good?*

A   No, I hate that. Some reviewer said, about the first *Pennington* book, did I think I was trying to show the young the error of their ways. That really annoyed me, because I would hate to think this is why I wrote books. I do think my own attitudes must show through, and what I disapprove of. But I would never consciously try to influence them. In fact, I think that's an awful thing to do.

Q   *But children are going to be influenced by what they read, obviously.*

A   Yes—I think they are going to be. Well, in a sense I wouldn't write anything which I thought could be harmful, so in a way—in a negative way—perhaps I do it. I'd rather they were reading my book than a harmful book. But on the other hand, I wouldn't stop *my* children reading what I thought were harmful books. They've had quite a wide reading experience, and I would never stop them reading even those really horrible American comics —you know, at a certain age they get them, I don't know where from; they aren't sold in shops, or certainly not in our village.

Q   *Sex or violence?*

A   Those awful American mags published for teenage illiterates, they're really nasty—war comics mostly, Japanese prison camps, that sort of thing—sadistic, not just rubbish. I don't mind *Jackie* and *Mirabelle*. I just used to say "Ugh, how could you read those things?" I used to show them that I disapproved of them, but I didn't take them away. And the same with unsuitable adult books. It might do them harm, but I don't know. The trouble is, you can never know what *is* doing harm, because you can think back to your own childhood; you don't tell your parents the things that are frightening you or disturbing you, do you? I wouldn't like to disturb children, but it's inevitable; they can't go through life never being disturbed, and you don't know what's going to disturb them. It never seems to arise in my own books; I can't remember a time when I've stopped writing something because I thought it's unsuitable. And if I did, I think I would start saying, "All right, you're not writing children's books." I'd be going into another sort of market alto-gether. And another thing—books are written today even for the so-called children's market about things like drugs and homosexuality; it's not because I don't particularly want to put them in, but because I don't know anything about drugs, not much about homosexuality, so it doesn't really arise. I wish I did know more.

Q   *Perhaps as a result, I got the impression reading the* Pennington *books that although it seems a rough, tough world on the surface, it is in fact nicer and simpler than reality.*

A   Could well be. You see this is my romantic wretched business coming out again. Anyway, I can't get away from my upbringing, can I, and my own environment? I haven't really suffered all that myself, it's been done through the imagination. This is how *Pennington* came about; the first *Pennington* book I wrote after I'd finished the *Flambards* trilogy, and I wanted to write something absolutely different from *Flambards*, and also some-thing that would be, I thought, very very difficult. I thought, *Flambards* came out all right, people said they were good, so now let's try something ridiculous. *Pennington* started out to be a ridiculous book, but I don't know what happened to it—I was going to write it for a lark and make everything much larger than life, the bucket of goo falling on the teacher's head and all the rest of it—I didn't expect anybody to believe in it. Perhaps the fact that it was taken seriously was my fault, because as I was writing it, *I* started to take *him* seriously. So I think it's a bit of a hybrid, really, that book. And I certainly have no personal knowledge of that type of person, only from what I can see and hear. This boy was modeled on a boy—I don't usually do this with characters consciously, but this one was particularly modeled on a boy who used to go on the train, the same train as I used to go shopping in, and he used to come home from school with his friends; they were real louts, they used to play cards and swear and talk about girls; and whenever I was in this train I used to go and sit right behind them so I could hear all this—because I thought it was quite fascinating. Quite a while ago. This particular boy was an enor-mous great thug, and he wore a little school cap—of course they don't wear caps any more. The book's dated anyway, because of the hair thing and everything. This was about six or seven years ago. That's how the book started, and I must admit I got rather involved, I enjoyed it. And I liked the music side of it, listening to records for hours and hours and saying I was working. I didn't know a lot about music when I started, but that was the driving force of the books really. I learned to play the piano! I took it very seriously, and had it vetted by some musical people; they were all very helpful.

Q   *Pennington in the first book is really only a rebellious schoolboy, and he hates playing the piano; in the second two he has developed into a serious artist.*

A   Probably perfectly true. He calms down, gets far more responsible—but whether it's successful as a piece of character drawing, as a picture of growing up, I wouldn't like to say—perhaps not entirely.

Q   *I wonder if it works for people who are today's Penningtons? Even if it does for people who aren't.*

A   Yes—I wonder about this myself. People like me think it's all right, but people like Pennington don't read books anyway. This is what annoyed me about this reviewer, who thought that people like Pennington were going to read it, but they're not. And in a way I think it's more for a girl's market anyway.

Q   *Why particularly for girls?*

A   Not particularly; I was just thinking of this one reviewer who annoyed me, assuming that the book is *written* for the type of person it is *about*. Put it like this—I would think it was just as *much* a book for girls as for boys. I think girls at that age, fourteen or fifteen, are reading fiction, whereas boys are reading science fiction, or have gone onto books about things they are interested in. You don't see that age boy in a public library looking at the fiction shelves, do you? Not in my experience. I know a lot of adults read them, because I get a lot of letters from them—schoolteachers, parents, they enjoy them.

Q   *Do they find them helpful?*

A   I don't think I write to be helpful. I would like to think of them as entertaining. You see, I've just abandoned a book because it was so miserable. It was a good book as far as it went, but it was getting so miserable, and I didn't see any point in offering it to people.

Q   *Your books are generally optimistic—this is self-censorship?*

A   They're often quite sad, sad but optimistic, but this one is sad and pessimistic, and this is why I stopped it. At Oxford they wanted me to go on with it, but they said "Oh well, if you do feel like that about it then leave it." It was a murder story. Again, I chose something I hadn't done before, and it was going to be difficult; but you see once you really start thinking about such a thing, with children involved, it really gets very, very depressing. And I didn't see how I could possibly end it the way it was built up. The plot was made, and I didn't see how I could change it. I thought, what's a difficult problem to tackle? Children solving a murder mystery—it's a children's book classic, isn't it?—without bringing adults into it. And for what reason would they not bring adults into it? In this day and age, again, you have to have rather hopeless parents who aren't very helpful anyway, and reasons why the children won't tell another adult. In this story the reason was that they found out who the murderer was, and it was the person they respected and admired most of anybody they knew. After that it all got so really sad. I could have gone on writing this book quite happily for myself, but this is one case where I abandoned it. I've read books like this which have left me feeling shattered, *The Children of the House* by Philippa Pearce for instance; it just left you crushed, absolutely crushed. I thought my book might come out the same as that, and I just didn't want to write that sort of book. I still think—though it's a bit crummy, I know—that books are supposed to bring you pleasure.

Q   *Although you can get pleasure out of a sad book. . .*

A   Apparently, yes. This is what my editor said at Oxford; she said it wasn't a reason for abandoning it.

Q   *Look at* Wuthering Heights. . .

A   It's *my* favorite book! When I saw the film on telly with Laurence Olivier I just sat there weeping. . . but it's not the same as being crushed. Gracious, I wouldn't have told Emily Bronte not to go on with her book because it was too sad, you mustn't get me wrong! This book wasn't a great work of art, this is the difference. But I wouldn't say I merely set out to entertain people; that makes it sound too trivial. I wouldn't like to say *what* my intentions are when I set out writing a book; I don't think they are aimed at the market at all, they are my own intentions, what I want it to come out like. But in this case I did think about the market—perhaps I shouldn't have. It was from the point of view of what I was doing to the readers that I cast it off. I haven't been able to go back to it.

Q   *Did you abandon it in favor of anything else?*

K.M.Peyton

A   I am writing a book at the moment, though it's not very worthy. It's just another pony one. There's one called *Fly-By-Night*—one of the minor ones, and it's just to round off that story. Which doesn't necessarily need rounding off, but it's about Ruth again; it's purely written for pony addicts, when she's just thirteen and terribly horsey. But I wanted to write it, because I am at the moment the secretary of the local pony club, and I'm very interested in it—well, I have been; I'm withdrawing this year, thank goodness. I think the material is good, it's good rich stuff, because there are some funny people. It's a very straightforward plot, it isn't what I would call an ambitious book at all.

Q   *Is that the kind of book you read when you were young?*

A   When I was young I was an avid reader, but not at all an intellectual reader. I'm afraid my reading was very trivial really. I read all these 1930's pony books, there were some quite good pony books in those days. There was the woman who I think wrote the best pony books that have ever been written, Joanna Cannon, and she's the mother of the three Pullein-Thompsons who write pony books today. She wrote a lot of novels, and I liked all her books, but her pony books were *superb*, I thought. I liked *Biggles* books. I read them all passionately as they came out, I devoured them, I loved them—*Biggles Flies North, Biggles Flies South, Biggles Flies West, Biggles in the Baltic*—oh, yes, wonderful. I had a friend who was also very keen and we used to read them all together.

Q   *How did the people at Oxford react when you offered them a pony book, having left your past behind you when you moved to them?*

A   They were quite happy, because I've promised them an ambitious book next.

Q   *Any idea what it's going to be?*

A   Yes, I have—it's set in Regency times, which is what makes it difficult for me, because I've got to do a lot of research. I don't think it will be written in a great hurry, if it's ever completed at all. At the moment—I don't know whether it's me, my age or my health or whatever, but I'm in a sort of state where I don't really know what I'm going to do next. I've got plenty of ideas, but I can't decide what I want to do.

Q   *Having rounded off* Flambards *and* Pennington, *and got such a lot of acclaim for them, it must be difficult to know what to cap them with.*

A   I'm not worried about the fact that they've been a success. But you wonder whether you're going to repeat yourself, and how much there is to say and whether you want to say it. But I'm sure this must happen, and in fact I'm amazed it hasn't happened before.

Q   *There is a kind of progression in your books up to now—from the past to the present, and from younger heroes and heroines to older and more mature ones, and from quite lightweight books to more ambitious ones about more serious questions. It's difficult to know how the series will go on.*

A   I do feel I've come to the end of something, though I'm not quite sure what I've come to the end of. It could be anything. This has lasted quite a long time now; generally I'm absolutely crazy about writing, I can't wait to get at it. I more or less leap out of bed thinking "Writing today, goody goody," because I enjoy it—and all of a sudden I don't. I keep staring into the distance and thinking what am I doing and why?

Q   *The sort of thing some writers would put into a book.*

A   I think writers are apt to put this sort of thing into books too often—their own predicaments—and when you think about it, most of the readers aren't writers anyway. There's a bit of a preponderance of this sort of thing in modern fiction. I don't think children are particularly interested in the worries of a middle-aged writer, are they?

Q   *There's one recent book which is rather outside the series,* A Pattern of Roses. *The interlinking of past and present was a new thing, wasn't it? What set you off?*

A   I got the idea because we actually moved house ourselves; in my mind I see their place in the book as quite different from our place, but there's a little churchyard like that, where we've moved to—they've ruined it a bit, all the elm trees are dying of elm disease and it's all been cleared out by a very keen man new to the village—but before he started messing about with it it was lovely. I got the idea of the two stories running together, and the parallel between the old couple and the modern couple; now this was an ambitious book, and I found it very difficult to write. I think I probably worked harder at this book than at any I've ever written. It was technically very difficult, to have the two stories running, without jarring when you went from one to the other, and what to leave out and what to put in. But I think if you were to ask me which is my best book, I'd say that one. It wasn't so enjoyable to write, though; the others rather rush along. This one didn't rush along at all—perhaps that's what I ought to do more often.

Q   *It's a much more contemplative book, isn't it; and it has a definite moral point about what the best life is, and whether it's a mindless laboring life or a life of compromise between yourself and your job.*

A   Yes, it definitely has. That wasn't what I thought of first; but this dropping out is happening to so many of my friends' children. I'm at the age now when you wonder why, why, why? And you see the reason. I mean do they want to grow up like we've grown up? I don't think they do, and I can't blame them, I honestly can't. That eventually became the point of the book.

Frontispiece, by K. M. Peyton, to her book *A Pattern of Roses.*

K.M.Peyton

Q   *Tim doesn't actually drop out, though, does he? Advertising
     doesn't suit him and his job in the smithy does lead him
     somewhere.*

A   Perhaps I should have been more honest and just had him com-
     pletely dropping out, which is more common today. I must say,
     on the whole I'm on the side of drop-outs today. Although I
     hate them when they sponge—the society which they so despise,
     they expect to support them; that I don't like. But there are
     a lot who drop out who at least keep themselves; they don't
     want to compete, perhaps that's the way to put it. A lot of
     them get laboring jobs, don't they? And their parents go berserk
     because they've got so many "A" levels and they've been to
     University and then—there's one in the village who's a fork-lift
     truck driver, and he's ever so happy, but his parents go raving
     about it. I think, if he was yours, would you worry? I would
     worry, but I'd say: well, what's gone wrong? It's not entirely
     him, I don't think. In fact I don't really think it's him at all.
     I'm on Tim's side. Actually I cheated a bit with Tim: I made
     his parents really horrid. These sort of people exist, but they
     probably wouldn't have had a boy like him, who goes into crea-
     tive things. Tim is fighting for his art, which is not a commercial
     proposition. If you've got that, or the brain that can pass "A"
     levels and so on, I don't think you're going to be satisfied with
     being a fork-lift truck driver for long. I'm at the stage where
     I'm wondering—quite a lot of my friends have boys who have
     done this drop-out and gone to Afghanistan, and this is going
     to be very interesting to me; they've been there for two years
     and they're on their way home, and I want to know what they're
     going to do next. This is a problem that has not been solved
     yet. You do change in your views, I'm afraid; I can hear myself
     saying things to my children now, and I say: "I'm sounding
     just like grandma," and they say "Yes, yes you are." As you
     grow old it's inevitable that you retrench a little. I see things
     differently. I don't say I was a hippie, because they didn't exist
     then, but my husband and I—I don't think we conformed very
     well, and yet I consider I conform very well now.

                                                        London, 1974

K. M. Peyton's books include: Windfall (1962); The Maplin Bird (1964); The Plan
for Birdsmarsh (1965); Thunder in the Sky (1966); Flambards (1966); The Edge of the
Cloud (1969); Flambards in Summer (1969); Pennington's Seventeenth Summer (1970);
The Beethoven Medal (1971); A Pattern of Roses (1972); Pennington's Heir (1973).

20 *Lucy Boston*

Interviewed by Emma Fisher

Lucy Boston is in touch with a much deeper spring of natural morality. She did not start writing for publication until she was past sixty. This late creativity would probably have been impossible without her house in Huntingdonshire, the Manor at Hemingford Grey. She first saw it in 1915, when it appeared to be no more than a derelict Georgian farmhouse. Twenty-five years later, after a life spent as a painter, mostly abroad, she came back and bought it. It took years of guesswork and restoration to uncover the twelfth-century shell and the Elizabethan fireplace and chimney, and to put the house together again. She has kept the best of the features added by each age, so that it contains a continuous record of eight centuries of domestic life.

She first began writing to celebrate her love of the house, which appears, as Green Knowe, in almost all her children's books. She herself appears in the books as Mrs Oldknow, the wise old woman who lives in the house and provides the security behind the sometimes light-hearted plots of the children—assorted orphans and relations who have found a haven at Green Knowe. But her books are also very serious. She feels the beauty of the world is threatened, by pollution, progress, and human crassness, but that part of the answer lies in the right attitude to nature. She seems to feel an almost Wordsworthian "one life" with her surroundings, even thinking of her house as a living thing. Its walls are blocks of stone, three foot thick, laid one on another without any mortar; she has described herself, existing between them, as "the heart within living ribs." Those of her books not set in Green Knowe are also linked to this theme: *The Sea Egg* is a celebration of the sea as it should be, but is no longer.

Lucy Boston was born in 1892 in Lancashire. She was educated in a Quaker school, a Paris finishing school and Somerville College, Oxford. In World War I, she nursed wounded soldiers in a French hospital. She married in 1917 and had one son, Peter, who has illustrated many of her books. She has related the story of her house and of her writing in *Memory in a House* (1973).

277

Lucy Boston

Q *You said in* Memory in a House *that* A Stranger at Green Knowe *was a particularly important book for you, on a big subject—the way one should treat nonhuman nature. Does the book also tell us something about the house, in that Hanno has nowhere to go—he's an outcast—and Green Knowe does provide him with a refuge from modern life, the nearest he can get to his African Eden?*

A Well, oddly enough, it seems to be the theme of nearly all my books—when it isn't Hanno, it's Tolly, who was a temporary orphan, and Ping who was a refugee. It's not even a thing I had realized, but it does seem to be my permanent theme. It comes in *Persephone* too. And I suppose in a way it's a reflection of my own life, since I landed up here when I had nowhere to be. My marriage had broken up and I was in a flat in Cambridge, and then I found this; and it was a completely new life, and I have never wanted to be anywhere else. I can hardly leave it for a day!

Q *It's more than just somewhere people end up at the end of the story, isn't it?*

A It's between past and future, and always aware of both. There's nothing temporary about it.

Q *It's not in the present, though, is it?*

A Oh yes. Absolutely in the present. I think that's the extraordinary thing about it, that it's totally contemporary. There's a great deal of the past in it, and when I bought it, I thought there was just as much future. But now one doesn't believe in the future at all.

Q *Not at all?*

A Well, there's such a question mark, one can't feel any certainty that there will be any future.

Q *Why not?*

A The hydrogen bomb; pollution; overcrowding. Pollution in particular, pollution terrifies me. And at the moment, I know, it's considered rather disgusting that one person should have a house like this. Or even that anybody should. But I hope that's temporary; we've had Levellers before. But there's nothing one can do about the overcrowding, except hope that nature, as usual, will restore the balance in some violent and drastic way. But that takes away the future too.

Q   *In* Memory in a House *you said that as long as one can feel that the earth is immortal, one can die happily.*

A   But one can't even feel that any more. I mean one doesn't now feel even temporary security.

Q   *Is the house threatened by people?*

A   Very few people hate it. But quite a lot of people are frightened of it, as though it was a threat to *them*. I don't know why, I can't understand why it should be frightening.

Q   *It's become almost a show house now, hasn't it? Does your wish that everyone should know and love it ever run out?*

A   It just holds good. It's a very private house, but since I wrote *Memory in a House* people have been coming two or three times a day, every day, and without making appointments, everybody just walking in and saying, "I do hope we are not intruding," which of course they are doing, though you can't say so. But I so love it, and never never never get used to it, that I hold out. I don't send people away unless it's really impossible. Big parties, associations, institutes and so on I now write off, because they behave so badly. They lose all their manners—one finds men coming out backwards, feet and bottom first, out of one's wardrobe, and things like that which one doesn't expect. I never have such huge parties, and I never take more than ten people at once round the house, because it's too small, and they can't see anything but each other. So if fifty come, that means that I have to do the whole round five times, including the stairs up to the attic and all that. And it's a day's work. But as a rule they enjoy it, and I suppose it's some security for the house that it's so well known.

Q   *In* Enemy at Green Knowe, *you have a magical contest with a witch who wants to destroy the house. Some critics have objected that all you offer to overcome the witch is general niceness and some nursery rhymes. But in* Memory *you say that the spell they use during the eclipse of the sun, to overcome Melanie. . .*

A   The one which is like a collect, which says "Be thou what thou art and what thou willest to be"?

Q   *That's it. That you find it the most powerful thing to overcome the force of evil.*

A   Yes. Because if evil is a necessary opposite of good, which belongs to it, then "what thou willest to be" might appear evil. And therefore evil has been taken in and dealt with. I think it's a tremendous thing. I don't know where it comes from; I know it comes out of Solomon's book, but what scripture that comes out of I just don't know. I think it sums up everything one might have to believe.

Q   *Is it addressed to us, to individual people? "What thou willest to be" might be wrong from another person's point of view.*

A   No, one is invoking the unknown power; *that* is to be whatever it wishes to be. It's not a command to people. It's an invocation.

Q   *To God?*

A   To the greater power.

Q   *To a good power?*

A   To the total power.

Q   *So you just have to accept it, whether it seems good or not.*

A   Yes, take it, remembering the whole.

Q   *And that is enough to explain the unhappiness in one's life.*

A   Yes.

Q   *But one can't know that, can one?*

A   One can find it out by being unhappy enough.

Q   *Perhaps the critics of the book haven't understood this.*

A   No; they complain as if all that I'd offered was these nursery rhymes backwards.

Q   *Do you find that grownups, or critics, tend to think a book ought to be an allegory?*

A   Yes, they always start psychoanalyzing and say, "What do gorillas mean to you? Is he a father figure?" when I have tried, summoning whatever powers of writing I may have, to say *exactly* what a gorilla seems to me to be like, himself, as a gorilla. It just means that I have seen something like *this.*

Q   *A* Stranger at Green Knowe *was touched off by your being transfixed by the experience of seeing Guy, the gorilla at the London Zoo, wasn't it?*

A   I was utterly astonished that there could be such a thing, yes. And he just met the case of something that could stand for a total misuse and abuse of life, that everybody does now, as if no life except human life mattered. Whereas I feel, like the Buddhists, that the whole of life, whatever it is, matters. And certainly sentient and intelligent life like that ought to be treated exactly as we treat our own.

Q   *Hanno in* Stranger at Green Knowe *is also a half man-like figure, isn't he?*

A   That is what makes him a perfect bridge.

Q   *It was interesting that the Zoo wouldn't let you dedicate the book to the gorilla's keeper. And yet they think they are on the side of the animals.*

A   Yes, because they're preventing them from being extinct. But they don't notice that what they've got in their cages is to all intents and purposes extinct by being there. You get a completely false impression of them. Not of Guy, my gorilla, because he was untameable; but the keeper of the Bristol Zoo once told me that he considered that all animals in cages were mad. Nothing that they did gave you any idea of what they would normally do. Those—what should be beautiful cranes, in muddy patches, who've learnt parlor tricks in order to get things thrown to them, which they do on their muddy patch all day long—it's enough to make you cry. Every time I see a tiger, it's a case of "my heart leaps up when I behold." Even though they are mad, even though they are in a cage. The way they move—such a comment on what the universe can do.

Q   *In* Stranger at Green Knowe, *Hanno dies rather than go back to captivity. Is there any solution for him in real life?*

A   There's no solution for Hanno; however, he has got a wife now. A friend of mine was at the zoo the other day—said Guy and his wife were lying out in the sun, and every now and then, to amuse the spectators, Guy would pull his wife's leg. He has a great sense of humor. What I missed in my study of gorillas was hearing them sing. They sing—I imagine it's high tenor, like dogs, but I don't know. When he became of marriageable age and there was no wife for him, the keeper said he sang in the morning before he was let out, raising his voice, and I'd love to have heard that. A wonderful thing to hear.

Q   *But you saw him dance.*

A   Extraordinary, extraordinary—like Samson. It was quite a stylized dance: He had his arms above his head, clasped, and he turned round and round, with rather the same kind of bottom-upwards stamping movements that African natives do, except it wasn't so bottom-upward because he was reaching to the heavens.

Q   *Does the point you were making in* Stranger *go right through nature to include inanimate things?*

A   Yes, it goes right through, and one is always horrified at a tree being cut down. I have a tremendous feeling for the sea, and a really cutting grief about its being dirtied. People don't mind. And the rubbish is indestructible. No, it's all quite revolting, and that's why I get pessimistic. People don't really seem to care about anything. Except money. Money and cars seem to be the only things people care about. The Torrey Canyon disaster came immediately after the publication of *The Sea Egg*, which is my favorite book. It's set more or less in Kynance cove, which was obliterated in oil. But apparently the threats about the death of everything living in the sea were not borne out: there are still sea anemones and seaweed. When I wrote *The Sea Egg* the threat to the sea had not been brought to our notice; it was only after the Torrey Canyon that all these reports came pouring in. And now of course after the cholera in Naples efforts will be made to clean things up a bit.

Q   *Since coming to the house, and publishing books about it, you've branched out and written books based on other places. Had you written anything before you came?*

A   I wrote a lot of poetry before, entirely for myself. It's a very good discipline.

Q   *Observing things?*

A   Well, I always do observe things; I can only think in the form of observed things, as you've probably noticed in the books.

I wrote ghost stories to amuse my son, but they didn't.

Q   *In* Memory *you describe how* Yew Hall *and* The Children of Green Knowe *were accepted by Faber, were going to be put in their adult list, but the fact that* The Children *had pictures meant that it had to be a children's book. Had you thought of yourself as a children's writer before then?*

A   I meant *The Children* as a children's book, though I was very pleased when they thought they could put it in the adults. Like Mayne, I write for the child I was. If you write for the child that was, in your own mind there's no division between that child and yourself now, so that it should be valid for both. Children I know literally live in my books. Green Noah has been seen to move on my lawn, and the other day a small boy got very excited when he found a nest in my yew castle and I told him *The Castle of Yew* was coming true. But reviewers often say "for intelligent children only," as though this were a black mark. I don't think it's even true. Somebody I know—she was a school teacher—decided to try some of my books out on what she called deprived children. She didn't mean defective, but children who could have had no experience at all of what was in the books, and she said they absolutely loved them. I was rather hurt when a reviewer called my books irrelevant and precious.

Q   *Have you ever been particularly inspired by another writer?*

A   No. No. It's rather hard to explain, but only the writer knows if he's said what he meant to say. And I don't see how anybody can help you with that. There's no library here, and I haven't got a car, so I tend to read the same books over and over and over—*The Tale of Genji*, in eight volumes. And Ivy Compton Burnett I read again and again; I think they're wonderful. I love Thomas Hardy; I used to love Henry James, but I'm off him now, because I don't see any point in tying the language up in knots. Language should be crystal-clear. And also I feel that very often, or at any rate in the short stories, he doesn't even mean what he's writing. It's like playing spillikins: he thinks of an idea with which you could make a pile of spillikins, and then move them one by one. For one thing it's a terribly catching style, and for a writer, to be avoided.

Q   *How do you get on with the more "realistic" children's books that have appeared recently—those of J. R. Townsend, for instance?*

Lucy Boston

A Well, I know he hates mine. He's written nicely about them in one of his books about children's stories, but he says quite firmly that they're not his cup of tea. I'm against all theoreticians, especially about writing. No original writing could result from a theory, could it? I myself am totally unprofessional, and never go to any of these conferences. After all, I only write in the winter; in the summer I do my garden, and take people round, which has now become a full-time job. I'm trying to brew up a book for this winter—I have hopes that it may work—but usually the plot comes from nowhere, it comes out of the blue and comes complete with first sentence and last sentence, and all the key sentences in between. No such idea has come, so I've got to work one up, which is not so good. I've got an idea for a good story for children, but that isn't enough; you see, it's got to be a good story for *me*, it's got to have shape and it's got to have something I mind about. It'll have to be about the house, because I no longer go away anywhere; *The Sea Egg* was after a visit to Kynance, and *Nothing Said* was after a visit to Yorkshire. I think if ideas are to come out of the blue, perhaps one really ought to keep moving. And now I don't. This is old age, it's too static. I now feel too adult to write children's books—on the other hand I am out of the contemporary world, and therefore would get it all wrong if I wrote an adult novel. I haven't got an idea that's burning to be written—but I feel I should be happier writing for adults than for children now. It's the optimism that's lacking.

Huntingdonshire, 1973

Lucy Boston's books for children include: The Children of Green Knowe (1954); The Chimneys of Green Knowe (1956); The River at Green Knowe (1959); The Enemy at Green Knowe (1964); A Stranger at Green Knowe (1961—winner of the Carnegie Medal); The Sea-Egg (1969); Nothing Said (1971); The Horned Moon (1971); The House That Grew (1972); The Castle of Yew (1972). *Her books for adults include:* Yew Hall (1954); Persephone (1967); Memory in a House (1973).

21 Rumer Godden

Interviewed by Emma Fisher

The Doll's House (1947), Rumer Godden's first children's book, was widely acclaimed, and she followed it with several other stories about dolls and doll's houses (sometimes inhabited by mice). The doll's world, with its delicate makeshifts and human rivalries, is consistent from one book to another, and a charming pair of Japanese dolls appears more than once. In *Little Plum* miniaturization goes a step further when they are given their own ceremonial dolls, made from matchsticks. The dolls' owners often learn from them; the little girl in *The Fairy Doll*, who is clumsy and backward and in despair, gains confidence through the fairy doll until she can manage without her—a resolution to encourage any awkward child.

Rumer Godden is a very versatile writer. She has produced several other children's books, such as *Operation Sippacik*, about a donkey in Cyprus, and *The Kitchen Madonna*, about two children who make an icon. Some of her many 'adult' novels are now highly regarded as children's books, in particular *Greengage Summer* (1958). This brilliant story of four children left in a provincial French hotel in summer, and their relationships to the seedy or mysterious characters in it, is an incredibly acute picture of growing up and the discovery of sex and love. It has far more passion and authenticity than most later books written specifically to encompass these subjects from an adolescent's point of view.

Rumer Godden was born in 1907, and spent part of her early childhood on her father's estate in Bengal, a period of her life she has described in *Two Under the Indian Sun* (1966), written with her sister Jon. She has married twice and has two daughters. For many years she has lived in Rye, Sussex, first in Hartshorn House and then in Lamb House, where Henry James wrote many of his novels; now in Mermaid Street, where she moved after the death of her husband. She is the author of many plays, poems and translations and has contributed to journals and periodicals.

Rumer Godden

Q   *You wrote about your childhood in* Two Under the Indian Sun. *After you left India, England must have been an exile—the emotion of homesickness often appears in your books.*

A   You say "after I left India." I've never left India, I keep going back; but the first time I came to England was when I was five and was left with my grandmother, and then mercifully my parents took me back again. I didn't come back to England until I was twelve and my sister was fourteen. Then they clapped us into an Anglo-Catholic convent, and that was murder, both for the nuns and for us, because we were not accustomed to English life or school life, or school ethics. If anybody said "Who did this?" we would say "Mary" or "Emily," because nobody had ever punished us; in India you're not treated like that. Children are not subject to the same kind of discipline at all. It never occurred to us that Emily or Mary would mind, and that we were sneaks and we weren't sports. We had a most terrible time. We didn't know any of the answers; I always remember in *The Constant Nymph* when they went to Church and didn't know you had to pay—we didn't know we had to pay. We were always disgracing ourselves. We didn't know what were Conservatives and Labours and Liberals, we didn't know Oxford and Cambridge, we didn't know anything. We were plunged into the school milieu and about 300 people tried to bring us up at once. So it was very miserable. My mother and father were here, but that was the hardest thing to bear, that they suddenly turned Judas on us. When we told them we were unhappy we expected them to come and take us away, and of course they just said "It'll wear off." And it seemed to us the utter betrayal.

Q   *Did it ever wear off?*

A   We only lasted a bit of a term at that school; it never wore off. I went to five schools, I think, in six years; but eventually settled at the last one, more or less, because they separated me from my sister. I had to. Also it was a more—a liberal school, Moira House in Eastbourne, and it didn't run to pattern; it was very individual. The vice-principal was a remarkable woman called Mona Swann, who was very interested in the stage, and theater and writing; and after my first week there, she took me out of school, and I only learnt French, and literature, and music. She let me work with her. And did she make me work, in no uncertain terms! I spent two terms doing Anglo-Saxon poetry. I spent a term reducing the *Times* leader to fourteen lines. I know all about *précis*, I can assure you! And what I owe to her is beyond words. She gave me a really thorough training in English, and technique.

Q *Did you go back to India when you left school?*

A I went back to India straight after that, and I've been going backwards and forwards ever since. Last time I went was in 1972, to research on a book—but it's a perpetual to-ing and fro-ing.

Q *What was the book—a new novel?*

A It's not written yet. It is a novel, but for the last eighteen months my husband was so desperately ill that I really could not work. I had to put it aside. Then we moved house. At the moment I'm saying that I haven't written anything but checks for about a year! It's been ghastly—he was my business manager, and I didn't even think about money. I always remember my small granddaughter coming back from Cyprus, where she wasn't used to shops and things, and I took her shopping in Rye, and she came back and said to her mother, "I don't want to tell you, but I think you ought to know that Grandmother goes into shops and buys things and doesn't pay for them!" She thought it was a beautiful kind of magic. But that's what I'm doing at the moment. I also have a children's book; I've been exiled in Scotland during the winter with a very badly broken ankle, and I was rather bored, so I wrote the draft of a children's book. But of course one never knows in draft if it's going to turn out, even with my age and experience.

Q *Is it written according to the pattern?*

A Do you mean my pattern or every writer's?

Q *I mean that the children's books do have certain common themes, and the doll books go together.*

A Yes, I think it goes in cycles; the last books I've done for children have been rather in the same category as that latest book of Joan Aiken's—they're for older children or grown-ups. Like *The Kitchen Madonna.* But then I wouldn't say any of my books are for very little children; I think seven is round about the age, for the doll ones.

Q Greengage Summer *could be read by older children, although it was written as an adult book.*

A Well, now it's a school textbook, for children from twelve to

287

sixteen; so is *The River*, which is very puzzling. So is *Episode of Sparrows*; they've turned them into textbooks because of the English.

Q *How autobiographical was* Greengage Summer?

A That was founded on fact. I was Cecil, my sister was Joss, we did actually go there and we were left all on our own by accident. My mother was a very romantic person, and we were so odious that she thought it might do us good if we went to see where Joan of Arc was burned, and the battlefields of France. And she quite unknowingly took us to this luxurious part of France where the champagne is made; we went back—I always write my book first and then do the research, I never do the research first, it spoils the story—we went back, it was Chateau Thiéry actually, and of course it had been very badly bombed; I only recognized the house by a little strip of paper, blue satin paper that had been in the dining room. But the orchard was still there, going down to the Marne, and the greengages were ripe—I'll always remember that.

Q *You turned it into a kind of detective story—or was that real?*

A There really was that man; actually there were two men, Eliot was compounded of two men; the woman who owned the hotel had a lover, who was a Canadian. And there was an Englishman staying in the hotel, a mysterious Englishman like Eliot, with a wife and small child; and they were very very kind to us when my mother was so dreadfully ill. And one day he disappeared; they went, overnight, and were not his wife and child at all, and he was an international bank thief. It was rather fascinating—we had to persuade them in Chateau Thiéry to open up the police records for us. Of the compound of the two men, one of whom fell in love with my sister—the French Canadian, the lover of the lady—I made Eliot; and there they all were, in the police records. But they didn't catch this man Martin, ever. My sister lent him a little attaché case which was very precious to her, because it was made out of a crocodile my father had shot in India (she liked this Englishman very much) and about three months later this little attaché case came back; not a word said, it just came back. Did you see the film? The film is beautiful. So often they're not, but that really is absolutely lovely. Jane Asher takes the part of Cecil—they rolled Cecil and Hester into one, because they thought there were too many children—and she gives a most remarkable performance. She must have been thirteen then. She stole it from Susannah York. It was Susannah's first big film, and she is enchanting in it, but she can't measure up to Jane Asher. In that drunk scene, Jane is extraordinary. That film made me very happy; if you do a film of your book, it's really very dreadful, because you've got to go back to a book finished some time ago. For instance, with *The River*, I went right through it with Jean Renoir, and it was nearly two years, over the same book again, and there's nothing more boring than being on a set. And yet if you're going to do it at all, you've got to do it properly.

Q   *As you said in, I think,* Swans and Turtles, *once you've finished a book you lose interest in the whole subject.*

A   Completely. You're like a cat with kittens; once the kittens are grown up you don't want to know them. So it is really rather dreadful to have to do a film; on the other hand if you don't do it, then they make something like *Black Narcissus*. Which really was too awful.

Q   *What went wrong with it?*

A   Oh, it really was too dreadful for words, really a travesty. The whole conception was wrong. First of all, for my young Rajput prince they had Sabu, the coolie boy from South India; that's who Sabu is by origin; he's a very charming creature, but he's no more like a Rajput prince than. . . then the beautiful Tibetan background; it was all made in Pinewood, with white muslin mountains; and then in their anxiety not to offend the Church, they became really offensive. The scene where the little nun falls in love with Mr. Dean was shocking, it even shocked me—the scene where she runs out of the convent and goes to him; they took her out of her habit, and it was absolutely shocking. I had no protests about the book, but I had endless protests about the film. I said I'd never have another film, but then Renoir came along with *The River* and persuaded me, and that was a very enriching experience, because after all he is a great artist. I learnt a tremendous amount from him. But it was two years, during which time I couldn't do any writing of my own. At the moment we're doing a musical of *Holly and Ivy*, which should be rather charming, I think. David Heneker is doing the music; it's really his idea. He did *Half a Sixpence* and *Charlie Girl* and *Irma La Douce*. I think it should be rather fun.

Q   *To go right back to the beginnings of all this—what was the first book you had published?*

A   It was about a Pekingese; it was the third book I'd written, and it was called *Chinese Puzzle*. In those days I was very precious, and I wrote it in longhand—and I used capitals for the nouns. I suppose I thought it would give a sort of Chinoiserie context to it, and of course when it was printed it looked too terrible for words. It absolutely killed the book, though it got very good reviews. I blame my publisher—he should have told me. I couldn't correct the proofs because I was having a baby.

Q *It must have looked a bit like* Omar Khayyam.

A Exactly. That was the first novel I had published, and then I wrote one with an Indian background called *The Lady and the Unicorn*. Which did quite well. Then I wrote *Black Narcissus*, which burst both sides of the Atlantic; I remember going in a bus up Charing Cross Road—I didn't even know it had been published, but I was so humble then, they never tell you—and I saw a great banner with *"Black Narcissus* by Rumer Godden" on it. I simply couldn't believe my eyes. It was the first book I had published in America, and it was a runaway, they couldn't keep up with it. But of course it's not very good for that to happen to you early in your writing career, you really just want a steady climb. I remember my agent, a very wise gentleman, taking me out to dinner and saying "Well, what are you going to do now? Are you going to write *White Chrysanthemum* and *Purple Pansy* or what?" But of course that is part of my trouble—that I do spot. I think the English particularly like you to have a vein and keep to it, so that they know what they're getting. And they are awfully puddingish. They don't like you to spot. Either you write novels with an Indian setting, or you write novels about religious life, or you write about children; you keep to your vein; whereas I don't. They never know what's going to be in the next book, and they don't like it. In America they do like it, because their minds are not so stiff. They are infinitely more receptive. If I have to give a talk to English people, I hate it; but the Americans, yes.

Q *The English find it embarrassing to talk about themselves?*

A They're such puddings. This lack of response, being brought up abroad, I find absolutely devastating in England. They don't react. You mustn't talk, you mustn't cry, you mustn't mention this or that—I find it very difficult. But I do know that that is part of the reason why I'm not as well-known in England as I am in America; because I'm unpredictable. But of course it's much more interesting for me. I couldn't go on writing the same kind of book. As for writing a series! I can understand the fascination of sequels, but it's when they write the same kind of story again and again. I must admit that I myself began

to realize I was haunted by this twelve-year-old girl who appears
two or three times in books of mine—Cecil, Harriet in *The River*,
Caddie in *Fiorita*— and I realized that I must not go on doing
this; so I decided I'd write a book with no children at all, that's
why I wrote *In This House of Brede*, my second book about
nuns. In the days when I wrote *Black Narcissus* I thought that
if you lived in a convent and rang the Angelus, you were a
nun—then I wrote *Brede*, when I did know about nuns, but
of course *Black Narcissus* is the better story, from a story teller's
point of view. It has more of a shape, After *Brede* I promised
my husband I'd never write another book about nuns; he said
write about a brothel if you like, but not about nuns!

Q   *In the adult novels, there's often violent death, perversity, hatred;*
    they're often very frightening, whereas in the young children's
    books something good usually happens, they are much more
    reassuring. Enemies become friends, the lost doll is found. Is
    this something to do with the fact that you are writing for young
    children?

A   I don't think it's anything to do with writing for children. It's
    not true of the first one, *The Doll's House*, which I think is
    the best of those. It is a complete novel set in a doll's house.
    That's what made me write it. It was the first book I ever wrote
    for children, and that wasn't because I had to or told them
    stories or things like that; they were grown up; I wanted to
    see if I could write a real novel—it's a murder story—in the
    tiny compass of a doll's house, and make it acceptable for
    children. Nobody ever detected it, but it is definitely a murder
    story. The only person who spotted it was John Betjeman; he
    wrote to me about it. After that they became less strong, perhaps;
    but there always has to be drama, there has to be conflict, and
    I suppose if conflict is going to be acceptable for children, you
    have to watch your ethics a little bit. I don't think it's done
    to write books for children where—this may sound awfully
    prissy—where evil triumphs.

Q   *Though in reality it does sometimes.*

A   It does triumph, but it's beaten in the end. And if you look
    at all the best children's books, you'll find it's always beaten
    in the end. It may be horrifying, scarifying while it's going
    on, but it's beaten. And I suppose unconsciously we want
    children to believe that good is stronger than evil. You've got
    to do it without being preachy or prissy. For instance, in *Candy*
    Floss, one couldn't let Clementina Davenport win. To start with,
    the children wouldn't have liked it. They'd have felt it was

291

very incomplete if she had defeated Jack and kept Candy Floss. It is a story of conflict, and naturally you want the one you are involved with to win. Practically all good children's books have a very strong moral, even though you don't say it. I do believe that a children's book must be ethical. For instance, I don't think a successful children's story could be made with "The Emperor's New Clothes" if the little boy hadn't seen through them. And I don't think "Cinderella" would have been in the least satisfactory if the ugly sisters had triumphed over Cinderella and got the prince. Whereas in a novel probably the ugly sisters *would* have triumphed.

Q   *Do you think it's difficult to have a happy ending in a novel nowadays, without making it sentimental?*

A   People don't believe in it. But now and again you must have a happy ending, because it comes like that. When you come to examine it, *In This House of Brede* is exactly the same story as *The Doll's House*. Or as in any of the children's books. It usually is the person saying he will not do something, and in the end he does it, he brings himself to do it.

Q   *In* Brede *it's learning humility and obedience.*

A   Or even more than that. You become different, you change, and people do change all the time. And I think that is perhaps the strongest thing to do in writing, to present this continuity in people. People are not fixed, they do change. You say, "I will *not* do something"; sure enough a year later you find yourself doing that very thing—almost always. If you're growing. But with the happy ending for grown-up people—for instance, I made a very bad mistake in giving *Episode of Sparrows* a happy ending. I realize that now. It doesn't fit on, it should have ended unhappily; it would have been a much better book. Lovejoy should have gone to the school and been left there. It was slightly sentimental; wrong, quite wrong, and contrived.

Q   *The ending of* Greengage Summer *leaves you in the air—there is a note of triumph though you know Eliot will be caught.*

A   That one *must* be unhappy. It had to be.

Q   *To go back to the doll books, which mostly do end happily; in all of them, you portray the dolls as people, who can think and feel, but definitely as dolls as well; they can't move, they are always the same age, their tea is made of paint water. A doll is real but always only a doll—*

A   —held in its dollness. That's how I thought of them; though I was quite convinced they would move if I wasn't looking at them. I think either you're fascinated by dolls and miniature things or you're not. None of my sisters liked dolls, and of my children, only one liked a doll. It seems to be something either in a child or not in a child, and I don't think it's anything to do with being maternal, because children who are very maternal take it out in animals, not dolls.

Q   *Perhaps the fascination is that one is creating another little world, in which you can make them do whatever you want.*

A   I think very much so. I think one finds a true artist's release in this world; which is why people take dolls so seriously. I like miniature things altogether, miniature boats and model trains, anything like that.

Q   *What do you think of some of the uses to which children's books are being put; for instance, giving information in the course of telling a story?*

A   I think children's books should either be information, straight, or else they should be for entertainment. I think you find this worst of all in pony books—they teach a child how to look after a pony through a story. And I always think that's pretty horrid. But then I have a dislike of this mix-up of things; for instance I dislike historical novels intensely. I like my history straight and my novels straight. Katherine Mansfield's life was turned into a novel recently. It's not true and it's not fiction: it's a hybrid, and a very uneasy hybrid.

Q   *Novels for young adults have recently appeared in publishers' lists. What do you think of this kind of categorization?*

A   As soon as anyone tries to write a novel with a target, he's bound to fail. A book *must* spring spontaneously; you can't write with a target. I particularly hate these ghastly books in simplified language—over and over again in America I've had a young author come to me almost in tears, because they've been told to write a book using only these words: for instance they mustn't say forest, they've got to say tree. What they call limited vocabulary books. A novel that is simplified for children will always fail. I never try to make my books simple, I never prescribe my words; children adore words. *Viz.* Beatrix Potter: "Lettuces make you somnolent." "The sparrows flew to Peter Rabbit in great excitement and implored him to exert himself." They would no more let you write that, these people, than they'd fly over the moon. All the richness has gone. When I give talks on writing for children I do an imaginary correspondence between one of these publishers and the ghost of Beatrix Potter; "Lippity-lippity"—not in the dictionary, you can't use it. "Kertishoo" for sneeze—"Tishoo" is more usual. And these novels are written for eleven to twelve-year-olds who are perfectly capable of reading *anything;* I remember the shock I got when I went to school at twelve to find I wasn't allowed to read *Jane Eyre,* which I'd read three times already. All children over the age of eleven, unless they're pony mad, are perfectly capable of reading adult books—some of them. As soon as you apply any limitation, to books for children or for grown-ups, then you're going to fail. It's almost unimaginable that you'd get a good book from it.

Q   *There's a technique I've often noticed you using in your books, of making the characters break into the narrative and say something, as if the story was being told to them.*

A   Yes—that is one of the ways I do it, to give depth. Another thing, this I learnt when I was doing a study of Hans Andersen; I read all my books aloud when they are finished. To see if they bind. I can't imagine why more writers don't do this, for it is the audio age; it almost goes without saying that your books will go on Jackanory or one of the children's programs, teachers read aloud, the libraries read aloud; how it sounds, the naturalness of the dialogue, is to me very important. And this building up, "interjecting" you might almost call it, I think is a technique I learnt when I tried to do the Time books like *China Court* and *Fugue in Time.* It gives enormous depth and naturalness to it; you suddenly see the person through another character's eyes. It seems to work. They endure, and that is the big test of a book. I am very lucky in that almost all my books are in print. They go on selling. *Black Narcissus* is now nearly forty years old; and it still goes into new editions all the time. It happens with most of them. I think it is because the books are what I would call hand-made, and I'm not prolific, when you think how long I've been at it. I started when I was very young, and I'm now sixty-six; I don't think there are more than thirty books.

Rye, 1974

Rumer Godden's children's books include: The Doll's House (1947); The Mousewife (1951); Impunity Jane (1955); The Fairy Doll (1956); Mouse House (1958); The Story of Holly and Ivy (1959); Candy Floss (1960); Miss Happiness and Miss Flower (1961); St. Jerome and the Lion (1961); Little Plum (1962); Home is the Sailor (1964); The Kitchen Madonna (1967); Operation Sippacik (1969). *Among her adult novels are:* Chinese Puzzle (1935); Black Narcissus (1938); Gypsy Gypsy (1940); Fugue in Time (1945); The River (1946); Kingfishers Catch Fire (1953); An Episode of Sparrows (1955); The Greengage Summer (1958); China Court (1961); The Battle of the Villa Fiorita (1963); In This House of Brede (1969).

22 Maia Wojciechowska

Interviewed by Justin Wintle

One explanation for the recent growth of the "young adult" novel could be that meeting the demands of the adult market has become harder and less rewarding for the writer whose concern it is to be an arbiter of morality, a midwife to society in the older phrase. Maia Wojciechowska is one of several authors interviewed who could be used to make this point. *Tuned Out* (1968), her most controversial book, looks at drug-taking in adolescence from a general perspective of individualism within the family. She shies away from what has been the usual function of marijuana or LSD in recent contemporary fiction, a means of titillating the fancy of bored adult audiences. When her characters experiment with drugs, they do so to find out about themselves and their relationships within immediate situations rather than in a hedonistic pursuit of pleasure. Ignoring the new culture drugs have created, Wojciechowska concentrates on older traditions in which individual destiny is still a matter of importance. *Shadow of a Bull* (1964), which is about a bullfighter's son who is expected to emulate his father's prowess in the ring but is unwilling to do so, is a more conventional children's book with a clear and powerful story line. But each book in its own way handles a similar theme: adolescence grappling with its own identity.

Maia Wojciechowska is a Polish Catholic, born in Warsaw in 1927. She grew up in Poland, France, Portugal and England before coming to America in 1942. She has been a bullfighter, and held down an assortment of jobs ranging from waitressing to being an undercover detective. It is not suprising that she thinks courage, not wealth, is the best antidote to insecurity. Her first husband was Selden Rodman, the expert in Haitian affairs. She lives in New Jersey and has two daughters, one who is grown up and also a children's writer, and Leonora, a two-year-old whom she recently adopted, and whom she would like to educate herself. To accomplish this she intends to move to Mexico.

Maia Wojciechowska

Q *From all accounts you've had an extraordinary and busy life, beginning with the Second World War when you became a refugee from occupied Poland. Looking back, how much do you resent the war?*

A The War came at the right time for me. Wars are only good for young people who survive them. My mother and my two brothers escaped with me. The rest of my family were very old and most of them died out during the war. At least three million Poles who were not Jews died in the Nazi concentration camps. Very few people in this country know about that. In all about seventeen million Poles were lost.

Q *How did you escape?*

A We walked most of the time. I hate to talk about it for one reason: we were under the impression that we were doing a very dishonorable thing. It was not the time to leave your country, so my brother and I never thought it the cleanest phase of our lives.

Q *What would have happened though if you had stayed?*

A We'd probably be dead. I know I would be, because I would have done all kinds of crazy things—not because I would have wanted to be killed, but because under that kind of system the imperative was you couldn't stay alive. You had to fight it, and it was strong. I think all the really good Poles are probably dead.

Q *Where did you go when you left Poland?*

A We went through Rumania and Italy to France, where my father was, and where we stayed until 1942. We also went to London where we stayed about a month, very close to Baker Street. I was crazy about Sherlock Holmes.

Q *Are you one of the people who think he's still alive?*

A Oh yes. Conan Doyle or whatever his name was—he was a phony, some kind of impostor who got in there and fixed up the royalties! Sherlock Holmes was the one who wrote the books.

Q *Who looked after you all this time?*

A My mother was on my back constantly. We were unmanageable, but she did a pretty good job of impersonating a policeman which kept us amused and therefore quiet. She must have had a pretty tough time of it. My younger brother doesn't have any fantastically happy memories of that time. All you could do was fend for yourself against the shocks of being moved and transplanted. But I had myself a ball. It was like living on the crest of a volcano which you'd made yourself, and which was going to explode any time that you wanted it to. My brother and I had this gigantic hatred of the French, who are a defunct race. We fought them as well as the Germans. It's always more exciting if you fight a war on two fronts.

Q   *What was your father doing in France?*

A   He was a commander in the Polish Air Force. I don't know if it was then or later that he became Chief of Staff. In any case, on the second day of the War he went off to France and England to ask for reinforcements. Neither of those countries lived up to the pact that declared we would all come to each other's aid. I've never felt right about the English or the French since September 1st 1939. My father made a lot of enemies when he was in London. He used to sneak out secretly on bombing raids, which wasn't quite the right thing for a desk man of his position to be doing. He spent his life obeying orders, but really hated the discipline imposed upon him by military life. Also, he'd always fought against promotion, which was not characteristic of an officer. He was a Lieutenant Colonel holding the kind of job that a general ought to have had. He was very impatient and had a lot of quarrels with the British during the war, so he was sent to Washington to be air attaché to the Polish Embassy, where he wouldn't be so much trouble. In England we were third-rate citizens, and we were used. The R.A.F. learned an awful lot from the Polish Air Force. The Polish pilots were flying round the clock, more than they should have been. There was the feeling that all kinds of tactical things were not being done right, and yet we didn't have any say in the matter. All the Poles thought that the war was being deliberately prolonged. I remember writing Churchill several letters. I didn't know English terribly well then, so I had to use a dictionary a lot.

Q   *How easy has it been for you to become an American?*

A   I didn't know anything about America when I first arrived. The last twenty years or so I've come to realize that the seat of evolution is here, for better or worse. They're catching up with us in other countries. It has nothing to do with being an American. It just happens to be here, like other civilizations have been the seat of everything—Greece, Rome, etcetera. And how we blow it is just incredible! Because in this age Americans are so goddam important we should be teaching our kids some kind of historical imperatives. I went back to Poland for a brief visit about four years ago. It was when I returned here that I saw the danger of Americans not knowing how willing they are to surrender themselves to the bureaucracy of their government. Government was invented to destroy man the same as God was invented to love man. In Poland the fight is continuous; but here, where people have the luxury of time they still surrender, and they don't know what they're surrendering to. This country is so young and so naive. Every politician has to be watched very closely.

Q   *What were your first impressions of the United States when you arrived here as a teenager?*

A   The first day I got to America I was robbed. Whenever I crossed a frontier I played a little game. I used to take perfectly ordinary pieces of paper and wrap them up carefully in clothes so the customs people might think I was carrying secrets or money or something. Only when I came to America did I have a little bundle of money, and this was stolen from my hotel room the first night. I remember on the boat coming over I was the only person who didn't come out to look at the skyline and the Statue of Liberty. I liked to do things I could feel were individualistic or strange.

Q   *That certainly comes across in your books. Why is it though?*

A   I must have been a very paranoid baby—the fear being that someone would mould you unless you did it for yourself. I was always aware that if anyone was going to mould me it would have to be myself. That's why I guess I didn't talk until I was four and a half years old. I know now that I could have talked before then, but preferred to pay the price of being considered retarded. Perhaps I could get more candies or whatever I was settling for at that point.

Q   *What happened when eventually you did break silence?*

A   I thought about what I would say, wanting to settle on the right words and the proper occasion. Finally it happened when the whole family was gathered together. My brother, who was a year younger than I and writing poetry, was generally considered a genius by everybody. I had to be terribly bright if I was going to attract any attention from him. So at dinner I stood up in my chair and spoke my first words: "Why must the world be so cruel?" All the relatives who thought I was retarded started having heart attacks at this profound question! That was the first thing I said. It still took me another three years before I could wave goodbye.

Q   *Presumably you had practiced on your own?*

A   I think I must have rehearsed it. I know I wanted to throw some guilt on my relatives. I don't know why, but probably it was as a result of being in direct competition with my little brother. As long as I was not considered to be intelligent there was no chance of ever getting any profound attention. For years after everyone thought I was a very unhappy child (I wasn't), and was very nice to me.

Q   *Has your question about why the world is so cruel ever been answered for you?*

A   Yes, I think that for me it has been. I think that for the last two thousand years people have concentrated rather on the Crucifixion than on the Resurrection. The Crucifixion was a very cruel act, and brings out guilt and other kinds of things. We have that mentality not of being saved but of being punished.

Q   *You finished off your education in American schools. Was that a crucifixion?*

A   Oh my God, my education! It was just a prolonged fight. I don't know what was so compulsive about my fighting schools. By the time I arrived in the States I had already been kicked out of a couple of dozen places, and I didn't start schooling until I was twelve! In France we spent three years moving from one town to the next because I kept on running out of new schools to go to. I was never kicked out for insubordination or discipline; it was always my quarrels with the teachers, that they had no right to say certain things. History was my favorite subject. I was madly in love with the fact that you could write lies, but I didn't think that one should be forced to learn lies.

Q   *Did your record of expulsion continue once you got here?*

A   Oh yes. I guess I lasted about two hours in my first American school. I didn't really know any English then except Hail Mary, which I didn't think was a prayer, but a Declaration of Independence from Shakespeare or somewhere. But I did know my French, and the second lesson I went to a French class. The teacher

299

didn't know French at all. I told her she shouldn't be teaching a language she didn't know. She took me to the Principal's office and had her translate to me that I was to leave the school. What was said in English I don't know, but I'm sure she didn't raise my criticism. Then I went to a Catholic school, and then another Catholic school, by which time I was getting older and really didn't want to be kicked out any more. I had also met a man in Portugal by then who was the only adult who said anything to me that put any light in the darkness. He told me that the school years are the least important years in one's life. I didn't know that because children don't really have a concept of the future. This bolstered me, knowing that it was going to be over soon. I was also in love with Lord Byron at that time, and that helped. The last three years at school were completely painless. I wrote my term paper on Byron once. I got a fail mark of course. I wrote too much on his physical relationship with his sister, and as I said it was a Catholic school. My bibliography alone was seven pages long, more than the whole paper was supposed to be. Every boy I met I compared with Lord Byron, so naturally I never went out with any of them. Unless there was a club-footed man walking around I wasn't interested.

Q   *Are you still a Catholic?*

A   Just in the physical things of going to Church and the Sacraments. I think it's my personal weakness: I need the Church, but the Church doesn't need me. I think something of vital importance belongs to the Catholic Church—not in terms of what is happening today, but in terms of what happened when Christ was alive. I can make a physical rather than a spiritual union with Him. If I was a better Christian I wouldn't need the truth so much. I would be able to see Christ in everyone, which was His message. But I keep feeling that they're failing Him. I can only see Christ in people momentarily. That's the difference between us and God, that we cannot love people unconditionally—except babies.

Q   *Most of your children's books are focused on some point beyond childhood—what will happen to the child eventually, what job he will take and so on. Is this a reflection of your belief that the school years are not so important?*

A   Yes, I think so. It's very hard for a child growing up to realize that it's a passing thing. There's so much they sell out on for the expediency of being young; the girls go on about the popularity thing, and the boys go on about bedding and smoking pot or whatever it is that counts, as if there were no tomorrow. Often it's to their detriment. Once you've sold out it's very hard to buy back. It's not a preoccupation of the young to impose their own moral prerogatives as far as character and pride go, and the result is young people can sell themselves very cheaply. I think where it starts is the great amount of pressure put upon them to conform. If you conform to this today, you'll conform to that tomorrow, and to something else the day after. Although this might be acceptable, it doesn't mean that it's right, like legalizing abortion doesn't mean that abortion is right. We are in a time when we proclaim that we cannot legislate morality; but we are very much legislating a morality. I just hate to see the society I live in so readily cheapening itself. I think pornography is cheap. I think stealing is cheap, but no cheaper than cheating or lying. It's just not worth the price.

Q   *What price?*

A   The price is you, and how much there is of respect left for yourself. That's the only reason there is for being good. The less respect there is the less likely you are to like yourself. It's that materialistic.

Q   *People conform because it is one way to get a level of security. What would you suggest?*

A   I think when one is young one should be terrifically aware of the giant obligations history has put upon us all. I don't mean that everybody should study the Greek philosophers, but they should at least be aware that they existed. They should know that they were ready to die and died for things cerebral, and that they dismissed the body as being too shoddy to bother with. I had to go to a school to give a talk the other day. Because there was no cafeteria the kids were shut out during lunch. I arrived there and saw all these children pressing against the bars waiting to be let in. To me that was symbolically a terrible shock, because I had always been inside trying to get out. Then they gave me a very preselected group of kids to talk to—only three out of twelve of them were black, and it was a mainly black school. I was paid a hundred dollars to go there. I thought that whoever was managing this mini-grant was doing something highly immoral. It meant eight dollars a child, and I'm not worth that. The kids had been selected from those who could be trusted not to rip me off, or rip the library off. Anyway, trying to make some kind of moral stand for the hour I was there, I was told at the end that the school didn't have any of my books because they had all been stolen.

I told the teacher that I would have liked to have spoken to the kids who stole them, not to those who could be trusted never to steal anything. At one point I had asked my audience why it was that people sometimes sacrificed their lives for an idea. The blankness never left the faces of the preselected twelve. They will never be prepared to die for anything because they will never live for anything. So many kids don't know what they want out of life, that's the sad thing. The family is gone, or going, so where are people to get their ideas from? Not from school. Juvenile literature has opened up of course, but in general if I was brought up to read what's published today I think I'd just as soon watch television. Another thing is that if you're not curious you'll never find out; and curiosity is being killed off in our society. Children don't go off looking for themselves. In my generation you couldn't keep the rebellious kid away from books—and where else would we get our strength from to fight?

Q   *Do you try and provide some of that strength in your books?*

A   In the ones I care deeply about, yes—like *Don't Play Dead Before You Have To* or *The Rotten Years*, which was how I thought the world should be saved. My husband used to call it *Mein Kampf*.

Q   *In the light of what you were saying earlier, do you regard* The Shadow of the Bull, *your best-known novel, as a Resurrection story?*

A   I wrote that you just have to keep on going until you find some kind of answer for yourself, which is the oldest truth in the world. We all do it, or we all should be doing it. The imposition is that the forces against that finding out about yourself are overwhelming. The individual has every right to be paranoid because everybody's compelling him not to be an individual.

Q   *You almost imply that a successful society would do a minimum of teaching.*

A   What I'm implying is that at this point in our evolution we've got to be eased into an anarchistic frame of mind (in the best possible philosophical sense). Not disorder, but an order that is not imposed.

Q   *In the Author's Notes that preface* Tuned Out *you refer to drugs as a disaster; and yet in that novel at least they provide a form of anarchy which bring about some good as well as the bad.*

Maia Wojciechowska

Was that something the publishers obliged you to put in?

A   Oh, God no. What they did try and do was to get one to eliminate any reference to the specific time when it was all supposed to have taken place. Being an optimist I thought it would only be a year or two before young people left off drugs and moved on to something else, so I did want to pinpoint it in time. The age of the children was important too, an age when some sort of transition is necessary. Almost symbolically you have to free yourself in the mid-to-late-teens, even if it means having to "blow your mind." If you have never felt that you had a brain, and then you smoke a joint and feel something start to happen upstairs, then you should smoke a joint! But if you know it already then there's no need. Drugs can open a door to the mind, but not much else. You've got to move through and leave drugs behind, otherwise there's so much damage that you can do to yourself. Each individual has a treasure chest of unknown potential. Drugs can open that chest, but used too much they can also destroy a lot of the contents.

Q   *Is that why there are long tirades against drugs from even the most sympathetic characters in* Tuned Out?

A   That book was completely misunderstood. I read the reviews and was appalled by how unclear I must have been in my intentions. I think I must have been very devious! In any case Kevin, the boy who was on drugs, was at least doing something about his predicament, showing courage and fortitude, realizing that he was in trouble, and that whatever he was doing was wrong. But it's his brother who is worried about him who is the real problem in that book. By the end, when Kevin is beginning to find himself some clear air, Jim is beginning to realize that he's got that same journey to make. It could be drugs, or it could be something else. Jim is the weak person. Kevin showed strength by going into drugs. By this pursuit of an extreme where something might be revealed he was not simply blowing his mind because he had nothing else to do. Nobody understood that though. When I was young somebody threw the old cliché about reading between the lines at me. Well, that's how I write— between the lines. None of my stories are really there: the intent and the book are never the same.

Q   *When Jim, the younger brother smokes some grass the results are far more hallucinogenic than one would expect, more like LSD than marijuana.*

A   It was a close rendition of what I felt when I once had a joint

303

in Mexico at the age of thirty-four. I don't think it was laced with anything stronger than grass. I also had a twenty-four hour reaction, so I do not feel that I have cheated my readers. Admittedly, what happened to me as a woman is not likely to happen to a boy of fourteen. What counts though is your frame of mind whenever you're taking something you don't know about. I turned on several young people here in this house with ordinary grass cut straight from my lawn, without the slightest hint of marijuana. I put it into the oven to dry, cut it up, ground it, and rolled it into cigarettes. We all got stoned, me included! It was a marvelously pleasurable high. The attitude of mind is everything. In *Tuned Out* Jim was petrified about drugs, so naturally his worries came out in his trip as a magnified experience.

Q *Anyone who writes about soft drugs automatically puts himself or herself at risk. Either you say it's a good thing or a bad thing, and there will always be someone to call you a liar or a perverter.*

A I know a group of young people who took the same acid in the same room under the same conditions. One of them ended up in the museum, another at the hospital. Everyone goes their own way. When I wrote *Tuned Out* I did want to frighten people a bit, tell them that unless they knew themselves very well it would be dangerous to fool around with any drugs. I knew another boy who ended up in a mental home for at least two and a half years after one trip, so perhaps I was right to moralize. All that time he felt he was on fire. It's better to be catatonic than that. There's a right time and a wrong time in life for these things. I think if parents and not the kids had been on grass and acid then the changes might have been more beneficial. The lady whose biggest thrill in life is going to the hairdresser's once a week might stop going to the hairdresser's; and her husband might stop being vice-president of his advertising firm.

Q *You've talked about the mind as something that is both real and important to you. How do you react to the suggestion that, philosophically, the mind as a phenomenon may only be an accident or an illusion?*

A Just like the Creation? However it happened, it's a fantastic accident or a magnificent premeditation. Like the Greeks, I think that the mind is the soul, and I don't think it's just accidental. I think it's the presence of God in us, just as our bodies are the missing link with nature. I don't see any quarrel between Darwin and the Bible. Our bodies I'm sure evolved from the apes, but I don't think our minds did. Where the mind comes from doesn't matter. Whether God invented Man or Man invented God is such an unimportant question, like which came first—the chicken or the egg? They are both there.

Q   *Is this why you write almost high-mindedly about individual destinies, even though your audience is usually a young one?*

A   I don't know when you are too young or not too young to know about these things. I would imagine that the proper way of learning would be to make a demarcation line between good and bad, and put the good with God and the bad with the self that is temporal (the body). When a kid does something bad he should know that he does it for his body and not for his head. Right there you've got the beginning of teaching children about our duality, that we are truly schizophrenic. If the world is catering for our bad side by selling us a lot of clothes and so forth, and not catering to our minds, then the world isn't doing us too much good, and we have to be wary of that society.

Q   *At least one of your books,* A Kingdom in a Horse, *suggests a different kind of world, although its ending, when the old woman is reunited with her dead husband through the agency of a horse, is unusually sentimental.*

A   That's a terrible book. The only thing that's redeeming about it is that I loved that horse. I had it for two years. I thought it wouldn't hurt anybody because if you're horse-mad nothing hurts you. Anybody who loves horses could read that book, but anybody who has nothing going for horses should be kept away from it. The ending was wrong, but then I can't end a book anyway.

Q   *Is that why* Shadow of a Bull *is critically your most successful book, because it does have an ending?*

A   It has three different endings. The British version has a much better version than the American version, where they forced me to revise the final chapter. I did another ending for the French edition, and I just wrote a screenplay of the book, and that has a very logical ending. The boy, the reluctant torero, goes out there and kills the bull, and then apologizes to his friend (who had wanted to be a bullfighter all along). There is no real way out of the situation that the boy was caught up in except to go through the door. Having thought about it over the years, that is the only way to end it.

Q   *In both the original version of* Shadow of a Bull *and* A

Kingdom in a Horse *the young heroes find their way to the path of medicine: they will become either doctors or vets. Why?*

A   Really? I haven't read *A Kingdom in a Horse* since I wrote it, so I don't remember. The only thing about that book that I do remember is that in the first draft the story was simply about the horse and the old lady. My editor asked me if I was writing for old ladies or for horses. If a book's for children it's got to have a child in it. So I went ahead and invented this obnoxious child. Is that prostitution in writing? I don't think I would be capable of doing that kind of book today. It's an example, though, of how publishers can be dangerous. None of us are so clean that we can't whore, given the opportunity.

Q   *Your well-known objections to a book like* Ferdinand the Bull *point to a different kind of selling out . . .*

A   Not the brave bull—the homosexual bull! Ferdinand who smells flowers. I though it was unfair of Munro Leaf to even ask whether Ferdinand was brave or not, just because he gets stung by a bee! Bulls just aren't like that. I'm so against animals being done that way in picture books. They invariably pervert the nature of the animal, and it's not as if this was being done for the edification of the child. They're just stupid, those books. We have a gigantic proliferation of mice books on the market in America. All these mice do all sorts of things that no self-respecting mouse would ever do. Then they're read to all those black kids who are being bitten by rats. I don't know what happens in the head of a kid who's absolutely petrified of getting another bite and then reads about this rodent playing Beethoven in her Dior dress. It's all insanity. I love animals, but I hate people who write picture books about them. Animals just don't talk like bad writers.

Q   *Which of your books did you most enjoy writing?*

A   *A Single Light*, because it was so difficult. It turned out a beautifully written book (I say it dispassionately), although the ending is an incongruous as ever. Also *The Rotten Years* I suppose, in which I set out to write a textbook. I discovered there are no courses in American schools in which the teacher has to be a human being. When I talk to kids at school one of them invariably comes up and tells me I'm the only human being he or she's ever met. I thought maybe they could invent a course and use *The Rotten Years* as a source. But again I compromised. It's not a novel, nor is it a textbook. It's a textbook that passes for a non-textbook. I got everything I wanted to say in it though. But when it was published as a paperback it had this jacket that, if you didn't already know what was inside, would make anyone think it was a novel about lesbians.

Q *Do you always write with a moral purpose?*

A So many kids have so many vacuous things in their lives, including their parents, that I think a book can and should give something more than entertainment. I think we are in trouble, and I think children's books can clarify the troubles. I don't mean that children's books should all be written about the troubles which beset the adult world. I just mean the essential troubles everybody's been in, like forgetting that there is a soul. Then you can be of use to your reader—you can make something click. If a kid with problems is reading your book, the problems you write about don't have to be specifically his. The click, I think, can happen between the lines.

New Jersey, 1974

Maia Wojciechowska's books include: A Single Light (1964); Shadow of a Bull (1964, a Newbery Award Winner); The Hollywood Kid (1967); Tuned Out (1968); Hey, What's Wrong With This One? (1969); Don't Play Dead Until You Have To (1970); The Rotten Years (1971); The Life and Death of a Brave Bull (1972); *and* Through the Broken Mirror with Alice (1972).

23 *Judy Blume*

Interviewed by Justin Wintle

If there is an *enfant terrible* in American children's writing today, her name is Judy Blume. Blume's books explore the private problems of East Coast suburban adolescence with a candor that some critics have found genuinely provocative. Her strength lies in an ability to reflect the discomforts of young individuals in the prosperous background she shares with her characters: the boundaries of her own experience are mirrored in the limitations of her plots. Intruders are rarely allowed to question New Jersey values; rather, those values are questioned from within.

Judy Blume's relationship to the society she lives in is best expressed in an anecdote. She was once accosted by a local mother who was so upset by two pages in *Then Again Maybe I Won't* about wet dreams that she had ripped them out of her son's copy. "What if they had been about a girl's menstruation?" Mrs. Blume asked her, "Would you still have torn the pages out?" "Oh no," the mother replied "that's normal."

Judy Blume was born in Elizabeth, New Jersey, in 1938. In 1959 she married John Blume, an attorney, by whom she has two children—Larry and Randy. They live in New Jersey.

Q   *How did you begin as a children's writer?*

A   I wish you wouldn't ask me that because I really don't know.
It was an accident. My kids were about three and five and I
wanted to do something, but I didn't want to go back to classroom teaching, which is what I was qualified for. I read my
kids a lot of books, and I guess I just decided—Well, I could
do that too. So when I washed the dinner plates at night I
would do imitation Dr. Seuss rhyming books; and each night
by the time I'd done the plates I would have a whole book.
I would send some of them in to publishers and they would
be rejected. They were terrible. That's how I started. Then I
thought it would be fun to do a longer book. I graduated from
New York University, and they used to send me these brochures
on courses they ran for graduates. One of these was a course
on how to write for children. I thought that must be an omen,
so I tried it. I didn't believe anybody could teach one to write,
but I needed professional encouragement, as I was on the point
of stopping altogether. My low point was when I had six or
seven rejections in one week.

Q   *What did you do in the course?*

A   What I did was write like crazy so I had something to turn
in every week. My teacher gave me a lot of encouragement.
She would write me little notes telling me I would get published
one day. I don't know what the other people did. We never
did our writing in class. Class-time was divided between the
teacher lecturing on things that really didn't mean too much
to me, and letting us in on the professional world—things like
how to prepare a manuscript, how to write a covering letter,
and about agents. Occasionally we had guests come in and talk
to us—established writers or publishers. It just made me feel
that in this field I was suddenly developing an interest, for at
least I was getting to know what's going on. I loved it. I even
went back. I took the course twice because I didn't want to
lose that contact. I still had no other contacts as regards other
writers or editors. But before I left the course, after two semes-
ters of basically the same thing, I had sold a couple of stories
to magazines, and I had written at least a version of *The One
In The Middle Is The Green Kangaroo*, and finished my first
real book, *Iggie's House*. I wrote that chapter by chapter, week
by week, the second semester that I took the course. It was
like homework.

Q   *How large was the class?*

A   Very small—under ten.

Q   *And have any of the others become "professional" writers?*

A   I've never heard.

Q   *Do you enjoy meeting publishers and editors and agents and librarians, and being a part of the industrial side of books?*

A   I love it. That's just me. But then I like to meet new people all the time. I look forward to meeting other writers and going to conventions and seeing the whole thing. I like to meet librarians, and I like to meet the kids.

Q   *Were you interested in writing at New York University?*

A   I always read a lot, and I wish now that somebody had encouraged me earlier or had discovered that I could do this thing. In my day it was different. You had to be practical. I think my college education reflected my mother's feeling that you went to college basically to find somebody to marry, and you get a degree in education so that you can always teach if quote God forbid unquote you should have to work. I never thought any further than that. Now I see so many different things I would have enjoyed doing, all connected with publishing. I think it would be fun to be an editor or a library promotion person. I have suddenly met up with all these people, and it looks like a very interesting and pleasant way of life. But you can't do everything! All the editors say they'd really rather sit at home and write. Sometimes I do get a bit frustrated and think what fun it would be to go out every day on a nine to five job, because when you have a family and work at home the family tend to think "Oh well, she's not really working, so she can do this and that and the other thing too."

Q   *Hence, perhaps, the importance to you of the business end of writing?*

A   Yes, yes.

Q   *I know that you work very closely with your editor. What does this mean in practice?*

A   We talk a lot over each book. When I finish a manuscript I send it in to my editor and he reads it, and hopefully he'll like it and want to publish it. One time he really didn't like the book and asked me not to publish it. It's in the bottom of the closet now. I'm glad it's there now—he was right. Anyway, after he's read the manuscript I go to his office and we sit together all day and talk about it. First we talk about general ideas—the plot and the characters. I take notes furiously. Then we go over the book page by page, scribbling all over it. After that I take it home with me and work on it for several weeks at least. I usually wind up rewriting at least half. In *Margaret (Are You There God? It's Me, Margaret)* I think there were seventy-five pages that I totally rewrote. But a book grows. I love the rewriting—that's the best part of it. The hardest part is the first draft—that's torture, and always takes the longest. And when it's done I think I'll never be able to do it again, I'll never get another idea. The second draft is lots of fun, because it's all there, and all I have to do is get it right.

Q *What do you find has to be changed the most when you rewrite a book?*

A It's never the dialogue. It's usually showing more of my characters. My editor says I always know much more about them than I let on. It's confusing for me—I don't know how it works, but it just does.

Q *Are you ever upset by anything your editor says?*

A Never. I rarely assert myself, although if I really believed in something I think that I would. But my editor is very tolerant and sensitive, and I think that he's usually right. He doesn't give me specific ideas. New scenes will come out of our meetings that neither of us had ever discussed during the meetings, new and better scenes that show something important. I get nervous if you ask how does it happen between us, because it's something that happens naturally. It's like when kids ask me where my ideas come from. I get upset about that because I don't know where my ideas come from.

Q *Your books are, however, usually about the same thing—the problems of early adolescence in a comfortable middle-class America.*

A Because that's what I know best. That's how I was raised and that's how I live, and I think we write best about the things we really do know about. I set most of my books in suburban New Jersey because this is where I grew up. And I think that when it's very real to you it's very real to your readers. I like to see something before I can write about it. I think I am a very visual person. Specifically I can run down the books and

311

tell you exactly where the ideas came from visually. *Margaret* came right out of my own sixth-grade life, except for the family situation. Her feelings, her actions, her friends, her concerns— they were all the things we were interested in in sixth grade. I never wrote it thinking it would be widely accepted as the way kids think today, but apparently they do.

Q   *Some of your main characters come across as problem children—one thinks of Deenie obviously, but the others too. Your young readers identify with them?*

A   All children are problem children, because anybody can have problems. Many of my readers identify with Margaret. They write to me and say "You don't know me but you wrote this book about me, and I *am* Margaret." If you ask me what do I do besides entertaining and making reading fun, it's creating characters with whom the kids can identify. I think it's the feelings they recognize more than anything else.

Q   *You certainly convey that general sense of panic that goes with being an adolescent. More than that, you convey the suspicion, which is a large part of that panic, that perhaps other kids don't share one's own insecurities.*

A   That's the whole thing, to let the kids who read the books know that it's okay, that other children *do* feel the way they do. Everybody feels alone sometimes. I'm always relieved when I read in a book, whether it's for children or for adults, that somebody else feels the same way about something as I do. I really love that. I know just how it is.

Q   *So you write to make children feel less isolated in their problems?*

A   Yeah, but I don't start out that way. I start with the character. I don't know everything about the character when I start the book. I'm surprised along the way myself. *Deenie* of course, was a deliberate idea, to write a book about a child with scoliosis, because I met a kid with scoliosis. That required a lot of research, while all my other books required none. That was a very special experience, and I couldn't write about it until I'd seen it, the way I said. I went to the hospital and watched these kids being molded and fitted for body-braces, because I couldn't visualize it on my own. My favorite scene in the book is the scene in the plaster-room. All of the dialogue in that is real. I sat in there with a pencil and a paper and wrote down everything the nurse and the doctor said. The children were very frightened and said nothing basically. Then I had to become Deenie. That's what I do whoever I'm writing about: I become that person for those few months.

Q   *The adults in your books don't emerge too brightly. The parents of your protagonists never really seem to have the first idea of what's going on in their child's mind.*

A   I don't really feel that way now. In my new book, *Blubber*, which is coming out in the Fall, the parents are very nice; and in the book that I am doing now I think the parents are really special. I don't think it was deliberate, what I did. For instance, I liked Margaret's parents. I thought they were nice people and I thought of her as having a happy home life. She was secretive about all those things because that's how I was. Most kids are that way. In *Then Again Maybe I Won't* the boy has a lousy mother, sure; and in *Deenie* my feeling was that if she had very warm, accepting, understanding parents, the story that I wanted to tell wouldn't have been there. It was not just about what was happening to her, but about the feelings and reactions of everyone around her as well. But I think it's a mistake to think that I always make adults come out that way.

Q   *Certainly the fathers come out rather better.*

A   That's probably because I had a very close relationship with my father.

Q   *Each of your books, it seems, selects and deals with a particular problem or experience of early adolescence. Why is this?*

A   I'm going to fight you here. I don't think of them as problems. There are a lot of librarians who refer to "Judy Blume's Book About Menstruation," or her "Book About Wet Dreams," or her "Book About Masturbation." That makes me very angry and it makes my editor very angry, because if you ask what the books are about I'll tell you: one is about Margaret, one is about Tony, one is about Deenie and one is about Karen. They're about kids, and not one specific problem.

Q   *Nevertheless your main characters are all very obsessional. With Margaret it's God and the bra.*

A   Yes, but only for a very short period of time. Okay—so I'm writing about Margaret for one school year. And for one school year those were her obsessions. But I think that if you saw her in seventh grade it would be totally different. It's a short period of time.

Judy Blume

Q   *Why have all your characters so far been around sixth grade?*

A   I'm not sure. That's what I know best. I remember everything from third grade on. I can tell you what I was wearing on certain days—I really do have this almost total recall. I'm not sure why sixth grade has been so important to me. It's difficult for me to talk about it because at the moment I'm immersed in a book about a whole other generation, eighteen-year-olds, who are a world away from sixth grade. But I will go back to sixth grade. I like them at that age.

Q   *Do you find writing about sixth graders for sixth graders involves you in any special responsibilities? Are there things you wanted to write about but weren't able to?*

A   Not any more. The one thing I wanted desperately to do in *Blubber*, which is about fifth graders, was to let them use the language they really use. I think kids reach their peak of nastiness in fifth grade: they're very cruel to each other. Up until that point I hadn't really tackled language as kids use it. Publishers would have been frightened by it. But in *Blubber* they do talk the way I feel they talk to each other. Children in America who ride school buses use all the four-letter-words freely. I've tried to show that in *Blubber*. We had a little problem over that. The solution was that if the language was not important to the character or the plot we would use another word. If it showed characterization then it stayed, so there are a couple of "phrases" in *Blubber*. I'm afraid it's a book that's going to make a lot of adult readers uncomfortable because it shatters the myth that kids are sweet and innocent. They just aren't. But I'm writing for the kids, and the only problem is that they're not the ones who buy their own books, or usually even choose them. What is available to them in the libraries is there because an adult has selected it. It is only with paperback books that they can get what they want.

Q   *One of the themes of* Then Again Maybe I Won't *was the sexual awakening of the young boy, mainly through an act of voyeurism as his neighbor's daughter undresses without pulling the curtains. But you shied away from any suggestion of masturbation.*

A   That's right. I wasn't as brave as I would be now. I think it's very important, and more so in *Deenie*, because female masturbation is something that up until now nobody would admit to.

Q   *I remember—you refer to her as "touching her special place," but nothing more specific.*

Judy Blume

A   Anybody who's reading *Deenie* and who is masturbating is going to know what she is doing and is going to feel relieved to know that it is fine to do. Again, I wrote that out of my own experiences; and the reason that I called it "the special place" is that that's what we called it. We never heard the word "masturbation"; we just said "can you get that good feeling?" There was a seventeen-year-old girl here the other evening interviewing me for a school report. She told me that she didn't know what I meant by that passage in *Deenie*. I was shocked that a girl of that age should know so little about her own body.

Q   *Not to eschew mentioning masturbation is one thing, to extol it is another. Is there a responsibility there?*

A   I think my only responsibility is to be truthful to the kids. In *Deenie* I didn't set out to refer to masturbation: it just grew out of the girl's character. I felt I knew her well enough to know that this is what she was doing. I do feel kids worry about masturbation because it's not something the average American parent is discussing. Boys I think are a little more outgoing, and talk about it among themselves. I wanted to let girls know it's okay. It's not something they should go and do, but if they are doing it then that's fine. It can't hurt you.

Q   *There seems to be a general feeling among the aficionados of children's literature in America that "Judy Blume provokes . . ."*

A   Is that it? The kids of course do not feel that way at all, and I don't set out to provoke—reviewers or librarians or anybody else. I just think kids have certain rights, and they've been denied those rights for a long time.

Q   *Your characters of course are going through experiences that they would be going through in almost any society. A child can have scoliosis anywhere, just as he can have sexual hang-ups anywhere. Do you think the society you describe is particularly neurotic about these things?*

A   I think that a lot of adults in our society are uncomfortable with their own sexuality, and therefore their children's sexuality is a threat to them. That's not true of everyone of course. I have had some very negative responses from adults, but I've also had some very wonderful ones. The negative responses don't usually come to me directly, but through a librarian or some other intermediary who tells me about some parent who comes in carrying a book of mine demanding that it be removed from the shelves. I do feel these are people who feel uncomfortable with themselves.

Q   *I gain the impression from reading you that the East Coast must be a particular hothouse for inhibitions.*

A   I don't think it's just East Coast America at all. It's spread across the board.

Q   *You are sometimes almost satirical when dealing with adult responses. The mother can be relied upon to break down in the worst possible way at the worst possible moment.*

A   The books are all told in the first person so the reader can only know what the narrator knows. I'm not sure that kids really know their parents as people at the age of twelve or thirteen, or even sixteen. One part of growing up is realizing that your parents are ordinary people and that they have the same kinds of hopes and fears as you do. The kids in my books only know their parents as a mother or a father. I don't think I ever meant to be satirical. I know I've been criticized once or twice for showing very whole children and very superficial adults.

Q   *Which comes of writing through the eyes of a child in the first person.*

A   Possibly. I write in the first person only for one reason, which is it comes naturally that way, and what comes naturally is best, at least for me. With *Blubber* I decided to go back to writing in the third person. I did about forty pages of it like that. My editor saw it and liked it very much. But then my children saw it and said "This is awful. Tell it like you were Jill." So I did, and it's much better.

Q   *There are limitations in writing first person though. In* Then Again, Maybe I Won't *the boy next door, Joel, comes out pretty badly. He's sneaky and he shoplifts. I'm sure one could write the book from his point of view, and he would come across sympathetically. The morality of your books is bound to be the uncorrected morality of the individual.*

A   I don't know what to answer you. Sure it would be a different book, and then I would be feeling sympathetic toward Joel, because whatever character I'm writing about I feel sympathetic toward. I don't think I'd write it otherwise.